Sex, Drugs, Rock & Roll, and Musicals

ALSO BY SCOTT MILLER

From Assassins *to* West Side Story:

The Director's Guide to Musical Theatre

Deconstructing Harold Hill:

The Insider's Guide to Musical Theatre

Rebels with Applause:

Broadway's Groundbreaking Musicals

Let the Sun Shine In:

The Genius of Hair

Strike Up the Band:

A New History of Musical Theatre

In the Blood a novel

SEX, DRUGS, ROCK & ROLL, AND MUSICALS

SCOTT MILLER

NORTHEASTERN UNIVERSITY PRESS BOSTON

Dedicated to

SPARGER-BERGER,

for bringing so many of my rock musicals to life.

An imprint of the
University Press of New England
www.upne.com

Manufactured in the
United States of America
Designed by Richard Hendel
Typeset in Arnhem and Fresco types
by Keystone Typesetting, Inc.

University Press of New England is a member of the Green Press Initiative. The paper used in this book meets their minimum requirement for recycled paper.

Library of Congress Cataloging-in-Publication Data
Miller, Scott, 1964–
Sex, drugs, rock & roll, and musicals /
Scott Miller. — 1st ed.
p. cm.
ISBN 978-1-55553-742-5 (cloth : alk. paper) — ISBN 978-1-55553-743-2 (pbk. : alk. paper) — ISBN 978-1-55553-761-6 (e-book)
1. Musicals—Social aspects.
2. Musicals—History and criticism.
3. Rock music—Social aspects. 4. Music—Psychological aspects. I. Title. II. Title: Sex, drugs, rock and roll, and musicals.
ML3918.M87M55 2011
782.1'416609—dc23 2011018547

5 4 3 2 1

Contents

Overture

The American musical theatre as an art form has never been more vigorous or more adventurous than it is right now, and sex, drugs, and rock and roll have collectively become the lifeblood of this new postmodern golden age, an era rejecting the mid-century morality and modernism of Rodgers and Hammerstein, an era that began in the mid-1990s with rule-shattering shows like *Bat Boy*; *Rent*; *Hedwig and the Angry Inch; Songs for a New World*; *The Capeman*; *Bring in 'da Noise, Bring in 'da Funk*; *The Bomb-itty of Errors*; and others.

Sex, drugs, and rock and roll may be the most powerful cultural forces we know today. All three have always stirred up irrational fear in many of us because all three come from very primal human drives, and that reminds people of their animal side and they don't like that. We want to believe we've civilized out of ourselves those animal instincts and urges and appetites. Sex, drugs, and rock and roll all remind us that we still have a primal side. We still have those appetites. In sex we seek connection. In rock and roll, we seek emotional expression. And in drugs we seek altered consciousness, just as humans have done for centuries, going back through all the world's religions. But for many, the acknowledgement—or even worse, the *indulging*—of those primal urges means anarchy and chaos.

Broadway lyricist E. Y. (Yip) Harburg once wrote, "Words make you think a thought. Music makes you feel a feeling. A song makes you feel a thought. A song can degrade your culture, debase your language; can pollute your air and poison your taste or it can clear your thoughts and refurbish your spirit. It is the pulse of a nation's heart, the fever chart of its health. Are we at peace? Are we in trouble? Are we floundering? Do we feel beautiful? Do we feel ugly? Are we hysterical? Violent? Listen to our songs."

There are those musical theatre traditionalists who believe fervently that theatre music should all still sound more or less like *The Pajama Game* (1954). These purists still wish rock and roll would fade away and leave musical theatre alone. *The Pajama Game* has a nice, tuneful score, but it holds little relevance for today's world of urban violence, terrorism, and new media. Those just aren't our songs anymore. America was a different country with a very different culture when the classic musical drama (the Rodgers and Hammerstein model) and the classic musical comedy (the George Abbott model) were born and perfected. And then everything changed in the 1960s and 1970s, with Vietnam, Watergate, the sexual revolution, and so much more. America is no longer the same country Rodgers and Hammerstein and Jerry Herman wrote about.

Though many people still feel great affection for the classic Rodgers and Hammerstein musicals and their imitators, today most of those shows are more historical artifacts than living theatre. They once had their metaphorical finger on the pulse of American hopes and dreams and fears during the mid-twentieth century, and they certainly moved the art form forward, but it's a different world now, with different music, and America is a very different country.

Many Americans no longer feel a nostalgia for the turn of the last century or for the venerated "rugged individualism" that built our nation. No longer does ragtime or Broadway's longtime workhorse, the foxtrot, represent America's musical voice. Our world today is a mass of complexities and ambiguities, awash in moral and intellectual gray area, so those older shows and musical forms no longer have much relevance for most of us anymore. The homespun folk wisdom of Rodgers and Hammerstein doesn't speak to our very different American zeitgeist today. The old-fashioned musicals created during the questionably dubbed "golden age" of musical theatre (1943–1964) are as distant and foreign to us now as old-school, turn-of-the-twentieth-century operettas like *The Student Prince* (1924) and *Naughty Marietta* (1910). These older shows don't offer the same experience they once did to today's audiences, who live in an age of information and irony.

Though many people may still agree that *Show Boat* (1927) and *Carousel* (1945) are masterpieces, they are nonetheless pre-1960s masterpieces. The 2008 Broadway revival of *South Pacific* worked only because the production infused a dark, foreboding irony underneath the dialogue, giving it more complexity and ambiguity than its original production had, and refashioning it (without rewriting it too much) into a post-1960s work. The same thing happened with *Carousel* in 1994 and *The King and I* in 1996, but it required a fundamentally revisionist approach. What was daring in the 1940s is old-fashioned today.

In contrast, the musicals of the 1960s and '70s really did change almost everything and many of them still seem daring and relevant today, if done well—*Cabaret*, *Hair*, *Man of La Mancha*, *Anyone Can Whistle*, *Com-*

pany, *The Robber Bridegroom*, *Chicago*, *The Rocky Horror Show*, *Jesus Christ Superstar*, *The Best Little Whorehouse in Texas*, *Sweeney Todd*, and others.

The 1960s and 1970s were an explosive period for musical theatre as a serious art form and for our national culture. Once the experimental theatre movement exploded in New York in the '60s, commercial theatre began to borrow its devices and philosophy, and Broadway itself became more experimental. The influence of German director and playwright Bertolt Brecht took hold of the musical theatre around this time as well, with shows like *Cabaret*, *La Mancha*, *Company*, *Follies*, *Chicago*, and lots of others. The American musical theatre got adventurous and ironic in the 1960s, and it got subtextual in the 1970s.

The indomitable leading ladies of the classic musical comedy—Reno Sweeney, Dolly Levi, Mame Dennis, and Marian the Librarian—have given way to more real, complicated women on musical theatre stages today, like the deeply damaged Diana in *Next to Normal* or the abused Celie in *The Color Purple*, or the mentally disabled Clara in *The Light in the Piazza*. The simple, folksy, black-and-white morality of classic musical drama seems curiously quaint and out of touch in light of these newer shows. Today, we get ambiguity and gray area, from musicals like *American Idiot*, *Spring Awakening*, *Bloody Bloody Andrew Jackson*, *bare*, *Love Kills*, and *The Scottsboro Boys*.

This book looks at sex, drugs, and rock and roll, three massively powerful cultural forces, through the musicals that have explored them, along the way also catching a glimpse of how these forces have changed American culture over the twentieth century, from the roaring '20s (*The Wild Party*) through the cultural chaos of the '50s (*Grease*) and the sexual revolution of the '60s (*Hair*) and '70s (*Rocky Horror*, *I Love My Wife*), through the rebirth of the art form in the '90s (*Bat Boy*, *Hedwig*), up through the present, exploring where we've been and where we might be heading.

The Wild Party

It was the age of bootleggers, flappers, and talkies; the hard-won vote for women; widespread social upheaval; and the birth of organized crime. As unprecedented prosperity and sweeping social change dazzled the American public, the restrictions of the Victorian nineteenth century seemed to vanish, and many of the institutions, ideas, and preoccupations of our own age emerged. America became, for the first time, thoroughly modern.

Joseph Moncure March wrote the book-length poem *The Wild Party* in 1926, though it took him two years to find a publisher brave enough to publish it. A more vulgar, more destructive take on Shakespeare's *A Midsummer Night's Dream*, this notorious, streetwise work painted a vivid picture of a decadent and deadly all-night party in late-1920s Manhattan, capturing a potent cocktail of bewildered innocence and worldly cynicism, poised at the roaring, fiery peak of the Jazz Age, just before the Crash of 1929, when much in America would collapse.

It's the story of a desperately damaged relationship between vaudeville dancer Queenie and vaudeville clown Burrs, two vicious, reckless people whose lives are spiraling downward fast, filled to the brim with meaningless sex, drugs, drink, jealousies, and casual betrayals. Intent on hurting each other as publicly as possible, they decide to throw a party to end all parties, and as the guests arrive, we meet an assortment of people living on the fringes of society, New York's artistic demimonde, and we can taste the heady blend of tabloid sizzle, hot jazz, and show biz. After a long night of sex, heroin, and bootleg gin, Burrs's jealousy erupts and a romantic double-triangle ends in tragedy.

Some said the story was based loosely on the infamous Fatty Arbuckle sex scandal. The legendary Beat writer William Burroughs said of the original poem, "It's the book that made me want to become a writer." It's a morality tale, a fable, about how the single-minded pursuit of pure selfish pleasure leads to destruction, and about the death of common civility. When Prohibition was passed, lawfulness took a hit along with alcohol. The fact that millions of people routinely disobeyed a law that had been enshrined in our Constitution arguably encouraged a disrespect for the law in general. If Prohibition was a silly law, maybe other laws were silly as well, some people may have reasoned, perhaps unconsciously. And with their new disregard for law came a companion disregard for other formerly accepted norms of behavior. As it did in the 1960s, when an unjust war and prohibitions against hallucinogenic drugs produced similar results, much of urban America in the 1920s became a hotbed of unchecked sexuality and other behaviors which until recently had been strictly forbidden by Victorian morality. *The Wild Party* shows us a world turned upside down, where two brothers are gay lovers, and there's nothing shocking about a predatory lesbian targeting a fourteen-year-old.

This story is a Walpurgisnacht, an exorcism; the demons have been released and they must be cast out. Watching Andrew Lippa's musical version of *The Wild Party* is like watching a play by Edward Albee or Arthur Miller or Eugene O'Neill; it's the spiritual/emotional equivalent of a horror story. Instead of a vampire representing our uncontrollable sexual drives, here the sexual drives are the monsters themselves, right there on the surface, cutting the middleman out. Instead of a wolf man representing our savage animal side, in this tale the beast within needs no metaphor; he's also right there on the surface. Storytelling like this allows us to explore the darker corners of our own souls in the safety of a darkened theatre, much in the way the original (extremely violent) Grimm's Fairy Tales function for children. It's a roller coaster for the soul.

It was a story begging to be musicalized. Though actual music is only minimally involved in the original story, there's no separating jazz from the 1920s or from Prohibition. They called it the Jazz Age for a reason. The jagged, jumpy, offbeat, improvised anarchy of jazz music characterized this decade most accurately. Jazz was considered a social evil. Larry Stempel writes in his book *Showtime*, "Jazz represented 'devil's music': it corrupted body and soul. 'Hot' or 'sweet,' jazz exuded an unbridled eroticism—the very meaning of the term likely rooted in sex, understood as a transitive verb. Not simply because of its popularity was this music vulgar, but also because as John Philip Sousa put it, it 'excited the baser instincts.' " What language could be better for this story?

But the story craves music also because it's pure melodrama (literally meaning *song drama* in the original Greek), trafficking in outsized emotions and passions and climaxing with a fatal gunshot, and the inherently abstract language of music better communicates emotions than words alone can (which is why film thrillers use almost continuous underscoring). In Andrew Lippa's 2000 stage musical, this story becomes more than just dark fable; the tension and propulsion of the almost continuous music make it a suspense thriller, a film noir. We know from the first scene that violence, both physical and emotional, is the animating force here; and once the romantic triangle is completed, we know it can only end in tragedy. The suspense is in the details. When will the explosion be? Who will she choose? Who will get the gun? Who will end up dead?

Through its exploration into violence and emotional destruction, the show likewise indicts our current culture of rage, which sometimes mirrors this 1920s nightmare all too closely, for the same crimes. And to make sure we catch this resonance, this double perspective, Lippa sometimes uses a contemporary rock and pop musical vocabulary, intertwined throughout the mostly jazz score. This isn't just a story set in the 1920s, his music tells us, it's one that comes with a contemporary point of view, and since it's a story entirely about the power of sex, it's only fitting that rock and roll be a part of its musical language. Where Kander and Ebb (*Cabaret*, *Chicago*, *The Scottsboro Boys*) would have crafted a score for this story entirely in period idioms, Lippa's score marries a 1920s sound with a contemporary pop/rock sound, using period jazz but also electric guitar throughout the show. He uses period music for surface action and more contemporary sounding music for the interior emotional moments. There is lots of dissonance here, complex key changes, moments in the score that approach atonality, and other musical devices that definitely aren't period. The middle section of "I'll Be Here" is pure rock. Without our knowing it, the music shapes our perception of this story.

Likewise, the show itself operates in two opposing theatre styles—on the one hand, a kind of postmodern-Broadway ironic (think *Urinetown*) laced with classic vaudeville (somewhat like *Chicago*); and on the other hand, a show with moments of very honest, raw, naked emotion (think *Love Kills* or *Passion*). There are very intimate, gentle scenes and moments of terrible violence. It's Fosse and Brecht, with some Shakespearean heft thrown in. And it works because that odd mix is exactly what this story is. The poem has that same dangerous split personality, both self-mocking and earnest, and that duality mirrors both Queenie herself and her relationship with Burrs. *The Wild Party* explores the double-edged swords of love and passion and sex. Queenie and Burrs love each deeply, recklessly, but they're poison to each other.

The Wild Party is Shakespearean in its themes and its dramatic arc, as dark as Eugene O'Neill or Edward Albee, as vulgar and carnal as David Mamet. We watch Burrs disintegrate before our eyes and we watch his tragic flaw (jealousy/rage) chew away at him, just as we watch the same thing happen to Othello or Lear. Burrs even gets his own mad scene with "Let Me Drown," begging the party guests to let him commit emotional (or actual?) suicide. And they do. And so he does. Thanks to the heroin and weed and homemade gin, this is a room full of nothing but primal drives—lust, jealousy, revenge, hurt, ego—there is no higher thinking going on here. Lear goes literally mad; here drink, drugs, and desire do the trick for Burrs.

The Birth of the Blues

Andrew Lippa (who also wrote *john & jen* and the score for *The Addams Family*) began work on *The Wild Party* in the mid-1990s. The show went through nine workshops and readings altogether, including Manhattan Theatre Club (1996), the O'Neill Theater Center (1997), MTC again (1997, 1998), in St. Petersburg, Russia (1999), a longer workshop back in the United States in 1999, and another reading that same year, with help from composer Stephen Schwartz (*Godspell*, *Pippin*, *Wicked*).

The Manhattan Theatre Club opened the show off Broadway at the City Center Stage I in February 2000, with Julia Murney (Queenie), Brian D'Arcy James (Burrs), Taye Diggs (Black), and Idina Menzel (Kate), directed by Gabriel Barre. The show ran only fifty-four performances. Strangely enough, a few months later, another musical called *The Wild Party*, based on the same source, opened *on* Broadway, with a score by Michael John LaChiusa, directed by George C. Wolfe, and starring Toni Collette and Mandy Patinkin. That one closed after sixty-eight performances.

Still, the *New York Daily News* called Lippa's show "sizzling, vital and groundbreaking." The *New York Times* said, "Its strong suit is summoning the anxious restlessness behind the hell-bent hedonism of the days of Prohibition." Lippa's *Wild Party* won the 2000 Drama Desk Award for Outstanding Music, the Outer Critics Circle Award for Outstanding Off Broadway Musical, three Lucille Lortel Awards, and an Obie Award. It was nominated for twelve additional Drama Desk Awards, including Outstanding New Musical. A cast album was recorded but because of its limited run, only a single disc was recorded, preserving only about half of the brilliant score. Today the show enjoys regional productions all over the country.

Not everyone was ready for a musical this aggressive, this vulgar, this desperately dark. It's fearless in its writing, explicit in its sexuality, and uncompromising in its ugliness. Its score is as complex and sophisticated and subtle as anything being written for the theatre today. But audiences and critics were uncomfortable with it. *The Wild Party* never lets the audience off the hook, never softens the blow. Lippa's score is as challenging as the show's content. This is real jazz, and though it uses period devices and sounds, it's not 1920s jazz. It's contemporary, modern jazz, dissonant and driving and sometimes veering close to atonality for brief moments. Lippa uses devices from the world of opera, including sung conversations, arias, quartets, trios, complex counterpoint, leitmotifs (musical phrases that represent a character or idea in the story), and much more. Like Stephen Sondheim's musical thriller *Sweeney Todd*, the music almost never stops and often refuses the audience the release of applause after songs, building a kind of tension few musical dramas can muster. It's music that requires an audience to actively listen.

Queenie Was a Blonde

The *Wild Party* score starts with a trumpet solo of the show's primary leitmotif, which will soon accompany the words "Queenie was a blonde." A walking jazz bass line takes over, and an electric guitar wails out fragments of that same musical phrase, rising each time, building to a climax, and then abruptly pulling back to "reveal" the solo voice of Queenie herself, talking about herself in the third person, in lines directly from the source poem:

> Queenie was a blonde
> And her age stood still
> And she danced twice a day in Vaudeville.
> Queenie was a blonde,
> And if looks could kill,
> She would kill twice a day in Vaudeville.

Right away, within a minute of the show starting, Lippa has given us a lot of important information. First of all, from her very first word, we know that this show will include third-person narration (as *Ragtime* also did). We know that characters will be stepping in and out of the story, sometimes living inside the events unfolding, and at other times standing outside them commenting on them (as *Company* also did). We know she's in show business, and even in the modern 1920s, theatre performers were not considered respectable. In a couple minutes, we'll see that in reaction to that, she and her friends have created their own insular world, a mostly nighttime world with different rules, different rituals, and different morality. These first few lines also introduce the idea of violence, even if only in ironic metaphor. But people who work in show business will instantly recognize the violence of show biz lingo—winning over an audience is "killing them," or "slaying them," or "knocking them dead," or "slaughtering them." By the end of the show, perhaps we'll think back on this lyric and realize that here looks *can* kill. After all, the first thing Black notices about Queenie is her hair.

The next few lines do more for setting the period than any piece of furniture on the set:

She had gray eyes,
Lips like coals aglow,
And her face was a
Tinted mask of snow.

Women's makeup was extremely dramatic at that time, as part of the rebellion against the respectable female plainness of the Victorian era. Women's eye shadow was nearly black, their lips as hot red as possible, unnaturally drawn into the famous Betty Boop kewpie-doll look, and their faces were powdered to look vampire pale, perhaps with a small explosion of rouge on the cheeks.

The lyric goes on and tells us about her relationship track record:

With those shoulders,
What a back she had.
Her legs were built
To drive men mad . . .
And she did . . .
She would skid . . .

The men enter, and for first time we see her flirting, playing with them, using her sexuality to get what she wants. Right now, the idea that her body would drive men mad seems like a figure of speech. By the end of the show, we'll realize it's not. Later on the lyric, the men tell us:

She liked her lovers violent,
And she liked her lovers vicious,
But until she found the one man

Who could answer all her wishes,
Queenie was sexually ambitious . . .

And with that, Queenie's vaudeville number is over and it's time for Burrs's introduction. By using the vaudeville form to introduce the two leads, Lippa has created a clever shorthand to give us at least a sketch of their lives, friends, work life, and other details. Burrs begins with what we can assume is his usual act opener, a line that will come back in a much darker context later on:

Are you ready to laugh?
Are you ready to smile?
Are you ready to sing and dance for a while?

Like the song "Let Me Entertain You" in *Gypsy*, the return of these words in Act II will pack a real wallop because the context here is so innocent. Burrs goes on to tell us that he is a star, but he also shows us the dark side—he tells us he's "a very scary clown"—and we find out he is a violent lover. *Where have we heard that before?* The story begins to take shape and we see that this is a thriller, a film noir, the best kind of Hollywood melodrama, but told in the language of jazz and musical theatre, both forms that were blossoming in the late 1920s.

As the number continues, Burrs (and later, also Queenie) narrates the story of how they met, all in the third person. The relationship was built on sex and passion, but nothing else. We get the first hints that these two people are emotionally retarded and perhaps are incapable of real love. As they themselves tell us, "The one thing that they had in common was the fact they were so good in bed." And as the music explodes in fast lines of jazz, Burrs and Queenie jump in bed and start having sex. It's rough sex, but we can tell they both like it. It's consensual. For now. And as they fall asleep, the number ends with one last quote of "Queenie Was a Blonde." This phrase will become a leitmotif representing the danger of Queenie's sex appeal as it ensnares Mr. Black and slowly drives Burrs mad.

All that information, all that insight, all that backstory, all those themes and ideas, the visual and musical style of the piece, the use of narration, and detailed sketches of both main characters along with their tragic flaws, all introduced in this single opening number. It's a sterling example of Sondheim's Ten-Minute Rule, that a musical (or play or movie) can do anything at all, use any device, break any rules, as long as it does it within the first ten minutes, to set the ground rules for the audience. Lippa has given us lots of information we need, he has told us how this show will work structurally and stylistically, and has given us a musical foundation on which he'll build the rest of the score. It's masterfully crafted.

The Apartment

Now the narrative begins. In the first number, the ensemble was the vaudeville chorus for Queenie and Burrs's acts. From this point forward, they'll take on two alternating roles. The first is that of a Brechtian Greek chorus, standing outside the action (though still in character) to narrate or comment on events. The same device is used, though in a less fundamental way, in *Bat Boy* and *Urinetown*. The second function the ensemble plays is as the party guests and as participants in Queenie's great game, the Humiliation of Burrs. In both functions, they are still Madelaine True, Eddie and Mae, the D'Armano Brothers, et al., but sometimes they're standing outside the story, and sometimes they're experiencing the story in real time from the inside. And often, they switch between these functions on a dime, even within a single song. If it sounds confusing, it's not, in a good production. Lippa teaches the audience how his devices work as he uses them, and the audience accepts them all fully.

The number "The Apartment" first shows us the state of disrepair of Queenie and Burrs's relationship. Lippa lays out for us the powder keg that just needs lighting: it's incredibly hot, the papers are full of violent crime, and then Queenie starts complaining, which starts an argument. Before we can digest what's happening, he's calling her a "lazy slut," he's throwing her to the bed and raping her, she's kicking him in the groin, and then pulling a knife on him. "Touch me again and I'll kill you," she says.

That's who these people are.

And all of it happens to highly charged jazz music. As Burrs reads the paper, Lippa sets "murder, rape, and suicide" to an expanding tangle of counterpoint, letting it overwhelm us as it overwhelms Burrs. This is the zeitgeist. Prohibition had made cynics of everyone and criminals of many. *The Wild Party* shows us that this culture of lawlessness bled dangerously into personal relationships and social customs.

"Out of the Blue" is a classic musical theatre "I Want" song, in which the character tells us outright what her motivation is and what she wants.

Queenie reaches her Obligatory Moment, the moment toward which everything before it leads and from which everything after it results. Listen to the opening lyrics of "Out of the Blue" and notice how passive Queenie is—she wants something to happen *to* her. But as the song progresses, she recognizes this and she makes the decision to take action for the first time, to forge her own destiny. She considers the options and picks the worst possible choice. She gets the idea that in order to bring passion back to their relationship, she'll throw a big party for all their friends and then work to humiliate Burrs as publicly as possible. (It's George and Martha from *Who's Afraid of Virginia Woolf?*, but originally written, in poem form, decades earlier.) But notice that Queenie never talks about love here, just passion and excitement. Their relationship can't work because there's nothing real there, but neither of them knows that. After "Out of the Blue," the audience certainly knows it. At the climax of the song, Queenie sings, "No boundaries, no limits, no compromise!" This is the first of three times we'll hear that phrase, and each time it will get darker. It will serve as signposts along Queenie's journey. As it is in the very best theatre songs, Queenie changes during this number; she's not in the same place at the end as she was at the beginning, and the plot has gotten underway.

The real shame in connection to this show is that the original cast album doesn't include so much of Lippa's fascinating, complex score. This show is as close to a jazz opera as it can be without actually crossing that line. There is a fluidity and a sense of perpetual motion to the score that only a few shows, like *Sweeney Todd* and *Ragtime*, have achieved. But its full artistry has not been preserved.

What a Party!

In the darkly ironic number "What a Party," Lippa introduces the second most important musical leitmotif, a jumpy, syncopated jazz bass line that will always be associated with the party itself. Here it's used as accompaniment to the introduction of many of these characters to the audience, who literally tell us that "the game begins." This bass line alternates with other music that will also come back time and again throughout the show. But the lyric prepares us for the ugliness ahead:

Lightly, quickly,
Slightly sickly,
Pasty, tasty,

Like birds of prey
'Round the hors d'oeuvre tray
. . .
Panting, prying,
Loudly lying,
Raving, craving . . .

At the end of the number, Queenie appears, and Burrs and the guests treat her to a lavish Ziegfeld welcome—the secret dream of every vaudevillian, and Burrs surely knows that. It's a little gift from him to her.

We segue directly into the Latin-flavored "Raise the Roof," mirroring the 1920s' new interest in Latin America and Latin musical forms. And Queenie tells us exactly where she is emotionally. She's spoiling for a fight.

Let's raise the roof.
Let's make a scene.
Let's hope the Gods of Love
Will shine above
And show the way.
Let's call the shots.
Let's roll the dice.
Take my advice,
It always pays to raise the roof.

This is a call for chaos. *But be careful what you wish for.* Short dialogue scenes are interspersed throughout the song, introducing characters more fully through what seem like cheap vaudeville gags, but what are actually very clever ways of sneaking in character information. Burrs asks Eddie, "When's the next fight?" and Queenie answers, "Maybe tonight." She's already thinking about how to get these two into combat.

The Sound of the Bell

Burrs tries to pick up the fourteen-year-old Nadine, but Queenie gets in his way. The music shifts dramatically to a dark, moody underscore, and the psychosexual chess game between Queenie and Burrs begins. "The sound of the bell" and Queenie's plan to "come out swinging" are both metaphors and, later in Act II, they will become literal. Queenie makes her way through most of the men there and settles on Eddie, as we knew she would. But her fun is interrupted by the entrance of Kate, former hooker, sometime best friend to Queenie. Kate makes a characteristically loud, boorish entrance with "Look at Me Now," decrying Prohibition and endorsing hard drinking, in another example of the casual lawlessness of the urban culture. It's a high-energy jazz number and its lyric is overflowing with subtextual self-loathing, just as her later solo, "The Life of the Party," will be. Kate has also brought along an outsider, the reserved Mr. Black. Interestingly, he is the only one of the four central characters we meet talking. All the others we met singing. In other words, Mr. Black is different; he's not of this world.

The scene continues, somewhat cinematically, as we roam the room, catching snippets of various conversations, random party chatter, much of it set to music, and the rest underscored, all while the room takes stock of the newcomer. In a significant moment, Kate asks Burrs, "Don't you want to be the life of the party?" He answers, "I thought I was." Those words will come back in Act II in a much darker context. Finally, we pick up a conversation between Queenie and Black as they meet for the first time, and then between Black and Kate, as the second chess game, this one initiated by Kate, gets underway.

In the most operatic moment of the show, we get the beautifully constructed "Poor Child," a jazz ballad quartet of both emotional and musical complexity, and all four of our leads get a chance to tell us exactly where they stand now that all the various games are underway. There are four competing agendas here and none of them are compatible. We know from this point on that there will be some losers here tonight. This is the song that earns the show the weight of the tragedy to come. Up to now, the show has been cynical, flippant, sarcastic, but "Poor Child" is serious and deeply felt. This is where we can see for the first time how impossible this conflict really is, and how surely we are headed to a very dark place.

This is no musical comedy.

Intermission, Sort Of

We now leave the unrelenting intensity of the central story to give the audience an emotional breather. Lippa built the score so that it continually builds up tension but only rarely allows the audience to release that tension through applause. So many of the songs are interrupted or segue directly into the next number. Kate's showstopper, "Look at Me Now," segues directly into the next number, taking the audience's release away. Later in the act, "Maybe I Like It That Way" will do the same thing.

But now, a bit of a rest as we meet the others. First we get Madelaine's hilariously subversive "An Old-Fashioned Love Story," an old-school charm song laced with postmodern irony and twenty-first-century sexual frankness (although the 1920s were pretty sexually frank). It's a funny, rowdy song, but it's also (partly) about this woman wanting to seduce a fourteen-year-old girl. The whole show is full of that kind of dissonance. It reminds us that we are outsiders in this world as much as Black is and that sex is war.

Some more musical narration takes us into the first showstopping dance (which also will not allow the audience a release at its end), "The Juggernaut." It's a nasty, sexy, savage dance number, sort of fulfilling the role of a "new dance craze" number in a 1920s musical comedy, but also doing so much narrative and character work at the same time. Just as "A Wild, Wild Party" will do in a few minutes, "The Juggernaut" comments slyly on the events of the evening—this train that Queenie and Burrs have started is now unstoppable, a literal juggernaut. As we will see over the course of the show, the darkness and anger that have fueled this evening will not subside until it's too late. Just look at the lyric—it's a challenge issued both to the party guests and *also* the audience:

> Will you do the Juggernaut?
> Can you do the Juggernaut?
> Put your foot into the ring
> And just start swinging.
> Man and woman Juggernaut,
> Everybody Juggernaut . . .

And isn't that exactly what Queenie and Burrs—and later, others—are doing? They are putting their foot into the ring, the fight, the arena for this public display of dysfunction, and they're coming out swinging blindly, with no regard for who gets hit along the way. In Act II, "just start swinging" will become literal. Throughout the score, Lippa creates numbers that work both as period pieces and as modern dramatic pieces. During the course of "The Juggernaut," Queenie goes after Eddie, Burrs goes after Nadine, Kate gets jealous and knocks Nadine to the floor, and Burrs goes after Queenie. The gloves are off.

Just when Burrs is about to explode, the charmingly incestuous D'Armano Brothers rescue the party with a song they've written, and, in keeping with the dual realities of the story, their song is a fragment of "Queenie Was a Blonde," from the opening. Only after this fragment is there finally room for applause, but now it's only the party guests who are applauding—the audience has just seen Burrs come within a hair of beating Queenie.

The D'Armano Brothers (both gay lovers *and* brothers) proceed to announce a number from their new musical, the Bible epic *Good Heavens*. And just like all of Cecil B. DeMille's silent film Bible epics, *Good Heavens* has an orgy scene. But as we listen to the song "A Wild, Wild Party," we realize this isn't really a Bible story—they're singing about *this* party *tonight*. Burrs and Queenie are cast as Adam and Eve, and if you listen closely, this is a morality tale about the tug of war between pleasure and responsibility, about immediate gratification versus future consequences—in other words, about Burrs and Queenie. What makes a funny song even funnier is that none of the people singing seem to notice that the story applies to them. Just like Adam and Eve, Burrs and Queenie ignore the rules of decency and morality, and it will lead to tragedy. This song's main melody will return in Act II, representing the emptiness of this party. Most eerily, the last verse of the song has them literally partying in Hell and ends with the line "And we're inviting you!" This subtle involving of the audience in this moral indictment will return in the last song of the show. This will become a party in Hell, and the audience has already RSVP'd.

The deceptively innocent diversions continue with Eddie and Mae's "Two of a Kind," and again, it's an old-school charm song but it's vulgar and raw. Eddie calls Mae his "buttered bride," mangling the title of the popular opera of the time, *The Bartered Bride*. Mae talks about farting. Eddie calls her a "sexy gopher." This isn't the *Ziegfeld Follies*. But as we listen, maybe we realize that even though these two are simpletons, even though we may laugh at Eddie, who seems like he's been hit in the head too many times, at least these two have a loving, generally respectful relationship. The only other relationship in the room that could possibly be called happy (depending to some extent on how it's played) is between the incestuous gay brothers. What does that say about this world?

This Place and All This Fuss

The last two songs of Act I give us real, sympathetic insight into Queenie and Burrs. We understand in a deeper way how damaged they are, and this prepares us for the weight of Act II. Queenie and Burrs have a profound physical connection but they are too damaged to connect in a deeper way and too lost to understand that.

The last section of Act I begins with a lovely fragment of a song called "Of All the Luck." Black makes the mistake of trying to turn Queenie against Burrs, but she stops him, and the number segues into one of the most emotionally naked ballads in musical theatre, "Maybe I Like It This Way." In a desperately honest confession, Queenie tells Black (and us) that as awful as it is with Burrs, she's not sure she wants to leave. It's this lyric that raises the show above its careless vulgarity and gives it the credentials of a truth-teller. Queenie sings:

> I see his pain.
> I hear his cry.
> He pulls me to the edge,
> But I don't ask him why.
> I understand and I obey.
> Maybe I like it this way.

As underscoring continues, Queenie tells us, minus the show biz of the opening, about meeting Burrs, and in retrospect we can see the warning signs. It wasn't as perfect as they told us it was earlier. Then she sings:

> If I could change,
> If I could grow,
> I'd ask for nothing more
> And through that door I'd go.
> But if I'm through, why do I stay?
> Maybe he wants me . . .
> Maybe he needs me . . .
> Maybe he loves me . . .
> Maybe I like it this way.

It's that word *maybe* that encapsulates Queenie's great tragic flaw. Her commitment to Burrs is built entirely on *maybe*.

And her song segues directly into the Act I finale, Burrs's companion confessional piece, a bold, almost operatic finale, "What Is It About Her?" Burrs's first lines say it all: "What is it about her that makes me want her? What is it about her that turns me pale?" He *wants* her; he doesn't *love* her, and their relationship makes him sick. Soon, Queenie is singing counterpoint, and we realize now that these are not just nasty people; they are addicted to each other. They both are abusers and they both are victims; they both need rescue, but neither one will get it. This is a tragedy, after all. Burrs sings:

This woman makes me cry,
This woman makes me burn!
This woman's eye
Can cut me to the core.
The hatred that I see
Has been reserved for me,
Yet I want more and more . . .

And the act ends with a howl of despair from Burrs, "How loud must I scream *no?*" as Black kisses Queenie and *blackout*. The audience goes into the lobby knowing only one thing: there is disaster ahead.

The Life of the Party

As Lippa did early in the first act, at the beginning of Act II he gives Kate "The Life of the Party," a number that works on several levels at once. It's direct address to the audience, like the other narration in the show has been, but this is also a revealing character song, full of defiance, bitterness, and some self-mocking irony. It's a classic, though alcoholic, "I Want" song. Depending to some extent on how it's played, it's a one-on-one conversation with the audience, actually pulling us into the party, making us feel like we're just another guest that Kate has cornered. Sure, she may be the life of the party, but she's also alone. Her advances on Burrs have come to nothing and Queenie has stolen her date. She's challenging the audience, daring them to live the kind of fearless life she leads, betting that they don't have it in them, but both she and the audience know that none of us would want to lead her life. She pretends to cherish the role of "life of the party," but we can see how miserable she is.

This song slices through the fun of the first act to remind the audience of the danger behind the hilarity, and one of the ways this is done is by dropping more hints of violence in the lyric, for instance, "Don't you wanna be there running the show until it's time to go or till it's time to kill?"

A transition piece built on the main theme of "A Wild, Wild Party" (that morality tale about the consequences of our actions) takes us back to the plot and into the next song. The guests sing, "How many years have passed her by?" and we don't know if they mean Kate, who just finished her song, or Queenie, who's about to start hers. In between the lines of lyric, we hear in the band a slightly altered quote of "A Wild, Wild Party." Because it describes them both and invokes the idea of consequences, it transitions seamlessly into the next song, "Who Is This Man?," Queenie's companion piece to Burrs's Act I finale. Lippa has given them mirror image soliloquies, split across the intermission. And Queenie's piece is fascinating in its construction, made up of bits and pieces of music, representing her fractured, racing mind. She finds herself in classically dysfunctional relationships (though she wouldn't know what that phrase meant), with *two* men now, one of them abusive and codependent, and the other one a rescuer and willing victim.

Her song is an operatic aria and a solidly built Broadway soliloquy, but it's broken somehow, just like Queenie. Much of the music is based, sometimes loosely, sometimes exactly, on the music of "Maybe I Like It This Way." The last section is based on the melody of "Out of the Blue," Queenie's decision song. She ends with the line, "Who's it gonna be?" ironically quoting "The Life of the Party."

"The Gal for Me" is a song that was cut from the original off Broadway production, but remains in the licensed materials. True, the song could be eliminated without damaging the show greatly, but it offers the audience and the story several valuable things. First, Queenie and Black get a moment of respite, no fighting, no hiding. Black gets a chance to be charming and attract Queenie in more than just a physical way, and he is able to plead his case to Queenie that he was a player, that he was insincere, and that he has learned his lesson. Or is he telling Queenie's story, hoping to cajole her into a decision? Either way, Black is *charming* Queenie instead of *taking* her, as Burrs would. Though she is falling for him, she questions his authenticity, and he rises to the occasion with his big power ballad, "I'll Be Here," wherein he offers to make a serious commitment to her. In the process he becomes the anti-Burrs, emotionally available, romantic, protective, an adult. But Lippa complicates it just a bit because in both "The Gal for Me" and "I'll Be Here," Black is telling a story about "a man" and what "he" should say to the woman he loves. It gives Black and Queenie a thin veneer of safety, since neither one is actually declaring love, which both know would be dangerous.

Taken together, "The Gal for Me" and "I'll Be Here" form a beautifully crafted character scene, in which we get to know Black better, he and

Queenie get to take their relationship to the next level of intimacy (and thereby raise all the stakes), and they move forward Queenie's coming decision about which man to choose. Without both pieces, Queenie and Black's relationship doesn't get enough time to develop sufficiently to make the end as emotionally potent as it should be.

There's another transition piece called "Listen to Me" that is a four-way conversation, again arguably operatic, and it uses accompaniment from the opening number when Burrs and Queenie first met. Kate tries to inject a little of "The Life of the Party," but Burrs suddenly lunges out to choke Queenie, and when he's stopped by Black, he crumbles to the floor in tears. We segue into Burrs's great Mad Scene, "Let Me Drown," cast in the form of a terrifying fantasy vaudeville number. He tries to quote Queenie's pivotal moment when she decided to throw the party, the moment that led him to this: "I think we're due for a . . . I think we're due for a . . . I think we're due for a . . ." But with the clarity of a madman, he now sees what he couldn't see before and his brain suddenly careens off in a different direction. He asks to be allowed to commit suicide without rescue. Burrs warns the partygoers, "By tomorrow morning we could be dead drunk, or just dead." His lyric works on two levels. First, we can take "drown" to be slang for getting drunk (as in "drown my sorrows"); in other words, he's asking to be left alone to drink until he passes out. But he's also pleading for release from the surety of being rescued. Until now, Queenie has been his salvation; but he knows she's probably gone now and he has nothing left. He declares that he will now commit suicide—symbolically, if not actually.

The Fight

As he does throughout the show, Lippa uses music here as artfully as the best thriller film scores. The guests appropriate Kate's "Life of the Party" melody as Burrs literally becomes the life of the party, in a fight with Eddie, exactly as Queenie had predicted in Act I. But it hasn't happened the way she planned. Nothing has. Her plan is spinning out of control. At the end of the fight, Black breaks a bottle over Eddie's head and saves Burrs. Kate nurses Burrs's wounds by giving him heroin till he passes out.

Black's act is shocking to Queenie, that someone could be that decent—saving his rival—and it throws her. Might this really be a decent man? She sings to him, "I know nothing about you . . ." So Black opens himself up to her. "I wanted change. I wanted something to excite me," he confesses. He wants what Queenie already has—passion, excitement—but she knows now that's not enough. Black is still too young to know that. He's the same person Queenie was years ago when she first got to New York, but she's no longer that person. Queenie reprises "Out of the Blue," revisiting those original decisions and motivations, and she sees how wrong she was. She's growing. And Black wins her. They retire to the bed for sex, accompanied by the pulsating, aggressively carnal song "Come with Me," and ending with a full-cast musical orgasm. Afterward, their love is no longer pure.

Same rule as slasher movies.

Burrs wakes, and when he calls Queenie's name, the electric guitar echoes him with two melodies that have shown up several times in the show. First, there is the music from "Out of the Blue," when Queenie is singing about "all our differences"; also in the piece "He Was Calm," when Queenie sings, "And I can do it!"; and also when Kate first tells Black that "her name is Queenie." They're all moments that moved the game forward, and Burrs is about to make the final move of the game. The second melody quotes Burrs's confessional "What Is It About Her?" That is his trap and now he must try to escape from it.

Burrs finds Queenie and Black in bed together and after a scuffle, he pulls a gun on them. He sings to Queenie, "Who's it gonna be?" both echoing Kate's "Life of the Party" and paralleling Queenie's quote of the same phrase at the end of "Who Is This Man?" But now the question isn't about who Queenie will end up with; now it's about who will leave this party alive and who will end up dead. The music segues into Burrs's final breakdown, "Make Me Happy," a powerful trio in which both Queenie and Black try to talk him down. He sings, "In my hands, the future was golden. Now it's what I hold in my palm,"—his gun. That's his only future. Queenie sings a section quoting Burrs's vaudeville act back to him, trying to distract him, hoping this can reach him.

As the story comes to its tragic end, Queenie sings to the audience the moral of this fable, in her song "How Did We Come to This?" as she comes to a new self-awareness. If there is any glimmer of hope in this story, it is that Queenie *understands*. Like the decade of the 1920s itself, the party here is over. The price must now be paid.

The Wild Party works as metaphor or microcosm for those moments in American history and culture when anger and fear supersede reason and decency. It happened during the Depression (just months ahead for these characters) and during the 1960s, and in the poisonous cultural atmosphere of America today. Arguably, this isn't as dark a show as *Sweeney Todd* or *The Threepenny Opera*, because at least in *The Wild Party*, there is some clarity, maybe even redemption of sorts, at the end. As the show closes, Queenie asks the partygoers—and the audience—quite sincerely, "How did we come to this?" If there is a message here, maybe it's that those darker impulses and emotions are inside all of us, and we're not always conscious of when they take us over. It takes real effort and vigilance to keep those dark forces at bay, to keep them from destroying ourselves the people around us (a message this show shares with *Bat Boy*). It's not always easy to be civil, but when we give up trying, we get what we deserve. As Queenie sings:

> We're all so sure.
> We're all so wise.
> No limits,
> No bound'ries,
> No compromise.
> Laughing at our neighbors,
> Smiling through a hiss,
> How did we come to this?
>
> We're all amused,
> We're all inspired,
> So cunning,
> So clever,
> And so admired.
> Easy to be angry,
> Easy to dismiss,
> How did we come to this?
>
> Tell me I've been
> Living in a daydream,
> Tell me I've been talking in my sleep.
> If I've been awake,
> Pardon my mistake,
> But time is running low,
> And talk is growing cheap.

We play our games,
We place our bets,
No witness,
No weakness,
And no regrets.
Filling up with frenzy,
Killing with a kiss,
How did we all come to this . . . ?

With any good narrative work of art, you can always find parallels to our world today—our politics, our social issues, our culture. That's what good art does. As long as we recognize that other people in other times and places will see other parallels, there's no harm is particularizing the art. In *The Wild Party*, we can see both rabid, self-involved consumption, which mirrors America's recent fiscal and political history; and we can also see a stark morality tale about the dangers of allowing the death of civility in our society, which mirrors the crazy, culturally combative times of early twenty-first century America.

Many of the characters in *The Wild Party* are people who "perform" much of their daily lives. They are the kind of people who wear a conscious persona, who show the world a version of themselves that is not their real self. We all know people like that. People who perform being artsy and colorful, who perform being sophisticated or worldly, who perform being outrageous. It's an act, designed to leave a particular impression or elicit a particular response. Though in the Manhattan demimonde of 1928, it was for different reasons than it is today. In that context, it was about being more daring than the next person, about being a social and moral adventurer, about being "thoroughly modern." But just as it can be now, that constant performing could be destructive. It treats truth and reality as lesser values. It doesn't matter to Queenie (until it's too late) that she is destroying the man she supposedly loves.

While much of America today arguably prizes authenticity above almost anything else (thanks to the 1960s and rock 'n' roll), a small slice of Americans are so terrified of no longer controlling our culture that they have retreated to the social performance of their beloved 1950s. And perhaps more than the disagreement over actual issues, it's this cultural divide over the basic idea of how we talk to each other that seems most dangerous. If people with the two competing visions of reality can't talk to each other, then where do we go from here? We see in *The Wild Party* what happens when two people who have had an emotional commitment to each other can no longer talk to each other or even hear each other. And even though Andrew Lippa wrote *The Wild Party* in the late 1990s (tellingly, toward the end of the Clinton years), his work is truthful enough and universal enough to offer us a lesson for these times—that a complete breakdown in communication leads to nothing but darkness.

How did we come to this?

Grease

Adolescents tend to be passionate people, and passion is no less real because it is directed toward a hot-rod, a commercialized popular singer, or the leader of a black-jacketed gang.
—Edgar Friedenberg, The Vanishing Adolescent

The year is 1959, a pivotal moment in American cultural history, when rock and roll was giving birth to the sexual revolution and much in American culture was about to be turned upside down. Record companies were releasing more than a hundred singles every week and the country was about to explode. *Grease*, today often considered a trivial little musical, is actually the story of America's tumultuous crossing over from the 1950s to the 1960s, throwing over repression and tradition for freedom and adventure and a generous helping of cultural chaos, a time when the styles and culture of the disengaged and disenfranchised became overpowering symbols of teenage power and autonomy. Originally a rowdy, rebellious, oversexed, and *insightful* piece of alternative theatre when it opened on Broadway in 1972, *Grease* was inspired by the rule-busting success of *Hair* and shows like it, rejecting the trappings of other Broadway musicals for a more authentic, more visceral, more radical theatre experience that revealed great cultural truths about America—an experience largely forgotten by most productions of the show today. As Ben Brantley wrote in the *New York Times*, comparing the clumsy 2007 revival of *Grease* to its original production, "Given the choice between slick soullessness and rough-edged sincerity, I'll take the latter any day."

In his book *Broadway Musicals: The Biggest Hit and the Biggest Flop of the Season*, Peter Filichia writes, "The 1950s that *Grease* wanted on stage represented the first time (and not the last) that peer pressure trumped time-honored family values. The respect of your friends and acquaintances had become more important than that of your family, school, and church. Society had changed; *Grease* knew it, and told the truth."

It was in some ways a response to *Bye Bye Birdie*, which had introduced rock and roll (sort of) to Broadway in 1960. But *Bye Bye Birdie* and the depiction of its fictional rock star Conrad Birdie came at rock music from an adult perspective peppered with a big helping of condescension and a lack of understanding of this powerful new cultural force. *Grease* came at rock and roll from the perspective of the teenagers who lived it. Riffing on the crazy popularity of early rock and roll star Conway Twitty (not Elvis, like everyone thinks; just compare the names), in *Bye Bye Birdie* rock and roll destroys. In *Grease,* rock and roll heals, it bonds, it protects.

Like *Hair* before it and *The Rocky Horror Show*, which would come a year later, *Grease* is a concept musical, a fascinating hybrid of plotted book musical and conceptual revue, that's about sexual repression versus sexual freedom, about the clumsy, tentative, but clearly emerging sexual rebellion of the late 1950s, as seen through the lens of the middle of the sexual revolution in the 1970s. It's about the near-carnal passion 1950s teenagers felt for their rock and roll, the first art form that arguably *changed* human sexuality. The phrase *rock and roll* was originally African American urban slang for sexual intercourse, going as far back as the 1920s, and it made its way onto many rhythm-and-blues recordings before the 1950s. As theatre, *Grease* finds its roots in the rawness, the rowdiness, the lack of polish that made *Hair* and other experimental pieces in the 1960s such cultural phenomena. The impact of *Hair* on *Grease* can be seen even in the two shows' titles, both taking as their primary symbols the hairstyles of young Americans to signify rebellion and sexuality (and rock and roll), just as the musical *Hairspray* would do again years later. As the characters of *Hair* and *Grease* reject conformity and authority, so too do *Hair* and *Grease* as theatre pieces. Like *Hair*, *Grease* is an anti-musical, closer to the experimental theatre pieces of New York's off off Broadway movement in the '60s, and light years from other musicals running on Broadway at the time like *No No Nanette* (in a bloated revival), *Sugar*, *The Rothschilds*, *Applause*, or *A Little Night Music*.

Good-bye to Sandra Dee

Also like *Hair*, *Grease* is about *authenticity*, the watchword of that first rock and roll generation. Teen sexuality had been an issue in America since the invention of the rumble seat, always moving forward like a freight train, forever going faster and farther; and *Grease* is a snapshot of America right before teen sexuality exploded, examining the early cracks in the armor of middle-class respectability and repression, the fantasy American Dream that never was but that came beaming into Americans' homes over the television airwaves.

Movie star Sandra Dee becomes *Grease*'s overarching metaphor for the artificiality of adult American life, a symbol that needed piercing. Sandra Dee was a big star at this point, and just in the two years that *Grease* spans, she released *The Restless Years* (1958), *The Reluctant Debutante* (1958), *A Stranger in My Arms* (1959), *Gidget* (1959), *Imitation of Life* (1959), *The Wild and the Innocent* (1959), and *A Summer Place* (1959), jumping back and forth between empty-headed teen comedies and stark melodrama. Today, it may be hard to understand what Sandra Dee represented, but she was the poster girl for the big studios' attempts to make teen movies, a genre which was up until that point the exclusive territory of small, low-budget producers like the ubiquitous Roger Corman (*The Little Shop of Horrors*, *Bucket of Blood*, and others). But the studios' teen flicks were inevitably artificial in the extreme, creating a freakish—and clueless—adult imitation of the teen world, a kind of cultural Frankenstein's monster, that teens could see right through. To savvy teenagers, Sandra Dee was a teen sellout, and in a world where authenticity was the goal, there was nothing worse. She was a fake, in her life, in her acting style, and in her onscreen emotions. Teen audiences didn't want that; they wanted *High School Hellcats* and *Teenage Doll*. But adults loved Sandra Dee; she reassured them that *their* teen daughter was a "good girl."

Still, many American girls took Sandra Dee as a role model, just not the *real* Sandra Dee, the cheery public character Sandra Dee, confusing her onscreen persona with her real life personality. Millions of Americans in postwar America were trying to live an American Dream that was pure fiction, particularly for the working class; and Sandra Dee is the fiction at the heart of Sandy's story arc in *Grease*. But on another level, the metaphor gets even deeper—and this demonstrates the craftsmanship of this script—because Sandy's relationship with Danny mirrors Sandra Dee's difficult real-life relationship with Bobby Darin. As Rizzo taunts Sandy with "Look at Me, I'm Sandra Dee," she doesn't know how dark that dark underbelly really is. Daphne Merkin wrote in the *New York Times* in 2005 at the time of Sandra Dee's death:

> [T]he "darling, pink world," as she herself characterized it, that Sandra Dee was thought to inhabit by her fans had always been a grotesque mockery, plagued not by an overripened case of virginity but by childhood incest. The girl with brimming brown eyes and a fizzy lilt to her voice was born Alexandria Zuck in Bayonne, New

> Jersey. Her parents divorced when she was five; her father, a bus driver, disappeared from her life shortly thereafter, and her mother, Mary, married a much-older real-estate entrepreneur named Eugene Duvan within a few years . . . Worse yet, Dee's devoted but manipulative mother turned a conveniently blind eye to the defiled sexual appetites of her new husband. Duvan, who liked to tease his wife that he married her "just to get Sandy," started having sex with his beautiful stepdaughter when she was 8 and continued doing so almost until his death when she was 12.

As a result, Sandra Dee suffered from anorexia, depression, and alcoholism throughout her life. All this made her cynically manufactured façade of sweetness even darker and more complex. This was the conventional, repressed, hypocritical, manufactured life from which Sandy Dumbrowski must escape. Merkin wrote:

> The thing is, [her career] happened so fast, was over practically before it began, that we can almost be forgiven for misconstruing her as a cultural simulacrum: a blip on the monitor, a media invention, an adorable incarnation of a feminine ideal of the reluctant or unwitting nymphet, rather than a flesh-and-blood creature with needs and wishes (not to mention raging demons) of her own.

Grease looks at the '50s with twenty-twenty hindsight and it sees the darkness and deception of the decade's role models and authority figures. Sandra Dee wasn't happy in her real life because she was never allowed to be herself—to be *authentic*—and Sandy Dumbrowski suffers the same problem. Sandra Dee represents not just strict morality and virginity in *Grease*, but the entire manufactured mainstream culture of 1950s America, a culture the kids of *Grease* reject (which means Rizzo is pretty good at choosing metaphors). This was arguably the first time in history that parents' worldview no longer matched their teenager's worldview. American teenagers now had independent life experience, disconnected from their parents' experience, and so they were coming to new and different conclusions about how they saw themselves and their world.

Still, for many kids, the '50s were a time when America caught its breath. After decades of upheaval—World War I, Prohibition, the Depression, World War II, and the Korean War—suddenly times weren't so hard and the world didn't seem as dangerous. (Kids were told about the threat of a Cold War nuclear attack, but it didn't mean much to some of them and didn't really affect their lives.) Before the '50s, if kids worked it was for the family's survival. During the '50s, if kids worked it might be because they were saving up to buy a car or buy parts for the car they already had. It was a happy, playful decade for some young (white) Americans, as family cars transformed adult culture and rock and roll transformed teen culture. One of the peripheral points of *Grease* is that kids of the '50s could *afford* to worry only about their own trivial problems; there was no world war, no Hitler to fear anymore. Though *Grease* implies many complex ideas, it is actually about the ordinary, everyday lives of a group of teenagers. Their chief worries are whether or not they'll have a date to the dance and can they get the car; yet the implications of those lives speak volumes more.

Today, some conservatives idealize the 1950s as a time of moral clarity, patriotism, family stability, traditional values, a time to which America should return. To many American traditionalists, the 1950s are the Eden of modern America's superpower creation story, a time of unstained innocence and clear-cut rules. And *Grease* chronicles the cultural upheaval that conservatives perceive as the (avoidable) expulsion from Eden. But that mythological 1950s never actually existed. As Grace Palladino asks in her excellent book *Teenagers: An American History*, "Did the world really work better when girls had no choice in life but to get married, blacks knew their servile place, and working class kids, who lived outside the charmed circle of upper-middle class life, were invisible?" What traditionalists remember as patriotism was more like nationalistic terrorism, demagoguery, witch hunting. What they remember as family stability was really mind-numbing conformity and drug-addicted suburban housewives. What they label "traditional values" were nothing short of race, class, and gender warfare. And it all boiled down to two central bogeymen, inextricably linked in the minds of the mainstream: sex and rock and roll.

The story of *Grease* is set during the 1958–1959 school year, at a time when America was facing the preliminary rumblings of the sexual revolution that would arrive in the mid-1960s and blossom in the '70s, only to be ended by AIDS in the early '80s. And like *The Rocky Horror Show* did later, *Grease* shows us how America reacted to this tumultuous time though two of its main characters. Danny Zuko (along with Rizzo and Kenickie) represents that segment of American teens who were already sexually active in the 1940s and '50s, and it's Danny who ultimately frees the conforming Sandy to express her sexuality without fear or shame, leading her into a new life and a new decade of sexual freedom. This same theme is also at the heart, though far more cautiously, of the 1959 film *A Summer Place*, starring Sandra Dee and Troy Donahue. Sandy Dumbrowski (notice how ethnic all the character names are, to suggest that they are working class) represents mainstream America, reluctant to throw off the sexual repression of the conforming 1950s for the sexual adventuring of the 1960s. *That* is the story of *Grease*—the story of mid-century America—the way sex was changing and the part rock and roll and cars and drive-ins played in that messy, mystical transformation. With twenty-twenty hindsight, *Grease* knows that the '50s were only a brief window of surface respite before the dark, dangerous times would return, with Vietnam, race riots, the antiwar movement, Watergate, and recession, and all that darkness is bubbling just under the surface of these teenage hijinks.

In the clumsy movie version of *Grease*, the central love story might have been the point, but on stage that romance is just a device for making a larger, more interesting point. *Grease* onstage isn't about Danny and Sandy (which is why fifteen of the show's twenty songs have nothing at all to do with them); it is about how rock and roll changed sex in America. And those who criticize *Grease* for its "immoral" ending don't understand what this show is about—and they haven't really paid attention to the lyric of the show's finale, "All Choked Up." Sandy is no victim here; she's becoming a women's libber.

The "Word" Made Flesh

To a large extent, the 1970s marked the end of the Rodgers and Hammerstein revolution; their old-fashioned values and patriotism no longer seemed relevant. It was the decade that gave permanent berth to both the concept musical and the rock musical, both explored during the '60s but now taking their rightful place in mainstream musical theatre. These were shows that rejected the sunny optimism of earlier decades and instead revealed the feelings of rage and loss that pervaded America in this era of Vietnam and Watergate. The concept musical had been germinating since Marc Blitzstein's very political, very angry *The Cradle Will Rock* in 1937, but it wasn't until Stephen Sondheim and Hal Prince's *Company* in 1970 that the concept musical was in a position to change the art form. The rock musical had been born with *Expresso Bongo* in 1958 and became mainstream with *Hair* in 1968, but it became a fixture on

Broadway during the '70s, partly because the definition of *rock* was so pliable, so inclusive by then. A rock musical could be *Jesus Christ Superstar*, *Hair*, *Two Gentlemen of Verona*, *The Rocky Horror Show*, or *Grease*, none of which sounded anything like the others; and yet they all shared a disdain for authority, a taste for rebellion, and a sexual frankness to which only the language of rock and roll could give full voice. *Grease* found its roots in both of these movements, taking inspiration not just from *Hair* but also from *Company*. Like the early Sondheim/Prince shows, *Grease* gave us snapshots instead of narrative, a tapestry of impressions that added up to a bigger picture and a life-changing decision. At the end of *Company*, Robert chooses to commit; in *Grease* Sandy chooses to rebel.

The phenomenon that was *Grease* began its long life in 1971 at Chicago's Kingston Mines Theatre, where its authors, Jim Jacobs and Warren Casey, were acting ensemble members. Opening February 5, 1971, the show was largely based on Jacobs's experience at Taft High School in Chicago. *Grease*'s kids were based on the real-life Pink Ladies and Burger Palace Boys. The show, with a production budget of $175, made its premiere in a basement theatre where an audience of a hundred sat on the floor on newspapers. The set consisted of backdrops painted on brown paper. At that time the show had far less music, far less plot, and no central characters. But it did have infectious songs like "Greased Lightning," "Beauty School Dropout," "Those Magic Changes," and "We Go Together," and a solo for Patty Simcox that was later cut, "Yuck." New York producers Ken Waissman and Maxine Fox saw the show and recognized its surprising honesty and the appeal of its raw, rough edges. Two of the Chicago cast members, Dinah Manoff (Marty) and James Canning (Doody) would play their roles on Broadway. Manoff would continue her role in the film. The far grittier, early version of *Grease* was revived for the first time in forty years by Chicago's American Theatre Company in 2011.

Once the producers decided to bring *Grease* to New York, they set about finding a production staff. One agent tried to sell them on hiring the bright young director-choreographer Michael Bennett, but they didn't think he was right for *Grease*. They were probably right. They asked Gerald Freedman to direct, since he had helmed the original off Broadway production of *Hair*, but Freedman turned them down without even reading the script. They finally settled on director Tom Moore and choreographer Patricia Birch, who had created such interesting, *real* staging and choreography for *The Me Nobody Knows*, a concept musical about urban kids. The producers wanted everything about the show to feel rough, unpolished, de-glamorized—*honest* and *authentic*, like *Hair*—a concept the subsequent film and revivals did not understand. According to Adrienne Barbeau, who played Rizzo on Broadway, writing in her autobiography, *There Are Worse Things I Could Do*, the producers hired Moore to direct because "Tom's strength was getting performances that were so realistic the audience didn't believe they were watching actors. That's what Ken [Waissman] and Maxine [Fox] wanted for *Grease*. What they didn't want was a cotton-candy musical."

It's easy to hear on the original 1972 *Grease* cast album the raw, pure, untrained sound of 1950s rock and roll. *Grease* knows that sound because its creators lived it, the sound of Muddy Waters, Chuck Berry, Little Richard, and Bo Diddley. The earliest rock and roll was never about polish or precision; this was the punk rock of the 1950s, purposefully rejecting mainstream necessities like playing in tune, singing on pitch, keeping the tempo, staying together. It was a wholesale rejection of their parents' values and culture, an aggressive *fuck you* to Pat Boone and the like. Three decades later, American kids would rebel against the Reagan Era (The Neo-'50s) with punk rock. Just as the greasers sported leather jackets, engineer boots, crazy hairstyles, and other rebellious fashions, so did their descendents, the punks, have their rebellious fashion statements in tattoos, piercings, and occult symbols. Critic Michael Feingold wrote in his introduction to the 1972 published *Grease* script:

> The people of *Grease* are a special class of aliens, self-appointed cynics in a work-oriented, upwardly mobile world. We know from the prologue that history has played its dirty trick on them before they even appear. They are not at the reunion; they will not be found among the prosperous Mrs. Honeywells and the go-getting vice presidents of Straight-Shooters, Unlimited. Nor, on the other hand, did they actively drop out; that was left to their younger siblings and cousins. (Memory of a line too explicit, and cut from the script early on: "Course I like life. Whaddya think I am, a beatnik?") They were the group who thought they had, or chose to have, nowhere to go. They stayed in the monotonous work routine of the lower middle class, acquiring, if they were lucky, enough status to move to one of the more nondescript suburbs, and losing their strongest virtue—the group solidarity that had made them, in high school, a force to be reckoned with. It is appropriate that the finale of *Grease* celebrates that solidarity, with the saving of its heroine, and the reclamation of

its hero from the clutches of respectability—a good lusty razz at the sanctimonious endings of those Sal Mineo j.d. [juvenile delinquent] movies (*Somebody Up There Likes Me*, remember?) wherein the tough punk is saved for society at the end. Everybody knew you didn't go to those films to see that part.

After only three and a half weeks of rehearsal (again, in an effort to keep it from looking too polished), *Grease* opened off Broadway at the Eden Theatre on Valentine's Day 1972. The reviews were negative to mixed. One television reviewer said, "The worst thing I've ever seen opened tonight at the Eden Theatre." It ran 128 performances, then moved uptown in June 1972 to the Broadhurst Theatre, and it seemed to run forever. In December 1979, *Grease* broke Broadway's long-run record. It made several moves during its Broadway run and finally closed on April 13, 1980, after a total run of 3,388 performances. It was nominated for seven Tony Awards but won none, the first musical since the awards began to break the long-run record (nudging aside *Fiddler on the Roof*) without winning a single Tony.

Two years into *Grease*'s New York run, *Happy Days* premiered on American television, a sappy, happy, rose-colored 1950s world with a warm-fuzzy faux greaser at its center. *Happy Days* was cute and warm; *Grease* was true. Jacobs and Casey were among the first to ignite the pervasive nostalgia for the 1950s. It was a new kind of nostalgia for the younger generation, the first time that young Americans wanted to return to a time they were never part of. Thanks to *Happy Days* and *Grease*, the greaser became the new American cowboy, the loner, the outsider. The hero.

The original production of *Grease* paid back its investors four thousand percent. The show also ran for over two years in Mexico under the title *Vaselina*, becoming the longest-running musical there. Over its life, *Grease* gave starts to many now well-known actors, including John Travolta (who had begun as Doody in the first national tour), Richard Gere, Treat Williams, Patrick Swayze, Adrienne Barbeau, Barry Bostwick, Jeff Conaway, Marilu Henner, and Judy Kaye, among others.

The watered-down, kinder, gentler 1978 film version starring John Travolta, Olivia Newton-John, and Stockard Channing became one of the most successful movie musicals of all time. But that meant that millions of people got to know a very different *Grease*, one that transplanted the action from the working-class urban jungle of Chicago to the middle-class palm trees and sunshine of Los Angeles. Instead of a local, small-time deejay hosting the school dance, the kids in the movie version found themselves doing the Hand Jive on national television. Instead of the poor kids who come to school with a fresh can of sardines for lunch (but *only* on the first day of school), the movie showed us a Rizzo who owned her own car and Pink Ladies who could afford matching pink satin jackets, something the characters in the stage version would find unattainable, and therefore laughable. As *Grease* author Jim Jacobs notes, "These are Rust Belt kids. They live in Chicago, Pittsburgh, Cleveland, St. Louis." One source, the 1970s New York cable show *Midnight Blue*, reported that the producers of the film initially offered the role of Coach Calhoun to Harry Reems, star of the porn classic *Deep Throat*, but the studio heads shot the idea down. Instead the adults in the film were played by television icons of the '50s: Eve Arden, Sid Caesar, Edd "Kookie" Byrnes, Alice Ghostly, Fannie Flagg, and others.

But *Grease* wasn't done yet. After fifteen years of declining numbers, the teenage population in America began to grow again in the early 1990s—"They're Back," said one *Business Week* cover—and so a glitzy, brainless, neon-scorched revival of *Grease* opened on Broadway in May 1994, painfully misdirected and misunderstood by Tommy Tune's protégé, director-choreographer Jeff Calhoun (who would years later direct a brilliant revival of *Big River* for Deaf West Theatre). Completely ignoring (or just missing) *Grease*'s agenda as social commentary, this revival decked out its set in bright neon colors, turning it into a simple-minded cartoon, *laughing* at the '50s instead of telling the truth about them, and it added an actual 1950s song, "Since I Don't Have You," a song completely without the irony of the rest of the score and therefore completely out of synch with the rest of the show. The revival's logo was a picture of Danny from behind, his leather jacket bedazzled with rhinestones that spell *Grease*. Could they have misunderstood the Burger Palace Boys any worse? But despite the lack of taste or honesty, it was apparently perfect for the theme park Broadway had become by that point and it ran 1,503 performances. It was not, however, *Grease*.

In 2003 the British television network Channel 4 held a poll to determine the greatest musicals of all time. *Grease* won the top honor. But in 2007, NBC created a reality show (which got ratings in the subbasement) through which to choose the two leads for a new Broadway revival of the show helmed by Kathleen Marshall. But any hopes of authenticity from a new Broadway *Grease* were dashed; this *Grease* was no closer to the original than the other revival had been.

In reviewing this wildly misfired revival, Ben Brantley wrote in the *New York Times*:

> The reincarnations of *Grease*, first staged on Broadway in 1972, can be read as a map of showbiz devolution. That original production had the amiable air of a gritty spoof, enacted by a lively, raunchy ensemble of youngsters just old enough to understand what they were spoofing. The vastly popular 1978 film, starring John Travolta and Olivia Newton-John, was a slicked-up, cleaned-up frame for its teenage idols, not all that different from the campus-cutup frolics that starred June Allyson and Van Johnson. The long-running revival that opened in 1994, produced by Barry and Fran Weissler, was a mindless, trashy theme park of a show, which managed to prolong its life beyond all sane expectations with revolving-door replacement casts of celebrities in career limbo. The implicit message was that anyone who is famous could star in a big-time musical, an outlook that continues to inform the Weisslers' blockbuster revivals of *Chicago* at home and abroad.

Gerald Bordman's outstanding history book, *American Theatre: A Chronicle*, missed the mark on the 2007 revival, saying, "Kathleen Marshall's slick direction and choreography could not conceal the formulaic, mercenary inspiration for the revival." But the truth is that the slick direction and choreography were just symptoms of the problem. No one involved—including co-author Jim Jacobs—seemed to care about being true to the show, the characters, the story, or the themes of the show. Yet the tourists kept it running for 554 performances.

Perhaps it's time for *Grease* in its original form to return at last, in this new age of Ironic Detachment. In 2005, Norman Lebrecht wrote about the new postmodern musicals (*Urinetown*, *Bat Boy*, *Hedwig and the Angry Inch*, *Spelling Bee*) in his online column: "The music in each of these shows amplifies this element of separation, licensing us to stand apart from what we are seeing and enter a third dimension where each of us can individually decide whether to take the plot literally or sardonically, whether to take offense or simply collapse in giggles. This degree of Ironic Detachment is the very making of the postmodern hit musical.

Ironic Detachment would be unattainable in a Tom Stoppard play because I.D. requires musical inflexion; it is impossible in opera and ballet, which are stiffened by tradition against self-mockery. Its application is unique to the musical comedy, an ephemeral entertainment which has found new relevance through its philosophical engagement with 21st century concepts of irony and alienation." Still, Ironic Detachment isn't entirely new in musical theatre—we've seen it before, periodically over the twentieth century, in *The Threepenny Opera* (1928), *Of Thee I Sing* (1931), *The Cradle Will Rock* (1937), *Guys and Dolls* (1950), *The Fantasticks* (1959), *How To Succeed in Business Without Really Trying* (1961), *Promenade* (1965), *Cabaret* (1966), *Promises, Promises* (1969), *Company* (1970), *The Rocky Horror Show* (1973), *The Robber Bridegroom* (1974), and yes, *Grease*.

Sock Hop Baby, Roll Up Your Crazy Jeans!

Almost every American musical sets up the same challenge for the protagonist—assimilate or be removed. These central characters must make a choice to either change in certain ways in order to join the existing community or they must be removed from that community by leaving or by dying. In *Sweeney Todd*, *Jesus Christ Superstar*, *Bat Boy*, and *Evita*, the main characters will not (or cannot) change so they must be removed by death. In *Show Boat*, Julie and Steve will not play by mainstream society's rules, so they must be removed, and they leave the Cotton Blossom. In *Man of La Mancha*, Quixote/Quijana refuses to live by conventional rules of behavior, so he must die. In *The Music Man*, Harold Hill turns legit in order to join the River City community. In *Brigadoon*, Tommy decides he must reject his previous life in order to stay in Brigadoon and become part of the community. In *Grease*, Sandy ultimately assimilates into the greaser community, rejecting her parents' worldview.

Many people are uncomfortable with the show's ending because they miss the fact that Sandy doesn't actually *become* a slut in the finale; she just learns how to *dress* like one, finally letting go of the tendency of too many Americans to stigmatize sexuality as dirty and shameful. She gives up the desexualizing poodle skirt that hid away her female form and replaces it with clothing that reveals and celebrates—*and takes ownership of*—her body and its adult curves. This is not a descent into decadence for Sandy; it is a throwing open of the doors of her moral prison. The authors' intentions are clear in a stage direction in the final scene. After describing Sandy's new hypersexual look—the tight pants, leather jacket, earrings, wild new hair—the script says, "Yet she actually looks prettier and more alive than she ever has."

Sandy's clothing in "All Choked Up" is extraordinarily subversive. Teenagers' clothing was a major source of contention at the time. Grace Palladino writes in *Teenagers*:

> School authorities solved the immediate problem (teenage "delinquency") with dress and behavior codes. Tight blue jeans, ducktail haircuts, and excessive makeup were prohibited in school. "Dress Right" campaigns set appropriate high school styles that drew national attention in the late 1950s. Boys were required to wear shirts and ties, standard trousers (or neatly pressed khakis), and polished shoes (or clean white bucks). Girls were required to wear dresses or shirts and forgo pin curls, dungarees, and slacks. As an article in *Newsweek* explained the theory: "Bejeaned girls behave better when they're in ladylike dress."

The end of *Grease* suggests that a lasting, healthy relationship is only possible when both partners are openly and completely themselves, without regard for other people's opinions, social conventions, or personal insecurities—and also when neither of them is afraid of their own human sexuality. This was not the message of the conforming adult world; this was a uniquely teen perspective. Both Sandy and Danny have to learn to be themselves, to shake off the masks of "cool" and "respectable." If there is any question about who the protagonist of the show is, Sandy is primary; she's the one who has changed, who has learned something significant. The same may be true of Danny, but to a much lesser extent.

But the ending of *Grease* isn't a "moral" and shouldn't be read that way. It doesn't declare what we should or shouldn't do; it's an objective and accurate description of America in 1959. Sandy *is* America in its progression from puritanical repression in the '50s to sexual freedom in the sexual revolution of the '60s. And yet, as she tells Danny in "All Choked Up," she isn't ready to give up her virginity quite yet. In 1959 America was about to "grow up" sexually, into adolescence in the '60s (*Hair*), and into full sexual adulthood in the '70s (*Rocky Horror*). Too many people believe that the message of *Grease* is that to win the man you love, you have to be a slut. But there's not a single line or lyric anywhere in the show to suggest Sandy has changed anything but her looks. Like Eliza Doolittle in *My Fair Lady*, Sandy learns the secret, that anyone can fit in just by talking and looking the right way (and don't we all do that to some extent?), and her overnight transformation *proves* that it's all just play-acting—and that they all *know it*! She has learned what Rizzo and the girls have known all along. Sandy has become one of them just by changing her clothes! She allows herself the freedom of the coming 1960s, a refusal to fear her own sexuality or to see sex as dirty, the freedom to be able to talk and laugh openly about sex. But behind all the rest, there's a simpler, more subversive message. Sandy isn't saved just by how she dresses; she's saved by singing rock and roll. It isn't until she can achieve the authenticity and sexual frankness of rock and roll by singing "All Choked Up" that she can be healed.

Grease doesn't moralize; it just reports. *Grease* is set in 1958 and 1959 for a good reason—it's not just about the changing of decades but also the changing of *eras*. Sandy's triumphant line late in the show, "Good-bye to Sandra Dee," puts away not only Sandy's false good-girl persona but also the 1950s as a whole, a world in which the goody-goody Sandra Dee can be a role model, in which façades were cracking. We were moving on . . .

> **The ~~Fabulous~~ Fractious '50s**
> The Fabulous '50s. The Decade Deluxe. The Ike Age. These were the good old days, the happy days, the source of many an American's earliest, fondest memories and many of our postwar institutions. For the past two decades Americans had lived in the grip of poverty and war. Now they were ready for some giddy, goofy fun. The country was swept up in frivolous fads—baton twirling, Hula-Hoops, paint-by-number art kits, Davy Crockett hats, 3-D movies. Life seemed a wide-screen, stereophonic special effect.
>
> Culture popped—in shades of turquoise, pink, salmon, and, if one color wasn't enough, delicious two-tones. Madison Avenue created an unlikely world of perfect appliances and perfect families, of highballs and hi-fis, Bermuda shorts and backyard barbecues. In the ads, the wives are beautiful (mowing the lawn in peasant blouses and a hint of lingerie); the children above average (exuberantly joining in the Saturday morning car wash). Over the clink of ice cubes, Americans mingled and misbehaved.

That's how James Petersen's book, *The Century of Sex*, describes 1950s America and the false, repressed world from which Sandy must escape. There were three distinct cultures in America during the 1950s—mainstream middle America, New York City (including the Beat writers), and teenagers—and they rarely intersected each other, so none of them spoke the others' languages or shared their morality. Much of mainstream adult America lived a life of complete ignorance, happily watching safely artificial television sitcoms and carefully censored studio films, having little or no idea what was going on in teen America, in teen music, movies, magazines, social life, and, most significantly, teen sexuality.

In *The Century of Sex*, Petersen writes:

> The ethic, if that's what it could be called, was simply don't get in trouble. The sexually active lived in fear of pregnancy. The Kinsey Report had revealed that a large number of women were having premarital sex. A third Kinsey Institute report on Pregnancy, Birth and Abortion, which was published in 1958, would reveal that one out of every five women who had premarital sex became pregnant. Of those, one in five would be forced into marriage. The other four women had their pregnancies terminated by abortion.

Grease's subplot with Rizzo and her fear of pregnancy was a real part of life in the '50s for many unmarried, sexually active women.

After World War II, most adult women had been expected to leave behind the independence of their lives on the home front during the war and return to a life of near complete dependence again—no more job, no more money, no more sexual control or choice. Betty Friedan wrote of the times, "It was fun at first, shopping in those new supermarkets. And we bought barbecue grills and made dips out of sour cream and dried onion soup to serve with potato chips, while our husbands made the martinis as dry as in the city and cooked hamburgers on the charcoal, and we sat in canvas chairs on our terrace and thought how beautiful our children looked, playing in the twilight, and how lucky we all were, and that it would last forever." These were the real people behind the metaphor of the 1956 film *Invasion of the Body Snatchers*. As *The Century of Sex* says, "Conformity became a national passion, part of a return to sexual and political conservatism."

The Battle Over Sex has always been waged between the Haves and the Have-Nots in America. Throughout history, there has been great sexual freedom and little shame among the Have-Nots, since they have nothing that can be imperiled. But the Haves are always terrified of any kind of cultural change, especially sexual, because the fallout could endanger their position as Haves. Sandy is a Have; Danny is a Have-Not. The sparks are bound to fly.

All in all, the 1950s was one of the most interesting decades of the twentieth century—so much wealth, so much repression, so many massive changes in the culture, perhaps most significantly the invention of the suburbs, in which middle-class wives would be forever isolated and tranquilized. The characters in *Grease* were born around 1942, the last generation born before the Baby Boomers, and they went to high school from fall 1955 to summer 1959. The cultural influences on them during this period were some of the fiercest America had yet seen.

In 1951, J.D. Salinger's controversial *Catcher in the Rye* was published and became an instant, lasting hit among teenagers, with its profanity and frank discussions of teenage angst and sexuality. Then, just as these kids were hitting puberty, America was hit with *The Wild One* in 1953, starring Marlon Brando, the movie that started the whole leather-jacket greaser thing as well as the "teen exploitation" film genre. The central relationship in *Grease* between Danny and Sandy is a goofier imitation of the central relationship in *The Wild One* between Johnny and Kathie.

Exactly like the teen market they were targeting, teen exploitation films were full of sex and sin and booze and cars, but many of them also had a sanctimonious "moral" laid out explicitly, at the beginning or end of the film, often by a nameless authority figure behind a desk or podium, sometimes by a "survivor" of the "tragedy." These fake morals gave the raunchy stories the patina of respectability to placate parents and would-be censors. But for the kids, these movies mirrored the real world, in which teenagers were discovering they had a certain kind of power that just might be able to challenge the power of their parents. And the teen rebel was born. In 1954, just a year before the *Grease* kids would start high school, Elvis Presley burst upon the American scene with his first hit, forever changing notions of gender and sexuality, rebelling against the "strong, silent type" model of previous generations of men like John Wayne and Gary Cooper, in favor of a remarkably sexual, nakedly emotional new model of maleness embodied by the likes of Marlon Brando and James Dean. John Waters documented this cultural shift in his 1990 film *Cry-Baby* (later, also a Broadway musical), set just a few years before *Grease*.

While the *Grease* kids—and the show's authors—were in high school, the movies *Rock Around the Clock* and *Rock, Rock, Rock* were released in

1956 (the same year the mayor of Jersey City, New Jersey, banned all rock and roll within the city limits), giving some teens their first chance to actually see Little Richard, Chuck Berry, Bill Haley and the Comets, the Platters, and many others performing their songs. That same year the teen exploitation flick *Hot Rod Girls* was released. In 1957, Roger Corman's daring *Teenage Doll* (which still holds up pretty well) and *Eighteen and Anxious* were released. *Teenage Doll* was about a girl gang out for revenge after one of their members is murdered by a rival gang. The film ended with a giant rumble with girl and boy gangs fighting in an auto salvage yard. That same year saw Michael Landon in *I Was a Teenage Werewolf*, a much more serious film than it sounds, about a damaged, misunderstood teen and about American teenagers' feelings (reinforced by rock and roll) of us versus them. Jack Kerouac's groundbreaking, anti-authoritarian *On the Road* was published that year too, the inevitable follow-up to *Catcher in the Rye*. In 1958, two more teen movies were released that showed us the underbelly of American teenage life (real or imagined), *High School Confidential* and the girl-gang flick *High School Hellcats*. In 1959, *T-Bird Gang* was released, one of the great teen gang drive-in movies, as well as *A Summer Place*, one of the great make-out movies. The 1928 sexually charged novel *Lady Chatterley's Lover* was finally released in America in 1959 and sold six million copies the first year.

During the Greasers' senior year at Rydell High, in February 1959, another epoch-changing event took place, the plane crash that killed Buddy Holly, Ritchie Valens, and the Big Bopper—"the day the music died." The 1950s were coming to a close, and a decade full of chaos and controversy was coming fast, with a whole new kind of rock and a whole new kind of American sexuality. *Grease* is a prequel to *Hair*, every bit as well crafted, every bit as authentic, every bit as insightful and truthful about an incredibly volatile, fascinating moment in American history.

Michael Feingold wrote:

> *Grease* does not discourse about our presence in Saigon. Nor does it contain in-depth study of such other '50s developments as the growth of mega-corporations and conglomerates, the suburban building boom that broke the backs of our cities, the separation of labor's political power from the workers by union leaders and organization men. Although set in and around an urban high school, it does not even discuss one of the decade's dominant news stories, the massive expansion of the university system, and the directing of a

whole generation of war babies toward the pursuit of college degrees. *Grease* is an escape, a musical designed to entertain, not to concern itself with serious political and social matters. But because it is truthful, because it spares neither the details nor the larger shapes of the narrow experience on which it focuses so tightly, *Grease* implies the topics I have raised, and many others. So I think it is a work of art, a firm image that projects, by means of what it does contain, everything it has chosen to leave out. And between the throbs of its ebullience, charm, and comedy, it conveys a feeling, about where we have been and how we got to where we are . . .

Rock and Roll Party Queen

As it would be for decades to come, rock music was more of an authority figure than any adult could ever be. In his book *Fever: How Rock 'n' Roll Transformed Gender in America*, author Tim Riley writes, "Rock stars helped their young fans grow from boys to men and girls to women, by exploring and celebrating the nature of that struggle—the full range of sexual bewilderment, frustration, and longing." *Grease* chronicles exactly that phenomenon. The kids in *Grease* may well have seen their rock heroes in person, since deejays like Alan Freed (a likely inspiration for Vince Fontaine) frequently hosted live rock and roll concerts in Cleveland, Chicago, and elsewhere. Howard Miller, known as "Uncle Moo Moo," was the number one morning deejay in Chicago from 1947 to 1968, on WIND, where the *Grease* kids would no doubt listen to him every morning before school. In 1957, Miller produced the first live rock show in Chicago, featuring Tab Hunter, Charlie Gracie, Chuck Berry, Eddie Cochran, and the Everly Brothers. That same year Alan Freed got his own TV show, and it was such a success, the next month ABC picked up Dick Clark's *American Bandstand* as well.

This was a time when music was still special in America, before it became aural wallpaper underscoring every moment of life, a time before Muzak (which had already been invented but was not yet in widespread use). In the 1950s, the consumption of music was still a choice, not an inescapable soundscape that followed you from your alarm clock to the television to the car to the elevator to the grocery store to the doctor's office. Music wasn't yet taken for granted as mere environment as it is now. And it wasn't yet as cynical an instrument of manipulation as it is today. Because of all that, it was more emotionally potent, its power to heal stronger.

In *The Century of Sex*, Petersen writes, "Previously, teenagers had shared their parents' world—watching the same movies, listening to the same songs on the radio. Now they had their own teenage idols, their own films, music, fads, and fashions." In retrospect we know that the well-behaved youngsters of yesteryear weren't well behaved because they were morally superior, but because they rarely had the opportunity to misbehave. In the 1950s—and even more so in the decades to come—those opportunities would be almost limitless. Adults were no longer sources of wisdom; adults were now outsiders. Teenagers had power and, more importantly, they had their own culture.

Palladino writes in *Teenagers*:

> By the mid-1950s, however, *Seventeen* [magazine]'s respectable brand of adolescent culture had real competition—white, middle-class teenagers were not the only high school students with money to spend! Postwar prosperity had opened the door to an entirely different teenage world, one that was populated by working-class and black teenagers who had never participated in high school social life before. This demographic shift changed the nature—and the appeal—of the teenage market.

These two worlds are represented in *Grease* by Sandy and Danny. Rock and roll was the first music ever created specifically for teenagers, and many adults literally predicted the apocalypse when they heard it. Now all American teens would lose their moral compass, they wailed, they would abandon all ambition and drive, and drown in a morass of juvenile delinquency. These were the same arguments against swing music in the '40s and marijuana in the '60s, yet America kept plugging along. Sure, there were occasionally riots at rock concerts, but there had also been a riot at a Guy Lombardo concert in 1944.

Unlike their parents, rock and roll took teenagers seriously. It took teenage sex and teenage love seriously. It put teenage emotions on a level with adult emotions, and it made teenagers feel like adults. American kids were suffering from emotional and spiritual starvation, and rock and roll fed them. And the best part for the kids was that parents *hated* rock and roll. (One 1957 article in *Cosmopolitan* asked "Are You Afraid of Your Teenager?") Much of the authenticity of *Grease* lies in its songs, a virtual catalog of 1950s styles, structures, chord progressions, lyrical themes, distinctive bass lines, and unforgettable guitar licks, all as authentic as a 1954 Fender Stratocaster. By opening the show with the old-fashioned "Alma Mater," followed by the explosion of the hard rocking "Alma Mater Parody," the kids of *Grease* literally rebel against their older selves at the reunion, the past assaulting the present, reminding the adults in the audience that most of them have become what they once hated most—the establishment. The "Alma Mater Parody" blasts off with a slight variation on one of the most famous guitar licks of all time, created by Chuck Berry for the hit "Johnny B. Goode." Berry was one of the fathers of rock and roll, and so in this first scene, *Grease* instantly establishes its authenticity and its street cred as a rock and roll document.

The third song in the show, "Those Magic Changes," comments on rock's most important characteristic—aside from the beat—the treatment of teenage love and emotions as serious and legitimate. The lyric starts off as a classic '50s teen lament, but it quickly becomes self-referential, a postmodern '50s song. It's a song about falling in love but also about chord changes, about the comfort and familiarity of those four simple chords that undergirded the majority of early rock and roll. And those four chords open "Those Magic Changes"—C, A minor, F, and G7; or I, vi, IV, V^7. The singer here is Doody, a boy lamenting lost love but finding safety and happy memories in those same four chords that he hears in every song:

> I have never heard that song before,
> But if I don't hear it anymore,
> It's still familiar to me,
> Sends a thrill right through me,
> 'Cause those chords remind me of
> The night that I first fell in love
> To those magic changes.

(And notice the internal rhyming that gives the song such momentum: *before/anymore*, *of/love*, and the best one, rhyming *familiar to me* with *a thrill right through me*.) But Doody goes even further with the metaphor, now suggesting that it's actually teenage emotion that creates, that incarnates rock and roll. He sings:

> My heart arranges
> A melody that's never the same,
> A melody that's calling your name
> And begs you, please, come back to me.

Rock gives him those four never-changing chords, and his heart supplies the ever-changing melody. This ubiquitous chord progression wasn't simple because songwriters were untalented; it was simple to get out of the way of the emotions of the songs, just like the best of rhythm and blues did. Unlike other musical forms—and this was something the adults just couldn't get—chords weren't the point here. The point was the emotion. This boy has been jilted, but he's not in love with *her* anymore; now the object of his love is rock and roll itself. Rock and roll understood teenagers. It wanted what they wanted.

The fact that Doody plays the guitar is significant. The guitar was *the* symbol of rock and roll, and by extension, of teenage rebellion. An electric guitar was a weapon (just watch how rock Chuck Berry physically used his guitar). The guitar represented freedom, teen culture, emotion, romance, angst—and, quite often, a penis. The guitar instilled confidence! That also explains Johnny Casino and the Gamblers in *Grease*'s prom scene—every boy wanted to be a rock and roll star. Nineteen-fifty-nine was a pivotal moment for rock and roll. Up to that time, rock and roll addressed teen angst and misfired romance; but once the '60s arrived, rock songs would tackle war, injustice, sexual oppression, drugs, hypocrisy and authority, religion, and politics. The songs in *Grease* straddle those two worlds, posing as the simpler songs of the '50s while subtextually delivering potent social commentary and satire.

Feingold wrote in his *Grease* introduction:

> *Grease* is in possession of a truth, one of its strongest, about the media and how they worked on us. This is of course best seen in its superb, sharp-eared songs. The musical basis of '50s rock is fractured by comedy quite early in the enumeration of "Those Magic Changes." After that it is a matter of astonishment how many delicate subforms there were to the songs of the period, and how many different comic approaches Jim Jacobs and Warren Casey use to pin them down: Imitative homage ("Rock and Roll Party Queen"), outright burlesque ("Sandra Dee"), ironic, look-the-other-way dirty joke ("Mooning"), character satire ("Freddy, My Love"), improbable-situation parody ("Beauty School Dropout"), and, best of all to my taste, the quiet revelation of fact as an antidote to the sentimentality of the originals. Take "It's Raining on Prom Night"—truthful, admittedly, but pretty squalid. Small. Petty. Not the deep sentimental tragedy you will find in a prototypical "serious" song like "Tell Tommy I Miss Him" or

"Teen Angel." This song is easier to laugh at than some of the others because it is more firmly distanced—not a report of something that actually happens to our heroine, just a convenient index to her momentary emotions.

Jazz was made for the brain. It was about detachment, bemusement, cool. But rock and roll came straight for the heart and the groin. It was about primal feelings and desires. It stripped its sound of precision, elegance, finesse, training, just like punk. Real rock and roll was animal, outlaw. It was sweaty. It didn't float like jazz. It exploded. It pounded. Rock and roll was banned in major cities across America. It terrified white adult America. Listening to rock became the ultimate rebellion for white kids especially. Their parents saw it as the biggest danger to all that was decent.

Rock and roll was responsible for an emotional revolution in America. It began as "race music" (in other words, African American music) and was initially declared unacceptable for young white ears. But it fast became the first truly racially integrated American art form, coming from equal parts black rhythm and blues and white country music. (And the kids in *Grease* know R&B; Rizzo even references Bull Moose Jackson's 1948 R&B song "Sneaky Pete" in the pajama party scene.) This was the first time in America that blacks and whites shared the same culture, both consuming and creating it. And because of Elvis, rock and roll finally became (marginally) acceptable for white kids. For the first time in American history, kids were being open and honest—even *inappropriate*—about their emotions. This was the most nakedly emotional music most white Americans had ever heard. And it changed everything.

Soon after, in the 1960s, rock and roll would morph into pop and Top 40, and it would no longer be the exclusive domain of the young. The adult world could finally get a grip on it. Elvis had been sent overseas. Chuck Berry was sent to prison for sexual misconduct. Congress held "payola" hearings to ruin deejays like Alan Freed, who broadcast his last live radio show in November 1957. In the 1960s rock and roll would become commercialized and forget its roots. This would continue to happen to rock every decade or so. But *Grease* is about the beginning, when rock and roll was still pure, still naked, still dangerous, and America was still terrified of it.

The Stacks of Wax

The score of *Grease* is remarkable in its craft and authenticity, even referencing actual songs of the period. Many of the actual period songs that influenced the *Grease* score were not chart toppers, because the *Grease* kids didn't always listen to the most popular music; they were more musically and culturally adventurous than that. They listened to songs you could only hear late at night on Alan Freed's radio show, "race songs," *dirty* songs, songs that scared adults.

But it's important to note that the songs of *Grease* differ from real rock and roll songs in one significant way. The lyrics to real '50s rock and roll songs were the least important element of the song, often just dummy lyrics used as a vehicle for the artists' personal vocal stylings, or for sophisticated harmonies or melodic ornaments. As in rhythm and blues, a rock and roll song didn't have to convey information, just style and emotion, most of which was delivered through the abstract language of music. But theatre songs have to convey a lot of information or the show won't work (which is why it was such a mistake to put a real '50s song into the 1994 revival). Because sung lyrics take more time than spoken dialogue, musicals have to do a lot of storytelling in fewer words than a play. So in *Grease*, "Summer Nights" lays out the central backstory, as well as characterizing most of the members of the two gangs through their pointed questions. "Those Magic Changes" and "Rock and Roll Party Queen" lay out and explore the show's central themes. Most of the girls' songs provide psychological character details—Marty and Rizzo's cynical view of love in "Freddy, My Love" and "Worse Things"; the friction between Rizzo and Sandy in "Look at Me, I'm Sandra Dee"—but we also find commentary on '50s sexuality in "Greased Lightning," "Mooning," "Drive-In Movie," and of course "Worse Things." Every lyric contributes to the agenda of this deceptively sophisticated concept musical.

Grease opens with an authentically bland and properly pious "Alma Mater," the sound of the adult world, of authority, complete with archaic language (like *foretell*, *hovel*, and *thou shalt*) which then is ripped apart, deconstructed, unexpectedly exploding, invoking "Johnny B. Goode," as well as that audacious rejection of adult culture, "Roll Over Beethoven." Like Berry's "School Day," this parody "Alma Mater" is an assault, a declaration of culture war, a defiant *fuck you* to the adult world, as the teenagers literally steal away the adults' anthem, give it a driving beat, and twist it to suit their own purposes. And so *Grease* is off and running. This will not be a nice show, a tame show, a traditional show, the music tells us. This will be aggressive, even obnoxious. This will be rock and roll theatre.

We move into the second scene and "Summer Nights," the introduction of two of the leads and their central plotline, inspired by real rock songs like Huey "Piano" Smith's "Don't You Just Know It?," a song released in 1958 as these kids were starting their senior year. "Summer Nights" introduces the ten main characters, allowing each of them to ask questions that reveal their characters. Marty wants to know if this guy has a car, while Frenchy only wants to know if Sandy's in love. Kenickie wants to know if the sex was rough, while Sonny only wants to know if the girl could fix him up with a friend. We see here and in the scene leading up to the song who each of the ten leads are—Kenickie and Rizzo, both damaged, beaten down, angry young adults; Roger, the clown; Jan, the cynic; Doody and Frenchy, the innocents; Sonny, the "dangerous" one; and Marty, the material girl. And the song also establishes the central conflict of *Grease* and of the 1950s, that Danny is comfortable with sexuality while Sandy is lost—trapped?—in the fantasy of perfect love, thanks to the likes of Sandra Dee, her handlers, and the movie studios (which were losing all their previous power, due in part to the burgeoning teen market).

Some sources report that Rizzo's dismissal of Sandy's tale, "'Cause he sounds like a drag," was originally written, "Cause he sounds like a *fag*." It's certainly plausible, since Sandy describes a boy who barely touches her all summer, and in Rizzo's world, that might well mean the boy is gay (or at least it would be a solid, cynical put-down of Sandy's romantic story). After the song, Rizzo suggests Sandy's summer lover may be "a fairy."

Now that the characters are established and the story is underway, *Grease* takes a moment with "Those Magic Changes" to explore the show's central themes, to underline the importance and centrality of music in this story and also in the show's social commentary. Closely based on Paul Anka's "Diana" and its distinctive bass line (you can actually sing "Magic Changes" to "Diana"), it also includes distinctive falsettos vocal ornaments that pay homage to songs like the Diamonds' comic doo-wop hit, "Little Darlin'." Doody starts off solo, then the girls join in, then the boys join in, then two of the boys take off on those falsetto riffs, giving the whole song the tang of improvisation, as if these kids are just fooling around between classes. This is part of what gives *Grease* such a unique feel as a musical.

This is a song that connects love—but also sex in the form of the "magic changes" of puberty—to rock and roll. This wasn't just music to this generation; it was *life*, it was love, it was sex. This was *their* music. They charted their lives to the songs on the radio, the song they fell in love to, the song they first had sex to. And as "Those Magic Changes" reminds us, every song is every other song, since so many of them used those exact same chord changes, a chord progression seemingly invented just for them (though really coming from rhythm and blues). *All* of rock and roll is "those magic changes" that Doody dreams of returning to him every night. The idea that all you need is a guitar to be a rock and roll star (perhaps in tribute to Bobby Bare's satirical 1958 Elvis song, "All-American Boy") was a deeply ingrained part of teen culture.

The next song, "Freddy, My Love," is the show's female doo-wop number, with a lead melody and rich harmonic backup, closely based on "Eddie, My Love" by the Tea Queens, while also slyly parodying the Shirelles' "I Met Him on a Sunday" and Ronnie Spector's "Be My Baby," reinforcing old female stereotypes while also undermining and revising them. The driving triplet accompaniment here was a common beat in early rock and roll, invented by Fats Domino for "Every Night About This Time." They're living in the 1950s, but these are women of the '60s. The idea of the other girls becoming backup singers for Marty shows us how much they love the girl doo-wop groups, an entirely new phenomenon at that moment that would become huge in the '60s. The Ronettes were the first "slutty" girl group to make it big singing rock and roll. They were what the girls wanted to be (to get the guys) and what the guys dreamed about getting. "Freddy, My Love" is a song about early feminism, about women being sexual and aggressive. But it's also about the materialism of the 1950s, a mindset in which money is better than sex, and gifts are the only true expression of love. And the idea of Marty singing to a guy stationed in Korea references the fact that Elvis was still in the Army overseas at this point, a sad fact for many teenagers.

"Greased Lightning" combines two of the three major cultural forces of the '50s—cars and rock and roll. Possibly inspired by the Cadillacs' cocky "Speedo," or Chuck Berry's "You Can't Catch Me," this is a companion piece to "Freddy, My Love." This is the guys' perspective in the language of doo-wop: it's all about sex, cars, and sex in cars. An article on Answers.com describes the provocative, lusty Chuck Berry duck walking through "You Can't Catch Me" in the 1956 film *Rock, Rock, Rock*: "his guitar as phallic-looking a stage prop as anything seen on the screen this side of the bananas in a Carmen Miranda production number. Had a black man ever before been permitted such a degree of sexual expression (and you can see the delightful, proud smugness on Berry's face, knowing what audience the movie was aimed at) in a movie intended for white audiences?" This is the unfettered sexuality that terrifies the adult world, and it does the same to Sandy.

"Greased Lightning" is about America's love affair with cars and teenagers' love of *speed*. According to *Rolling Stones*' excellent history of music, *Rock of Ages*, "American automakers were asserting their products' virtues of speed and power, turning the 1957 models into rocketship fantasies with nose cones, chrome grills, and razor sharp fins." This song is not just a catalog of car accessories, but instead it provides real insight into the dreams of these guys. After all, this is not a *real* car Kenickie's singing about, but an unattainable fantasy car (which is why it may be better if we *don't* actually see it onstage), the ultimate luxury high-performance drag racing car, with high-priced accessories for speed and performance (lifters, fins, fuel injection), and also for automotive sex appeal (palomino dashboard, purple frenched tail lights, twin tail pipes). And it's clear from the details that this will be a car intended for drag racing, the gladiator sport of 1950s teenagers, an extreme and dangerous sport pitting one man against one man, in what was sometimes a battle to actual death. (Kenickie acknowledges this danger, and even knows how to diminish it with a fuel-injection cutoff, which stops the flow of gasoline in the event of a crash, in order to lower the danger of an explosion.) Drag racing was illegal, sometimes deadly . . . and really sexy! Skill and success in drag racing could always get a guy laid, as Kenickie well knows (or at least imagines).

But the song also tells us that Kenickie doesn't really know much about drag racing or about customizing cars. A true drag racing enthusiast knows that the accessories Kenickie dreams of don't all make sense together. For example, the "four-barrel quads" refers to a carburetor, but a car with fuel injection (as in his "fuel injection cutoff") doesn't have a carburetor—those two things would not be on the same car. And no one would chrome-plate connecting rods; chrome-plating was just for show and nobody can see connecting rods on a car. And though palomino leather was popular for car interiors, no one would put palomino leather on a dashboard. Finally, a kid in 1959 would either make his car look good or go fast; no kid had the money to do both (although you could argue that this *is* just a fantasy). In fact, a drag car that looked *too* good was the sure sign of a driver who wasn't really serious about racing. It's safe to assume that Kenickie probably knows very little about cars or drag racing, which gives this lyric far more complexity, humor, and character detail than it initially seems to have.

The last scene of Act I is set in a park late on a Friday night, where the kids have gathered to hang out, drink, smoke, and neck. Because the scene is one of the longest in the show, it's also a prime example of the supreme craft in the writing of the show's dialogue. The script of *Grease* isn't just a catalog of period references and influences; it's also a carefully constructed ensemble character piece, revealing so much about all the main characters, usually subtextually. As an example, when Roger calls Jan "Petunia Pig," she shoots back, "Oh yeah? Right here, lardass!" This seemingly trivial throwaway line tells us so much about Jan: that she's always been overweight (or at least for much of her life), that she's regularly picked on, that she's sensitive about her weight, and most importantly that over time she has learned to defend herself, to give as good as she gets. A girl who is never mocked about her weight would not be that fierce in her comeback. All this is confirmed later in the scene when Roger asks Jan to the dance and she responds, "You kiddin', Rog?" Her suspicious reply tells us that either guys never ask her out or maybe guys have asked her out in the past only as a cruel joke of some kind. She has to be reassured by Roger that he really wants to go out with her before she agrees. There's lots going on with her under the surface, and the same is true of every one of the main characters.

Roger and Jan's song "Mooning" may have been inspired by the Mello-Kings' "Tonight, Tonight" or the Skyliners' "Since I Don't Have You," and though the other songs in *Grease* proclaim a new worldview of sex and love, this one also trashes the old worldview, reducing the tepid moon-spoon-June romance of the '30s and '40s to a silly anachronism. It contrasts modern love (1959) with their parents' love, the physical versus the romantic, and the play between the old definition of mooning as an over-sentimentalization of young love, and the newer definition of mooning as the act of baring one's ass. Like "Summer Nights," this is a song about the difference between chaste love and carnal love, the love Sandra Dee falls into versus the more physical love of naked, sweaty bodies. But this song goes further, into wickedly funny social satire; "Summer Nights" is about two kids, but "Mooning" is about the whole generation. And for Jan, this is safe sexuality, vaguely explicit, but also safely not serious.

As a companion piece to "Mooning," Rizzo makes the comparison between old and new sexual moralities more personal with "Look at Me, I'm Sandra Dee," an assault on Sandy's false role models, a shot across the bow, making certain that Sandy knows that Rizzo knows that it's all bullshit. The music is a classic, brilliantly imitative 1950s novelty song, with a meter and an introduction lovingly ripped off from David Seville's "The Chipmunk Song," the surprise hit of the 1958 Christmas season. But the laughs get even darker when you realize that every male movie star mentioned in the lyric was a closeted gay man, forced to live a lie by his studio. This is a song about sexual repression, false lives, and false role models, and it's proof that Rizzo knows more than we thought, that she has genuine insight into the world around her. And this peek into her mind allows her to carry the weighty "There Are Worse Things I Could Do" later in Act II.

The act ends with "We Go Together," an archetypal Happy Teenager song, very closely modeled on the Kodaks' "Oh Gee, Oh Gosh" and Lewis Lyman's "I'm So Happy," maybe with a dash of Little Richard's "Tutti Frutti." (You can actually sing "We Go Together" to both "I'm So Happy" and "Oh Gee, Oh Gosh.") This is a song celebrating the nonsense syllables of early rock and roll, songs like "Gee" (the Crows), "Bip Bam" (the Drifters), "Oop Shoop" (the Queens), and "Sh-Boom" and "Zippity Zum" (both by the Chords). Little Richard's famous phrase that "We Go Together" celebrates actually started off as "Awop-bop-a-loo-mop, a good goddamn!" followed by "Tutti Frutti, *good booty* . . ." It was later cleaned up.

But the lyric of "We Go Together" succeeds as more than just a send-up; it is also an articulation and celebration of this created family that nurtures and protects these kids, an artificial but also very *real* family that has through necessity replaced their dysfunctional, possibly abusive birth families. It is this family at the heart of the show's plot that must survive the difficulties and obstacles of teenage life, and which must be sustained even as its leader, Danny, attempts to create a relationship outside the family for the first time. This lyric tells us—and these kids are telling each other—that these ties that bind are indeed strong enough to withstand the current conflicts, and the song's reprise at the end of the show reminds us of the importance of that strength for these kids. Perhaps it was also telling audiences in 1972 that those ties will help get them through the cultural chaos of the 1970s, a theme picked up in the 1977 musical *I Love My Wife*.

Shakin' at the High School Hop

Act II picks up where Act I left off, with "Shakin' at the High School Hop," a loving tribute to Little Richard's "Ready Teddy," as well as many other legendary songs, like "Shake, Rattle, and Roll" (Big Joe Turner, then Elvis, and others), "Whole Lotta Shakin' Goin' On" (Jerry Lee Lewis), "High School Confidential" (Jerry Lee Lewis), and "At the Hop" (Danny and the Juniors). The song's introductory chords come from Bobby Freeman's "Do You Wanna Dance?" In fact, "High School Confidential" actually contains the lyric "shakin' at the high school hop." There's also be a touch of Bobby Darin's "Splish Splash," a song that references other early rock and roll songs, just as "High School Hop" catalogues the dances of the time, including the Chicken, the Stroll, the Shimmy, the Cha-Cha, the Walk, the Hully-Gully, the Hand Jive, the Stomp, the Calypso, the Slop, and the Bop. It also names several songs of the period, including "Alley Oop" and "Mr. Lee," among others.

"It's Raining on Prom Night" is a Connie Francis-inspired number, combining attributes from several of her "weeper" songs, including "Frankie" (with a spoken section), "Valentino," "Carolina Moon," and "Happy Days and Lonely Nights," among others. The Latin beat recalls her fondness for recording Italian-language ballads like the hit "Mama," and "Frankie" even contains the idea of hiding tears, something that later shows up in "There Are Worse Things I Could Do." It also has echoes of the Diamonds' "Little Darlin'," with its Latin beat and one spoken verse. According to some sources, this was the first *Grease* song Jacobs and Casey wrote, even before they had conceived the show, satirically putting the trivial and mundane at the center of a big, emotional lament. Far more than any other song in the score, this is parody more than tribute or invocation. Its sly reference to Maidenform bras recalls the brand's long-standing ad campaigns that associated their bras with various female fantasy situations, like a romance novel in a magazine ad. Surely for the singer (or listener) of this song, the prom was a romantic fantasy as potent as any other.

The prom scene is the centerpiece of Act II and, not surprisingly, almost the entire scene is accompanied by dance music. This is a scene that's entirely about the rock and roll. And the centerpiece of the scene is "Born to Hand Jive," with its now universally famous choreography. The Hand Jive was invented for the Johnny Otis song "Willie and the Hand Jive," which hit the charts in 1958 and stayed in the Top Ten for sixteen weeks. This "Hand Jive" also takes inspiration (and its bass line) from Bo Diddley's self-titled song, "Bo Diddley," with its famous beat (the "hambone") that accompanied so many of Diddley's songs. The beat is relentless, dangerous, full of wild abandon—the beat of sex. Once again, rock and roll *is* sex. Johnny Casino and the Gamblers are an example of the thousands of garage bands that appeared in the '50s. The lyric of "Hand Jive" clearly tells us that *anyone* can be a rock star if they've got the beat in them, and the fact that *everyone* knows how to Hand Jive means *everyone* has the beat. This was the beginning of the democratization of pop music that would continue into the '60s. Grace Palladino writes, "If unremarkable kids like Dion DiMucci and his group, the Belmonts, who hailed from the Bronx, could make it on *American Bandstand*, [teenagers] reasoned, then anyone with talent and determination had the same chance to succeed."

"Beauty School Dropout," Frenchy's wacky nightmare of the misogynist mainstream "real world," was inspired (musically) by songs like the Penguins' classic "Earth Angel." But this scene also references the 1957 film *Tammy and the Bachelor* with Debbie Reynolds. Just before "Beauty School Dropout" starts, Frenchy wishes for a guardian angel "like in that Debbie Reynolds movie." In the film, Aunt Renie (Mildred Natwick) plays the role of Tammy's (merely metaphorical) fairy godmother, who transforms her into a captivating Southern belle, who looks just like the portrait of an ancestor in her elite Southern family. She even gives Tammy the ancestor's dress to wear, so she can win the heart of her love. *This* is the fantasy Frenchy wants. And of course, it's what will eventually happen to Sandy, who will be taken under the wing of other women, given new clothes, and taught new manners, though all in a hard-core, rock-and-roll kinda way . . . And it's also a smart parody of those psychological dream sequences in old-fashioned musical dramas like *Oklahoma!*, *West Side Story*, *Lady in the Dark*, and others, in which the leading lady works through her dilemma in the form of a dream. The joke in "Beauty School Dropout" is that Frenchy doesn't get the answer she wants from *her* dream, because *Grease* isn't an old-fashioned musical.

Danny's big character song (sadly replaced in the film), "Alone at a Drive-In Movie," is a delicious tribute to and parody of the teen laments of early rock and roll, including the Penguins' "Earth Angel" (you can sing "Drive-In Movie" to the original recording of "Earth Angel"), the Platters' "The Great Pretender," the Flamingos' "Would I Be Cryin'?," and Johnny Ray's "Cry." It is a classic male doo-wop song, with its independent bass line and falsetto tenor floating up above the lead melody. The song works both as a musical theatre "I Want" character song, and also as an authentic '50s rock lament. This moment couldn't be clearer: Sandy may want acceptance, (self-)love, self-knowledge, but Danny just wants *sex*. These two worlds have to find an accommodation, and they will in the show's finale. (The replacement song in the film, "Sandy," isn't a bad song, but it doesn't achieve half of what "Alone at a Drive-In Move" does, textually, thematically, or musically, and it's *far* too introspective for a kid like Danny Zuko.)

But this song also works on a second level, as a cultural commentary on the power of drive-in movies in teen culture in the 1950s. Cars had been changing sex since the 1920s, but by the '50s, more teenagers had more access to cars than ever before, giving them the privacy they craved on a regular basis. Drive-in movies had been created as family entertainment, and between 1943 and 1953 more than 2,900 drive-in theatres opened in America, reaching a high of 5,000 by 1958. But once television stole the family audience, drive-in owners targeted their marketing exclusively at teens, while small, low-budget studios started cranking out material specifically for this new niche market, creating "teen exploitation" films that drastically changed and radicalized teenagers' perceptions of themselves and each other. Drive-ins became a place to cruise for girls, hang with the "wrong crowd," get drunk and get laid, awkwardly, in the back seat. These films opened teenaged eyes to sex, violence, and other various vices like never before, creating a new, more sophisticated, more cynical teen market. The fake movie dialogue in the scene leading up to "Alone at a Drive-In Movie" lampoons the two most prevalent genres of drive-in films: horror movies (a comic mix of 1957's *I Was a Teenage Werewolf* and those paranoid 1950s science-run-amok flicks, like 1954's *Them!*) and drag-racing movies. Strangely enough, television had also come close to killing radio, in ratings and advertising revenue, until radio did what the drive-ins did by targeting teenagers.

"Rock and Roll Party Queen" is another song (like "Those Magic Changes" and "Hand Jive") that reminds us that *Grease* isn't primarily about Danny and Sandy; it's about rock and roll and how it impacted American sex. This is a tribute to the Everly Brothers and their perfect-thirds harmonies, modeled on "Wake Up, Little Susie" (a song about having sex at the drive-in) and other Everly Brothers hits, as well as songs like the Dell-Vikings' "Come Go With Me." The lyric says more than it seems to, describing a party girl that all the kids "know" (in the biblical sense?), someone they talk about, who stays out late with boys, and who will soon be seventeen (the age of sexual consent, which of course means she's currently *under* the age of consent). The Party Queen is the fully sexual girl that Rizzo is and Sandy may become. In context, the song both comments on Rizzo's fears of pregnancy and foreshadows Sandy's realization that she's too repressed sexually.

This scene also shows us another aspect of '50s teen culture, the basement party. Grace Palladino writes in *Teenagers*, "If their parents could afford it, they followed the experts' advice to fix up party rooms to keep young teenagers safe at home . . . complete with a television set, soft drink bar, and plenty of room for dancing." Jan hosts this party and Marty hosts the pajama party in Act I—their parents clearly know this philosophy. But the scene is important dramatically because it's the first time we see Rizzo and Kenickie grapple with real, serious emotions, revealing a vulnerability that is unfamiliar and uncomfortable for both of them.

Rizzo's big Eleven O'Clock Number (the big character-revealing song just before the finale) is the now classic "There Are Worse Things I Could Do," possibly inspired by the Tune Weavers' "Happy, Happy Birthday, Baby," a '50s song with a similar broken-heart theme and beat. Rizzo is (spiritually if not actually) one of the Beats (who were commonly—and derisively—called *Beatniks* by the mainstream to suggest that they were Communists), a group most famously represented by Jack Kerouac and Allen Ginsberg, who in the 1950s rejected mainstream values, morality, and art, trying to break through the façade of polite society to a more honest, more authentic way of living. "Worse Things" contains the entirety of 1950s youth (and Beat) morality in its lyric. Like everything else in *Grease*, Rizzo represents that transition from the '50s to the '60s. She'd like us to think she's as authentic as they come, but she hides Kenickie's paternity from him and she hides her hurt from her friends. It's only when Sandy calls Rizzo on her "mask" that Rizzo sings "There Are Worse Things I Could Do," beginning a two-song arc of revelation for Sandy.

Structurally, this song links these two women. In each of the three verses, Rizzo attacks Sandy for her perceived sins—being a tease (leading Danny on but not delivering), being self-pitying (most notably in "It's Raining on Prom Night"), and being judgmental (in the scene leading up to the song). As often happens in real life, the sins Rizzo sees in Sandy are Rizzo's sins as well. This is a song built on very real, raw emotions, a song that finally reveals the character of Rizzo late in Act II as vulnerable, insecure, easily hurt. The audience may not see this coming, but it fills out and explains everything Rizzo has done over the course of the story. Almost at the end of the show, we see that she probably *was* in love with

Danny (only to see him taken away), that she is now clearly in love with Kenickie (whom she has just cut off), and that she sees no happily ever after for herself. All she thinks she can do is put up a brave front and hide her insecurity. But that also walls her off from any real emotional connection to anyone. If she won't allow herself to cry in front of anyone, how can she ever get close? And the payoff of the last line is the most telling: none of the normal "crimes" of dating is the *worst* crime; the *worst* crime is showing vulnerability. That's really good writing and a really good character song. It's so sad and it says so much in such seemingly simple language without ever being simplistic.

"Worse Things" segues directly to its companion piece, Sandy's parallel self-evaluation, the reprise of "Look at Me, I'm Sandra Dee," in which Sandy finally sees and accepts the truth in Rizzo's metaphor, finally recognizing that she must reject artificial values imposed by others and find her own way. But Sandy only comes to this realization because "Worse Things" opened her up to the idea of authenticity as a fundamental value; now she can act on that newfound wisdom in her reprise (just like in all the ancient hero myths).

Tim Riley argues in *Fever* that early rock and roll delivered a powerful message to its listeners: "The challenge of building an original identity, rather than accepting a received identity predicated on the values of their parents, became a necessary life passage." Like all the best theatre songs, Sandy makes a *decision* in the "Sandra Dee" reprise, and the plot takes a turn toward its final destination. Sandy must decide who she is and what she values *herself*; she must embrace *all* of who she is, including her sexuality. She now realizes that only when she is true to herself can she be happy with Danny, and this final revelation will lead us to the show's rowdy, playful finale, "All Choked Up" (sadly replaced in the film by the less carnal disco number "You're the One That I Want").

In the "Sandra Dee" reprise we can see Jacobs and Casey's lyric writing craft here in their most conventional theatre song, as they effortlessly spin out multiple rhymes without ever disrupting a line or thought:

Look at me,
There has to be
Something more than what they see.
Wholesome and pure,
Also scared and unsure,
A poor man's Sandra Dee.

Poor even rhymes (unnoticed) with *pure* and *unsure* . . . The bridge is loaded with long *e* and long *i* sounds, with a close interior rhyme at the end, in *has* and *last*:

When they criticize
And make fun of me,
Can't they see the tears in my smile?
Don't they realize
There's just one of me,
And it has to last me a while?

And the rhyming accelerates in the last verse, giving the song real momentum as Sandy marches toward triumph:

Sandy, you
Must start anew.
Don't you know what you
Must do?
Hold your head high,
Take a deep breath and sigh,
Good-bye
To Sandra Dee.

Here again, there is some usually unnoticed treasure, in the powerful alliteration of *hold your head high*, as each successive line climbs musically higher and higher to the climax.

But this song isn't just about Sandy saying good-bye to her false idols; it's also about America saying good-bye to the false idols of the 1950s, saying good-bye to the turning of its collective blind eye away from the hidden horrors of the decade: rampant racism, sexism, homophobia, teen pregnancy and abortion, prescription drug abuse in the suburbs, and so much more. Sandy has to face herself and find her own authenticity, but so too does America.

The rowdy "All Choked Up," the show's finale, is clearly inspired by Jerry Lee Lewis's 1957 song "Great Balls of Fire" and perhaps also by Little Willie John's "Fever" (later recorded by Peggy Lee in 1958), not only paying tribute to the music but also to the content of "Great Balls of Fire," with the idea of love causing sickness. Here *Grease* shows us the turmoil ahead in the 1960s, as sexual roles are reversed. Now that Sandy is a sexual being, she can finally sing real rock and roll. Now *Sandy* is the aggressor, a lesson she learned from rock and roll, a social trend that would soon push boundaries further and further, from Tina Turner's "A Fool in Love" well into the 1970s. This is the beginning of feminism. Now American women could be sexual too. Many of those who still object to the show's ending might be missing the point of the show and may be unconsciously caught up in gender stereotypes from the '50s that remain pervasive today. If a boy is sexually aggressive (as in "Greased Lightning"), he's just a guy. If a girl is sexually aggressive, she's a slut.

Have we really come all that far since 1959?

But notice that in the lyric of "All Choked Up," Sandy tells Danny (and us) that she is still not ready to sleep with him. Sandy may have changed the way she looks, and she may now have a more progressive philosophy of sexuality, but no matter how dramatically Danny pleads, she's still not "going all the way" just yet; that part of her has not changed fundamentally. She has *not* become a slut.

But perhaps even more significant than Sandy's new sexualized rock and roll persona in "All Choked Up" is her line after the song: Danny asks her if she's still mad at him and she answers, "Nah, fuck it." That this is the first time we've heard Sandy talk like that is certainly important, but even more important is what her answer *means.* The phrase is not just obscene; it's also a universally recognized idiom with two related meanings. First, it says to the world that the speaker just doesn't care anymore. Sandy's not just cussing here; she's publicly rejecting all the values of her past life, in particular the idea that sex is "dirty." She's moving from the '50s to the '60s. The other parallel meaning is that, regardless of the consequences, the speaker is charging ahead, and that's part of this moment as well.

But it goes even deeper than that. *Fuck* is the granddaddy of all cuss words, the word that draws a line in the moral sand. Especially in 1959—but even today—*fuck* is a word that separates the "nice" (i.e., conforming) people from the "bad" (i.e., less repressed) people. Sandy has picked sides in one of America's great culture wars, and so her journey moves out of the personal and into the political, as she utters this infamous word that will stand at the very center of the counterculture of the 1960s, a word Lenny Bruce will go to jail for. It's a great way to end this story, and it's also why a cleaned-up *Grease* is worse than no *Grease* at all. . . .

Hair

It is an obscene and yet serene parade of shaggey-headed black and white people, coming, going, sometimes angry, sometimes sweet, sometimes bitterly truthful. Singing really good songs like "Aquarius" and "Let the Sun Shine In." People making love. Black people doing both their own thing and a white thing. White people doing their own thing, a black thing, and their forefather's thing. Sodomy. Love. Pot. Black/white/sex/love. Black-black love/sex. Homosexual love/sex. The flag, endeared and chided. The war, ignobled and dishonored. A mockery of self. People nude and spiritual. Spirited people in raggedy, kooky clothes. A love-knock at the Supremes. An immortalization of James Brown. Shiny, glittery costumes. Psychedelic lighting. A love affair between the cast and the audience.

—Ebony *magazine, May 1970*

On February 2, 1962, the moon, Mercury, Venus, Mars, Jupiter, and Saturn all aligned in the constellation Aquarius. All seven of these heavenly bodies had not come together for 2,500 years. Many people believed it was the dawning of a new age, the age of Aquarius, symbolizing a pooling of everyone's creativity, an age of communalism. The lyric to the song "Aquarius" talks of "harmony and understanding, sympathy and trust abounding, no more falsehood or derision, golden, living dreams of visions, mystic, crystal revelation, and the mind's true liberation." And it's not kidding. That stuff is real to anyone who's done *Hair*. And those of us who've gone there wish the rest of the world could go there too. Especially now. There's a reason *Hair* was called "The American Tribal Love-Rock Musical."

When *Hair* opened, John J. O'Connor wrote in the *Wall Street Journal*, "No matter the reaction to the content . . . I suspect the form will be important to the history of the American musical." It was, paving the way for the non-linear concept musicals that dominated musical theatre innovation in the 1970s: *Company*, *Follies*, *A Chorus Line*, *Working*, and others. And yet, some Broadway establishment figures refused then and still refuse today to accept *Hair*'s radical departure from mainstream musical theatre. Even now, some people can't see past the appearance of chaos and randomness to the brilliant construction and sophisticated imagery underneath. In 1996, while reviewing *Hair*'s godchild, the rock musical *Rent*,

Howard Kissel wrote in the *New York Daily News* that *Hair* had been nothing more than "formless amateurism."

Back in the late 1960s, the artists of off Broadway and off off Broadway had been complaining that the professional theatre was dead and, even worse, that it was boring. *Hair* was the revolution they had been waiting for. With very little plot, a unit set, plenty of four-letter words, explicit sexual content, rituals, drugs, lyrics that didn't rhyme, music that didn't follow the rules, and the sound of genuine rock and roll on the Broadway stage for the first time, in 1968, this musical knocked Broadway on its collective ass. The show rejected every convention of Broadway, of traditional theatre in general, and of the American musical in specific. And it was brilliant. Most surprising of all, it was an enormous hit. Director Tom O'Horgan said at the time that he saw *Hair* as a once-in-a-lifetime opportunity to create "a theatre form whose demeanor, language, clothing, dance, and even its name accurately reflect a social epoch in full explosion."

The show opened off Broadway first at Joseph Papp's Public Theatre in October 1967 for a limited, eight-week run. When its run ended, Papp and independent producer Michael Butler moved the show to the Cheetah, a New York disco. Papp then pulled out, and after massive revisions (including thirteen new songs), new cast members, a new director (O'Horgan), a new choreographer (they wanted the movement to look more spontaneous, less choreographed), and the addition of designers Jules Fisher and Robin Wagner, Michael Butler moved the show to Broadway, opening it in April 1968 at the Biltmore Theatre. Butler's astrologer picked the opening date to insure a successful run. It worked—the show ran 1,750 performances.

When *Hair* opened, Michael Smith of *The Village Voice* called it "downtown, dirty, ballsy, and outrageous." *Time* magazine wrote, "This musical is a cross between a Dionysian revel and an old-fashioned revival meeting. The religion that *Hair* preaches, and often screeches, is flower power, pot, and protest." *Saturday Review* said, "Director Tom O'Horgan is pushing the medium to new limits by moving away from the verbality of multisensual theater. Instead of finding conventional musical-comedy performers to impersonate hippies, he has encouraged a bunch of mainly hippie performers inventively to explore their own natures with song and dance." In *The Journal of Popular Culture*, Irving Buchen wrote, "*Hair* can not be cut short as mere sensationalism; nudity there is, but it is selective, functional, and even discrete. It is not the new drama of assault or insult, although the audience is never immune from incursions into its midst. It is radical but not violent; eclectic but not chaotic; sexually freewheeling but not perverse." He called it "an authentic glimpse into a pre-verbal state—perhaps, into the origins of drama itself as chant and dance."

Hair acted as a launching pad for the careers of Diane Keaton, Melba Moore, Donna Summer, Tim Curry, Nell Carter, Peter Gallagher, Joe Montegna, Ben Vereen, Cliff DeYoung, Meat Loaf, and many other performers who went on to great success.

Though a 1977 revival did not fare well, divorced as it was from the authenticity of the original, the show never lost its audience. Tours of the show crisscrossed the country periodically over the years and proved the show was still commercial. As with many works that tap into the current cultural zeitgeist, *Hair* went through a period in which it felt dated and quaint, but it eventually came out intact on the other side, now as a period piece. In 2009, a new production was mounted, which successfully tapped into the authenticity and innocence of the original again. There was no watering down here, no tinkering to make it more family-friendly; this was *Hair* exactly as it was meant to be, and it thrilled a new generation as much as it had their parents and grandparents. The show moved to Broadway and ran for more than a year, attracting young people as much as older folks who remembered those times, sending out a tour in 2010 and 2011. Maybe it was the election of Barack Obama that brought the '60s back, or maybe *Hair* was just finally distant enough from its original production that it could be fresh all over again.

The show still packs a wallop. *Hair* criticizes and satirizes racism, discrimination, war, violence, pollution, sexual repression, and other societal evils. It is a genuinely psychedelic musical, perhaps the only one ever on Broadway. The show is made up of a barrage of images, often very surrealistic, often overwhelming, coming at the audience fast and furious, not always following logically; but when taken together, those images form a coherent, unified, and ultimately comprehensible whole. At its best, the show really can cause the kind of euphoria in its audience that one usually associates with psychedelic drugs. As with most satires, *Hair* makes fun of racism, war, sex, and other things by carrying them to ridiculous extremes, as in the songs "Sodomy" and "Colored Spade." *Hair* shocks the audience (though that is not really its goal) by challenging what they believe, by showing how absurd, how offensive, how nonsensical, and, in some cases, how dangerous the behavior and language that society calls normal can be. And the show asks some good questions:

Why did we send American soldiers halfway around the world to Vietnam to kill strangers when there was no direct threat to our country? Why can't we talk openly about sex? Why are certain words "dirty" and other words that mean the same thing acceptable? Why are there so many offensive words for black people but hardly any for white people? Why are so many straight people interested in what gay people do in private? If the Constitution guarantees free speech, why can't we burn the flag? Is it right to protest and refuse to follow laws that are unjust?

The Hippies

The hippies of the 1960s were the second generation of the Beat movement of the 1950s. (Interestingly, most hippies didn't call themselves "hippies;" they called themselves "freaks.") Theirs was a counterculture movement that included many separate sub-movements—the drug culture, nudists and naturalists, vegetarians, "Jesus freaks," communes, environmentalists, Krishna followers, mystics, and many others. What united them was their rejection of mainstream culture, the culture of their parents. And they weren't all kids; the hippie movement started in the early '60s, and by 1969 many hippies were in their thirties and older. In fact, the older hippies were often revered as tribal wise men. The hippies were about nonviolence, individualism, a rejection of materialism, about spirituality but also a rejection of institutionalized religion, and above all about the desire to reach a higher, purer level of consciousness. Their drug use was not just an escape; it was a means to find the spirituality they believed their parents had lost in the meaningless hypocrisy of organized religion.

The serious hippies differentiated between "good" and "bad" drugs. The "good" drugs were mind-expanding, psychedelic drugs like marijuana, peyote, and LSD, which helped them find spirituality and opened up the mind. The "bad" drugs were those used only for escape, like alcohol, nicotine, tranquilizers (like Valium), cocaine, and heroin, which shut down the mind. The abuse of prescription drugs by adults is satirized in Act I of *Hair* as two mothers (played by men) bemoan their rebellious daughters and Berger responds by offering tranquilizers to several famous authority figures who were having trouble with rebellious kids—Rabbi Schultz (a high-profile Jewish political figure), the Rockefeller Foundation, President Nixon, Vice-President Humphrey, and the pope. The hippies condemned this kind of drug use. Notice that the drug-trip song "Walking in Space" in Act II of *Hair* says explicitly that the two reasons for taking the drugs are total self-awareness and meeting God. Paul McCartney said in one '60s interview, "God is the space between us. God is the table in front of you. It just happened I realized all this through weed."

It's not surprising that the hippie movement sprang up when it did. After World War II, America went through a very disorienting time. There was prosperity like the country hadn't seen in quite some time and material wealth was at an all-time high; but there was also the threat of nuclear bombs. In addition, many women who had learned during the war that they could work outside the home, that they could participate actively in society, were now thrust back into their old repressive roles as wives and mothers. After relative social chaos during the war, the already repressive American society now became even more repressive to try to restore the prewar social order—which was, of course, impossible. The genie could not be put back in the lamp. As there had been during other times of social upheaval (like at the turn of the century and during the Depression), there was friction between the demands for conformity and conservatism and the instinctive human need to express oneself, made even worse by the taste of freedom women had gotten while their husbands and boyfriends were off fighting the war. For women, there was also a new sexual freedom knocking at America's door, courtesy of the invention of the birth control pill. The "baby boomer" children growing up in the '50s had all the consumer goods they could want but found little to feed their souls. They had had permissive childhoods but were then expected to fit into a repressively conformist adult world. Their parents taught conservative values while those same parents' own social drinking reached heights not seen since the 1920s. Also, more kids than ever before were being sent to college, where they were learning to question everything, to form their own opinions about the world. They found that the liberal arts education their parents wanted for them turned out highly educated men and women with no real world skills, lots of unanswered existential questions, and no preparation to get a job and start a family. Even worse, these kids left college with endless possibilities before them—too many possibilities, it turned out. Whereas earlier generations had been locked into taking over family businesses, the baby boomers had more freedom in choosing their futures but they had no guideposts. In many cases, the wide array of choices proved overwhelming, and they "dropped out."

Along with all this, the black civil rights movement was gaining steam and all these disillusioned kids found a strong, viable model for social protest. Following the example of Martin Luther King Jr. and other great African American leaders, the youth of America, especially those on college campuses, started protesting all the things that they saw wrong with America: racism, environmental destruction, poverty, sexism and sexual repression, violence at home and the war in Vietnam, depersonalization from new technologies, and corruption in politics. The hippies' predecessors, the Beat generation, had been a far less political counterculture. But the escalation of the war in Vietnam, the expansion of the draft, more aggressively enforced drug laws, and increased anti-loitering sweeps in parks and public spaces forced the hippies to become political, and a new underground press sprang up. The hippies had great respect for America and believed that *they* were the true patriots, the only ones who could and would save our country and make it the best it could be.

One big difference between the Beats and the hippies was the audiences for their respective art. The Beats' chosen art forms were poetry and jazz, and they readily admitted that their art was elitist. The hippies, on the other hand, were determined to create art of the people, and their chosen art form, rock and folk music, was by definition populist. Due in some measure to Bob Dylan, country music also became a big part of the hippie music movement (as represented in *Hair* by "Don't Put It Down"). But possibly the biggest difference between the music of the hippies and the music of the Beats was that the hippies' music was often very angry, its anger directed at those who would prostitute the Constitution, who would sell America out, who would betray what America stood for; in other words, directed at their parents and a paternalistic government.

In 1967, twenty thousand people gathered in Golden Gate Park in San Francisco for the world's first "Be-In." (The term "Be-In" became very popular and was later parodied as the title of the TV show "Laugh-In.") Despite the hippies' anti-capitalist leanings and alongside their populist intentions, major record labels got the message and immediately signed several San Francisco bands to gigantic advances. In early 1967, Brian Jones of the Rolling Stones told one interviewer that things were changing, that the world "was about to enter the age of Aquarius. There is a young revolution in thought and manner about to take place." By 1968, high school teachers were teaching Bob Dylan's lyrics as poetry in English classes, and psychedelic artists like Peter Max were designing mainstream advertisements.

The creators of *Hair* gave their musical its title because long hair was the hippies' flag—their "freak flag," they called it—a symbol not only of rebellion but also of new possibilities, a rejection of discrimination and restrictive gender roles (as celebrated in one of *Hair*'s songs, "My Conviction"). It symbolized equality between men and women. In addition to the long hair, the hippies' chosen clothing also made statements. Wearing drab work clothes (jeans, work shirts, pea coats) was a rejection of materialism and a somewhat disingenuous identification with oppressed workers. Adopting clothing from other cultures, particularly Third World and Native American cultures, represented the hippies' awareness of the global community and their rejection of US imperialism and selfishness. Wearing simple cotton dresses and other natural fabrics was a rejection of synthetics, a return to natural things and simpler times. Some hippies wore old World War II or Civil War jackets as way of co-opting the symbols of war into their newfound philosophy of nonviolence. And yet nudity was also a big part of the hippie culture, both as a rejection of the sexual repression of their parents and also as a statement about naturalism, spirituality, honesty, openness, and freedom. The naked body was beautiful, they believed, something to be celebrated and appreciated, not scorned and hidden. They saw their bodies and their sexuality as gifts, not as "dirty" things.

Experimental Theatre and the Bantu

In addition to the social influences of the '60s, *Hair* also came from New York's experimental theatre movement. In the late '60s when *Hair* was created, this movement had been going on for quite some time, led by directors like Joseph Chaikin, Peter Brook, Jerzy Grotowski, and Antonin Artaud; writers like Samuel Beckett, Jean Genet, and Eugene Ionesco; companies like the Living Theatre and the Open Theatre; and theatre spaces like Joe Cino's Caffe Cino and Ellen Stewart's La MaMa Experimental Theatre Club. The work created during this time was based heavily on improvisation, on group creation, on ritual, on exploring new ways to communicate with an audience, and new ways to involve an audience directly in the act of performance. The creation process, often done in extended workshops, was as important—or, in some cases, more important—than the actual presentation of the work. They rejected many of the conventional notions of director, playwright, script, rehearsal, and character.

Ritual was important to *Hair* because of its roots in experimental theatre but also because of its spiritual roots. The show's opening number, "Aquarius," is a ritual summoning of the tribe, a formal calling together of the members of this group of hippies. In the original Broadway production, when the song began, the hippies were out mingling with the audience. At a certain moment, they all froze and then began moving to the stage in slow motion, coming together on stage and forming a large circle, a potent, primal symbol of life that would be used throughout the show. Ritual is used in many moments in the show, in the mock Catholic mass of "Sodomy," in the Be-In, in the passing of the joints before the trip, in the marching and chanting in protest that happens throughout the show.

The experimental theatre movement was also exploring the idea of words as sounds, as percussion, or as background noise, divorced from literal meaning, something Gertrude Stein had played with earlier in the century. In songs like "Ain't Got No," "Three-Five-Zero-Zero," and "The Bed," words come at the audience like a freight train, so fast, so quirky that no audience could ever catch it all or comprehend it all. But the purpose of these lyrics isn't just to be comprehended; they are to be enjoyed as abstract sounds. Toward the end of "Ain't Got No," the lyric deconstructs itself into a list of words and phrases based on the sound "pop." The words are no longer meaningful in a conventional sense; they have become percussion. *Hair* was the first impressionist Broadway musical, in which lyrics, dialogue, plot, and character were often not drawn conventionally—they were implied, suggested, often abstract. Just as the impressionist painters created only the impression of form and structure, left to be interpreted and synthesized by the eye and mind, *Hair* did the same thing with the art of theatre.

Hair director Tom O'Horgan was very directly involved in the experimental theatre movement (and after *Hair*, he would go on to bring that philosophy to the Broadway production of *Jesus Christ Superstar* as well). Gerome Ragni and James Rado, *Hair*'s authors, came out of this world too, although both had also had mainstream success as actors on Broadway and elsewhere. In fact, Rado's initial dream was to become a mainstream Broadway songwriter in the Rodgers and Hammerstein tradition. Neither Ragni nor Rado were hippies themselves (and only two of the original Broadway cast were), but the authors found the hippie counterculture fascinating, and once they decided to write *Hair*, they spent all their time in Greenwich Village with the hippies, doing research.

Off Broadway producer Eric Blau (who would go on to create the cult hit musical *Jacques Brel is Alive and Well and Living in Paris*) introduced Ragni and Rado to composer Galt MacDermot, who agreed to set their bizarre lyrics to music. Blau was the show's first producer, but when Joseph Papp guaranteed an eight-week run at the Public Theatre, Blau encouraged Rado and Ragni to take it; Blau could only guarantee an opening, no more. MacDermot had been born in Montreal but went to college at Capetown University in South Africa. He brought this African influence to the music of *Hair*, using the rhythms of the rituals of the Bantu tribe, the driving pulse of African music, and the habit of musically setting stresses on unexpected syllables (as in "What a Piece of Work Is Man," "Ain't Got No," and other songs).

A Really, Really Brief Look at the War

In its initial 1967 version, *Hair* was more about the war in Vietnam. It was only when the rewrites were done as they moved the show to Broadway in 1968 that other issues were made as prominent. Vietnam was a major issue in the hippie movement, and though its prominence was reduced somewhat in the revised version of the show on Broadway, it still formed the backdrop of the only real story line in the show, that of Claude going off to war; and an understanding of the background of the war is important to an understanding of *Hair.* Of course, it's important to remember that people still disagree not only on interpretations of the war and motivations for the war, they also disagree on actual facts about the war. It's impossible to find two reference sources today that tell the exact same story.

Vietnam had been a possession of France since the late nineteenth century. During World War II, the French gave Vietnam to the Japanese. Toward the end of the war, a Vietnamese leader named Ho Chi Minh established a government headquartered in Hanoi, in the northern part of the country, with a constitution based loosely on the US Constitution (he was an ardent admirer of Thomas Jefferson). But after the war was over, Winston Churchill insisted that Vietnam should return to French "ownership," against the wishes of the Vietnamese people, and the French invaded to take the country back.

In 1954, a Vietnamese Communist faction under the leadership of Ho Chi Minh rose up against the French and finally drove them back out of Vietnam. An international conference in Geneva, Switzerland, that year negotiated a cease-fire and decided to split the country in two, leaving the north half of the country to Ho Chi Minh. The conference also demanded that free elections be held in 1956 to reunify the country. But the leaders in the south refused to hold the elections because they knew how widespread support was for the increasingly Communist Ho Chi Minh. The US supported this refusal because there were politicians in the US who were so terrified by Communism, so obsessed with its perceived threat to America, that they believed they had to prevent the Communists from taking over Vietnam. They believed that there was a secret international alliance of Communist countries, and that if Vietnam fell to the Communists, they would then systematically take over the world, country by country, until the US itself fell to Communism. These politicians were wrong, of course. There was no such international threat or alliance.

Based on this unfounded fear, the US went in and set up a pseudo-democratic puppet government in the south of Vietnam in 1956, claiming rule over the entire country; but the North Vietnamese refused to recognize this government (which had very little power outside the city of Saigon). Meanwhile, many South Vietnamese saw the Americans as no different than the French, just another imperialist power who wanted to control them. In the early 1960s, a coalition of South Vietnamese Communist groups, called the Vietcong (which was essentially independent of the Communists in North Vietnam, though connected in some ways) rose up in the south against the US puppet government.

In 1964, President Johnson announced that the North Vietnamese had fired on US personnel in the Gulf of Tonkin (even though it was a lie) and Johnson convinced Congress to give him free reign to take "all necessary measures" to retaliate, with the infamous Gulf of Tonkin Resolution, an act that was unprecedented and arguably unconstitutional. Some historians believe Johnson needed the war to escalate in order to energize the political right wing, to jump-start dormant patriotism, and to galvanize the American people behind his social programs and his dream of the Great Society. Unfortunately, it would not end up working the way he planned. Johnson began the bombing of North Vietnam.

Soon he was sending in ground troops as well. On the morning of March 8, 1965, thirty-five hundred US Marines—the first ground troops of the war—came ashore near the Da Nang airbase, welcomed by Vietnamese girls and four American advisors holding a bed sheet proclaiming, "Welcome to the Gallant Marines."

Back home, antiwar protests, marches, and demonstrations began in America around 1967, due in large part to the fact that this was the first war ever broadcast on television; and the coverage wasn't what we're used to today, with correspondents reporting from the rooftops of hotels. During the Vietnam War, the reporters and cameramen were in combat with the ground troops, beaming home pictures of blood and carnage, bringing the full force of the horror of war into American living rooms. Most Americans had never seen war like this. War was real like it had never been before. The protests escalated and continued throughout the rest of the war. The Pentagon learned its lesson and never allowed such open access to the press again, and, not surprisingly, there have been no antiwar protests of that size and scope since then.

This is the world into which came *Hair*.

And the war would rage on. By 1969, with no victory in sight, President Nixon talked about plans for US troop withdrawal, promising to end the war within three years. In 1973, a cease-fire was agreed upon and most of the US ground troops left Vietnam, but the bombing of North Vietnam continued. Eventually, in 1975, the North Vietnamese took Saigon, the biggest city in the south (renaming it Ho Chi Minh City), and effectively "won" the war, forcing the US to pull out completely. Once the Communists took over, the US politicians were proved wrong. Instead of Communism spreading across Asia and Europe, the Communist countries started fighting with each other and Vietnam got into a bloody war with Communist China.

During the Vietnam War, more than 47,000 Americans were killed in action and more than 303,000 wounded in action. The South Vietnamese suffered about 200,000 killed and 500,000 wounded. The North Vietnamese and the Vietcong suffered about 900,000 killed and an unknown number wounded. More than a million Vietnamese civilians were killed. The combined financial cost of the war ended up being about two hundred billion dollars.

The legacy of the war was that America lost its innocence. It was no longer the unquestioned Good Guy in world affairs. The reception for troops returning from the war was not always friendly. Many Americans felt the war was immoral, and America's long-held image of itself as global champion of the oppressed was replaced by an image of America as bully, interfering where it had no business, killing innocent men, women, and children, and lying about it all to the public.

Interestingly enough, the 3,500 troops sent into Vietnam in 1965 may not be what the song "Three-Five-Zero-Zero" in *Hair* refers to. Jim Rado has said that the song was inspired by Allen Ginsberg's poem "Wichita Vortex Sutra," written in February 1966, which contains almost all the freaky, violent, surrealistic images in *Hair*'s song "Three-Five-Zero-Zero," and is often quoted word-for-word. In the poem, General Maxwell Taylor proudly reports to the press that 3,500 of the enemy were killed in one month. He repeats the number, digit by digit, for effect: "Three-Five-Zero-Zero." Ginsberg also refers to 256 Vietcong killed and 31 captured, which became 256 captured in the lyric. Though the song starts out somber and intense, spilling out Ginsberg's images of death and dying, it turns midway into a manic dance number, an absurdist celebration of killing that echoes Maxwell's glee at reporting the enemy casualties, commenting on the happy face that the US government tried to put on the ever-diminishing returns of the war in Vietnam. While our soldiers (and theirs) kept dying, Washington tried to whip up World War II–style support for the war among Americans. But we had seen the war on our TV screens this time, and we weren't celebrating.

Let the Sun Shine In

References to the war are peppered throughout the *Hair* script. The central dramatic through-line focuses on Claude receiving his draft notice and his dilemma over whether to go to war or burn his draft card. The war is an ever-present image in the show. During Claude's Act II drug trip, the images of war pile up in both comic images and disturbingly dramatic images. Berger gives Claude a "special" joint before the trip, one presumably laced with more powerful hallucinogens. Since the hippies believed that some drugs (LSD, peyote, pot, and others) opened and expanded the mind, increasing the power of the mind, helping the user reach higher consciousness and greater understanding, we can assume that Berger gives Claude a more powerful drug specifically to help him make up his mind, to clear away his indecision about Vietnam (in an apparently unconscious nod to *Oklahoma!*, in which Laurey is given special smelling salts for the same purpose). Jim Rado maintains it must be peyote in Claude's joint because Berger wouldn't approve of the synthetic LSD.

Claude's trip begins with the song "Walking in Space," most of which describes the sensations of being high, but there are a few references to the war here. Once the song has ended, everything else in the trip is triggered by Claude's fear of going to war. The first images are of young men, Claude among them, jumping out of a helicopter into the jungles of Vietnam. When Claude lands, he sees two American soldiers chasing a Vietnamese peasant. He turns around and sees George Washington and his troops, retreating from an attack by Indians. The next image is of Ulysses

S. Grant assembling his troops, which include Abraham Lincoln, John Wilkes Booth, Calvin Coolidge, Rhett Butler and Scarlett O'Hara, and General Custer, all symbols of war in Claude's mixed-up, trippy mind.

Also among Grant's troops is Aretha Franklin, a surrealistic non sequitur that might represent Claude's knowledge that the draft is racist—or it might just be the kind of random image a drugged-out mind conjures. Perhaps it's significant that Aretha sings "Indian Love Call," an old-fashioned love song from the 1924 operetta *Rose Marie*. Maybe this crazy vision of Aretha Franklin funkifying this operetta song is Claude's image of a new, more racially open definition of love and coupling. Grant's troops dance a minuet for a bit and then are attacked by African witch doctors (probably a reference to the black activist character, Hud, who is referred to as the boogeyman in Act I), and the witch doctors kill everyone but Lincoln. Hud becomes LeRoi Jones, the black social activist, writer, and publisher, and he confronts Lincoln (played by a black woman, by the way), threatening to kill him/her, satirizing the black separatists of the '60s who refused to allow whites to participate in the Civil Rights movement. Lincoln calms Hud/Jones down and proceeds to deliver a crazy, soulful Gettysburg Address. Complete with doo-wop backup singers.

The trip continues as the killing of war comes to the forefront of Claude's mind. A succession of comic stereotypes murder each other—first monks, who are killed by Catholic nuns, who are killed by astronauts, who are killed by Chinese people, who are killed by guerillas, who are killed by a Native American. This sequence is played three times, forward and backward as the trip spins out of control. The action continues as Claude's parents appear with a drill sergeant and have a conversation with a suit Claude has left behind, the only thing that remains after Claude is killed in war. The tribe begins playing children's games, which escalate until they all end up murdering each other. The song "Three-Five-Zero-Zero" begins and the tribe becomes the walking dead, advancing on the audience, accusing them of complicity in the horror of war. By the end of the song, everyone has died again, in agonizing, slow-motion deaths. Two tribe members have been watching all this from a platform above the fray and they sing "What a Piece of Work Is Man," an ironic tribute to the majesty and nobility of mankind, sung as the two singers walk though the battlefield of murdered bodies. A short section of "Three-Five-Zero-Zero" returns and the trip ends as Claude wakes up.

So why, after so much pressure from the tribe to burn his draft card, after his terrifying hallucinations about agonizing death during his drug trip, does he still choose to go to Vietnam? In a literary sense, he is destined to go. He's the Chosen One, the one who will sacrifice himself for the others. But on a personal level, Ragni and Rado have painted a portrait of a very real, very complex person. From the very beginning of the show, we find out that Claude is searching for fulfillment, trying to find himself and his place in the world. This is why he has joined the tribe. In his first song, "Manchester, England," Claude says that he "dropped out," as hippie and drug guru Timothy Leary advocated, but that his life is still unfulfilling. He asks Timothy Leary directly in the song why this is, why his life should still feel so meaningless when he has followed Leary's instructions. Like the title character in *Pippin*, Claude is on a quest to find the meaning of life, and like young men throughout the history of the world, Claude believes that war may just be the thing that makes a man of him, that shows him who he really is. Although for Pippin war is just a comic sketch performed by a troupe of players, for Claude war is very real. He may find out who he is, but he may also get killed. After the trip, Claude realizes that although war scares him, nothing else in life has proved satisfying.

But here *Hair* breaks the rules again. Instead of following the archetypal hero myth story, instead of Claude finding his true self deep in the jungles of Vietnam, instead of gaining elusive wisdom about the nature of life, Claude is dropped into Vietnam and instantly killed by a North Vietnamese sniper. There is no romance here, no literary devices, no triumph for our hero. He just gets shot and dies in the jungle, running away, screaming like a frightened child. It reminds us that war is not like a John Wayne movie or a romance novel. War is death.

The show's finale, "The Flesh Failures," summarizes the themes of the show, particularly the insanity of war and our consumerist culture, our collective obsession with comfort even while people are being murdered in Southeast Asia. We pass each other on the street, bundled up in our designer clothes, created and purchased specifically to display our level of wealth and success, too busy to stop and connect with each other, too busy to help the homeless lying on the street, too preoccupied with our superficial lives, our appointments, our scramble to accumulate possessions (a theme *Hair*'s descendent *Rent* would return to). The song tells us that somewhere inside, buried beneath all this, hidden deep down, there is greatness in the human race, that we have great potential, but that so far we have failed. We have failed by succumbing to comfort, to the demands of the flesh, instead of aiming for something higher. Claude comes forward, now dead, killed in Vietnam, invisible to the tribe—just as returning Vietnam vets were "invisible" in American culture—and as he reprises his theme song, "Manchester, England," the tribe sings in counterpoint "Eyes Look Your Last," a musical setting of a speech from *Romeo and Juliet.* The words are Romeo's, after he finds Juliet's (apparently) dead body, and just before he takes his own life. The last line of this section, "the rest is silence," is Hamlet's last line before dying at the end of *Hamlet.* We are killing ourselves, the tribe is telling us. After another verse of "The Flesh Failures," the show finishes with the iconic "Let the Sun Shine In."

But "Let the Sun Shine In" is not the happy song many people think it is. It's a call to action. The tribe is begging us, the audience, to change things, to stop the killing, the hatred, the discrimination, the destruction of our world. They are saying that we are in a time of darkness (as described in detail by "The Flesh Failures," "Easy to Be Hard," and other songs), that it is now time to let the sun shine in and change things. It's significant that the lyric doesn't say that the sun is already shining and everything is going to be fine. It says that we have to take action, we have to *let* the sun shine on the darkness around us, and the implication is unmistakable—if we don't let the sun shine, it will be the end of us.

The Tribe

The cast of *Hair* is called "the Tribe," and in each production of *Hair* around the world, the cast chooses a tribe name, generally naming themselves after a Native American tribe. The practice is not just cosmetic. This show, perhaps more than almost any other, really is an ensemble piece, one in which the entire cast must work together, must like each other, and, often within the show, must work as a single organism. All the sense of family, of belonging, of responsibility and loyalty inherent in the word *tribe* has to be felt by the cast. And the mere choosing of a tribe name begins that process in a very real way.

Like Stephen Sondheim and George Furth's musical *Company*, the characters in *Hair* are greatly—and intentionally—underwritten. Much of what is important about the characters is in the subtext, hidden below what feels like very casual, even trivial, conversation. It's the job of the actor and director to read between the lines, to discover the relationships, the loyalties, the tensions, the love, and the deep connections among the characters.

At the center of the tribe and the show are George Berger and Claude Bukowski (presumably named for Beat generation poet Charles Bukowski, though Bukowski is also Jim Rado's mother's maiden name). While Act I is Berger's act as he introduces the tribe, their philosophy, and their way of life, Act II belongs to Claude, his drug trip, and his decision about going to war. Berger and Claude are two halves of one whole. Claude is the intellectual half, the introspective one, the voice of reason, morality, spirituality, guilt. He's the one who tries to *understand* everything around him, including that which is not understandable—and that's his downfall. He says several times in the show that he is "Aquarius, destined for greatness or madness," but he is actually destined for both. His greatness is in forcing the tribe (through his death) to confront the evils of the world; his madness is his decision to become part of the machinery of war. If Claude is Aquarius (Jim Rado, who played Claude on Broadway, was also an Aquarius), then this is Claude's show, and the opening number is summoning him. Notice that the tribe's final good-byes to Claude are done while singing "Aquarius."

Berger, on the other hand, is the animal half, focused on instinct, pleasure, primal urges. But those primal urges are not just for food, water, and sex—they are also to protect the tribe, to be its leader. Only together do Berger (the id) and Claude (the superego) make one healthy person. (This is a common device in literature and film, used in the novel and 1999 film *Fight Club*, and also used in the late 1960s in "The Enemy Within," an episode of the original *Star Trek* series.)

With this in mind, it's interesting that both Berger and Claude want the young, idealistic Sheila, since they are two halves of a whole. Berger wants Sheila only for the physical pleasures of sex, nothing more; while Claude wants her for the spiritual pleasures of pure love. Only together do they make the perfect lover. Sheila loves Berger but Berger's only interest in her is physical. When she buys him a shirt in Act I, his reaction speaks volumes. He feels smothered by her. He doesn't want gifts. He doesn't want commitment and he doesn't want the depth of feeling he sees in Sheila. His reaction to the smothering love she offers is to treat her badly in order to get her to leave him alone. He explodes at her over nothing (and in an early version of the script, brutally rapes her), hoping that she'll hate him, hoping that she'll crawl away, licking her wounds, giving him at least temporary freedom. She tries to hang on, tries to laugh off his insults, but eventually, she lashes back with the song "Easy to be Hard." She doesn't understand him. To him, it's just sex. To her, it's love.

In the earlier, off Broadway script, Berger cares so little for Sheila (or maybe, so much more for Claude), he even asks Sheila to sleep with Claude before he goes off to war.

What a Piece of Work Is Claude

It's easy to see Claude as Hamlet, the melancholy hippie, prisoner of indecision. In fact, there are several Shakespeare references in the show. In the original off Broadway script, Claude recites a speech from *Hamlet* to Berger after the trip, a speech in which Claude/Hamlet marvels at the nobility and great potential of mankind but confesses that he sees the world as nothing but a barren wasteland. Galt MacDermot later set this speech to music for Broadway, called it "What a Piece of Work Is Man," and it was inserted into Claude's trip, still serving basically the same purpose, but now sung by two other members of the tribe as part of Claude's hallucination (so arguably it's still coming from Claude).

After the trip, as Berger and Claude are waking up, Berger says, "Face reality, Shakespeare." Is that just a coincidence or does Berger know Claude's trip included a speech from *Hamlet*? Does Berger possess some kind of Shakespearean magical powers that allow him to see inside Claude's mind? And if he does, was Berger manipulating Claude's trip like a latter-day Prospero to persuade him to decide not to go to Vietnam? "What a Piece of Work Is Man" also serves as proof of how literate Claude is—if *Hamlet* shows up in his trip, Claude must be familiar with the play and its themes. And of course, by this logic, Claude has read Allen Ginsberg's poem "Wichita Vortex Sutra," on which the other song in the trip, "Three-Five-Zero-Zero," is based.

But Claude is also clearly a Christ figure, and there are even more references to Jesus Christ in *Hair* than there are to Hamlet. Several times throughout the show, Claude talks about wanting to be invisible, wanting to know what people are thinking, and wanting to perform miracles. Midway through Act I, Claude enters saying, "I am the Son of God. I shall vanish and be forgotten." Is this a comment on organized religion losing touch with God and forgetting the true meaning of Jesus's teachings? Following this comment, Claude comes through the audience and the tribe, "blessing" people as he goes. Later, he compares his hair to Jesus in the song "Hair." At one point, the tribe mystic, Jeanie, says that "Claude is hung up on a cross over Sheila and Berger." After the trip he says he wants to hang on a cross and eat cornflakes. At the end of the show, when Claude returns to the tribe for the finale, he says, "Berger,

I feel like I died." Like Christ, Claude has died and has returned, and, like Christ, Claude is the Chosen One, the one member of the tribe chosen (literally, by the draft board) to give his life for the others. In the last moment of the show, Berger forms a cross over Claude as the final lights fade.

In addition to these very obvious moments, there are other less direct references. Like Christ, Claude is sent to his death by the government. Like Christ, Claude suffers through enormous confusion and conflict over what to do—throughout Act I and specifically in "Where Do I Go," Claude is just like Christ in the Garden of Gethsemane. Just as Claude's parents disapprove of him and his lifestyle, there is some evidence in the Bible that Jesus's mother and brothers thought he was out of his mind and an embarrassment to the family. And just as the second half of the Bible (the New Testament) focuses on Jesus Christ, the second half of *Hair* shifts its focus almost exclusively to Claude and the story of his death and (metaphorical) resurrection. The hippies' trip the night before Claude goes off to his death in war could even be compared to the Last Supper.

Furthermore, if Claude is Jesus, then Berger is John the Baptist, and Jeanie is Mary Magdalene. Even Claude and Berger's names, by accident or not, are similar to their biblical counterparts—Claude and Christ, George Berger and John the Baptist. Berger's first speech to the audience deals a lot with water, creating an arguable connection to John the Baptist. At one point, one member of the tribe actually cites John the Baptist as his hero. In fact, the historical John the Baptist was a lot like Berger—wild, out of the mainstream, roaming the countryside, a strong and harsh critic of the government and the church. Like the hippies of the 1960s, John the Baptist believed the church had lost touch with God, that he and his followers had to totally discard accepted mainstream religion in order to find God. John the Baptist wore camel skins and ate bugs and wild honey. He had wild, long hair and a long, unkempt beard. He was a first-century hippie, vigorously rejecting the establishment and the moral and political status quo. Just as Claude is drawn to Berger, so was Jesus drawn to the radical revolutionary John the Baptist, a charismatic young man declaring philosophical war on the church, the government, and other adult institutions. And like the hippies, most of the followers of John the Baptist were very young.

And like Mary Magdalene and Jesus, Jeanie loves Claude, but he can't return her love. Because Claude is the emotional and moral center of

Hair, Jeanie is by extension the most important female character in the show, even though it might not appear that way at first glance. She acts as Greek chorus several times throughout the show, explaining things to the audience, identifying characters and relationships, but she also gets a solo introduction song in Act I ("Air") along with the other leads. It's through her that we feel the tragedy and the anguish of those Claude will leave behind. There are cryptic references throughout the show that Jeanie may be psychic in some way (or at least some kind of hippie mystic), that she knows Claude will end up going to war, and that she may know that Claude will die in Vietnam.

It may even be that Jeanie is denying the fact that Claude is the father of her unborn child only to free him from any responsibility, since she knows he doesn't really love her. It's probable that they have slept together. Though there's nothing in the text that says this explicitly, Jeanie and Claude allude to this in their conversation before the Be-In. Though Claude is in love with Sheila, Jeanie is in love with Claude and, along with Berger, she will suffer the greatest loss when Claude dies. It's hard not to see parallels to Mary Magdalene, and since the discovery of "new" Lost Gospels in 1945, there may even be romantic parallels. These papyrus texts, discovered at the Nag Hammadi library in Egypt, have holes and gaps in them but some scholars maintain that these texts describe a romantic relationship between Jesus and Mary Magdalene. Unsurprisingly, this is hotly contested among biblical scholars.

Like Mary Magdalene, who was called both prostitute and saint, Jeanie provides a symbolic bridge between sexuality and spirituality, between the pleasures of the flesh and the cultivation of the soul. Jeanie is promiscuous, already pregnant when the show begins, but she is also the one who invites the audience to the Be-In, an event of spiritual exploration and awakening. She brings Claude a book on astral projection, and, as mentioned earlier, she seems to have mystical powers. But even beyond all that, the historical Mary Magdalene would have been right at home with Berger and the tribe. She grew up in Magdala, a small fishing village that was a hotbed of rebel activity against the Roman Empire. She came from a well-to-do family, just as many of the hippies came from upper-middle-class families. And Mary Magdalene was not a prostitute, even though she was characterized as such for centuries, just as the hippies were often characterized as sexual deviants and hedonists. Some texts suggest that she did have a considerable sexual appetite and, because she was well-off enough that she didn't have to work, she may have practiced what the hippies of the 1960s called "free love." And for that she was considered a sinner by her contemporaries. Like the hippies, Mary Magdalene was an independent thinker who met Jesus, a radical political activist, and joined his movement, a movement dedicated to finding enlightenment, rejecting old social norms and rules, and discovering the answers to the great existential questions; the parallels to the tribe in *Hair* are obvious. After Christ's crucifixion, and after Mary's subsequent preaching and evangelism, she retired to a secluded wilderness where she lived out her remaining years. Some accounts say that each day she was carried up by angels to listen to the music of the heavens, an experience probably akin to astral projection, a practice Jeanie is very interested in.

All There in Black and White

Hair challenges nearly everything we complacently accept as ordinary in life, all the things we just don't think about. It shoves them in our faces and demands that we look at them. Racism, obscenity, sexual repression, and other issues are all laid bare before us, rejecting the restrictions of "polite society."

Racism is the most American of all issues. It was an issue when the Declaration of Independence was written. It split the nation during the Civil War and again in the 1960s. In the song "Colored Spade," Hud lists every offensive, racist label and stereotype ever thrown at him, words as *weapons*, to make us see how horrible, how offensive, how dehumanizing they are. He assaults the audience with words and phrases and stereotypes they may have actually used (or passively allowed others to use) and he claims them for his own. When we hear them all together, when we realize how many more labels there are for blacks than for whites, they become ridiculous. They lose their power.

In the song "Dead End," the black tribe members list signs we encounter every day—DEAD END, KEEP OUT, DON'T WALK, NO STANDING, KEEP OFF THE GRASS, and others. And the fact that these warnings are being sung by black men and women raises them to the level of social metaphor. This is the world black Americans face every day, in employment, in housing, in pay, in opportunity, and not just in 1968 but still today.

At the beginning of Act II, two songs, "Black Boys" and "White Boys," make a powerful statement. It's surprising enough (especially in 1968) for women to objectify men the way men have been objectifying women for centuries, but it was even more surprising in 1968 to be doing it across race lines. Three white women sing about how much they love black men, and then three black women sing about how much they love white men. The songs are funny, seemingly harmless entertainments. But there were states in the 1960s where interracial marriage was still illegal. It wasn't until *Star Trek* in the late '60s that television saw its first interracial kiss.

The trip is an interesting commentary on race. When General Grant lines up his troops, not only are the genders reversed (women as Lincoln, Booth, Coolidge, Gable, etc.), but so is race in at least one case. A black woman plays Abraham Lincoln and a blond girl plays Lincoln's shoeshine boy. Like the song "Colored Spade," "Abie Baby" is another politically incorrect comedy number, in which three black tribe members sing joyously about being freed by Lincoln, in stereotypical Hollywood-black dialects.

Though it's common today to practice color-blind casting—ignoring an actor's race when considering him for a role—*Hair* forced this upon audiences, demanding that they think about the social roles separating the races, demanding that the audience sees these separations as arbitrary and ridiculous. It's jarring to see a white girl shining shoes, but had it been a black man, we might not have even thought about it. It's odd to hear a black woman recite the Gettysburg Address but there's no reason why she shouldn't. As she quite correctly points out, they are "*all* our forefathers." But most disturbing is that as startling as this must have been in 1968, it's still more surprising today than it should be.

In the Name of the Father

LeRoi Jones, the black social activist and writer, wrote in the 1960s, "God has been replaced, as he has all over the West, with respectability and air conditioning." And *Hair* reflects that view of American society in the 1960s. It exposes the dark underbelly of organized religion as it satirizes its hypocrisies. In the song "Donna," it's unclear whether Berger is singing about looking for a girl named Donna or, in fact, looking for the Virgin Mary, the Madonna. The song starts with a slight variation of "once upon a time" and the last line of the song actually replaces the words "my Donna" with "Madonna." Could Berger be talking about *the* Madonna, the "sixteen-year-old" Virgin Mary? Could this song be about his search for true spirituality as symbolized by Mary, his inability to find that spirituality in the hypocrisy and institutionalization of organized religion? And could that "disfigured" spirituality be represented by the "tattooed" Donna? After all, the song catalogs all his attempts to find spirituality in India, in South America, and through psychedelic drugs in San Francisco. In the second part of the song when he calls Donna psychedelic, perhaps he's telling us he found the Virgin Mary—and God—through psychedelic, mind-expanding drugs (which was the goal of many drug users, after all), and it was only through the drugs that he could "evolve" into a more spiritual being.

Just a few minutes after "Donna," the tribe performs the song "Sodomy," a mock religious ceremony cataloguing sex acts that organized religion condemns: fellatio, cunnilingus, pederasty, and masturbation. It satirizes religion's preoccupation with sex, with "unspeakable" acts that nonetheless fill the Bible (making it as R-rated as *Hair* itself), acts that continue to embarrass the modern-day Catholic Church. Today, the audience flinches when pederasty is mentioned, because we can't help but connect that to the Catholic Church's child molestation scandals. Before the song, Woof, as high priest, says, "This is the body and blood of Jesus Christ. And I am going to eat you. I swear to tell the truth, the whole truth, and nothing but the truth, so help me God. In the name of the Father, the Son, and the Holy Ghost. Amen." In one short speech, he mocks the solemnity of priests and religious rituals, the cannibalistic implications of communion, and the all too blatant exceptions to the Constitution's separation of church and state in America. "Sodomy" concludes with a reference to the Kama Sutra, an ancient text which celebrates sex rather than denigrating and controlling it.

The song "Ain't Got No" also makes two religious references in its list of things the hippies "ain't got," with responses shouted out by the tribe. When the soloist sings that he has no faith, the tribe shouts out "Catholic," suggesting that the Catholics have lost touch with God in the morass of man-made ritual that defines the church. At the end of the song, when the soloist sings that he has no God, the tribe shouts, "Good!" But we learn throughout the show the tribe is in fact very spiritual, so this reference means only that it's a good thing to lose God *as defined by modern religions*, a false God, a God loaded up with man's baggage and distanced from real spirituality and faith. *Hair* rejects religion but embraces spirituality. The mantra chanted before the song "Don't Put it Down" ("*om mane padme hum*") is a scared Buddhist mantra to Avalokiteswara, the Buddhist Savior and Protector.

As evidence of the spiritual side of the hippie culture and of *Hair* (and despite, or perhaps because of, the show's criticism of organized religion), the original Broadway cast celebrated its third anniversary in May 1971 by holding a very special mass at the Cathedral of St. John the Divine in New York City, presided over by Jerry Ragni's brother and other clergy. For the occasion, Galt MacDermot wrote a new Mass in F, and instead of hymns, he used songs from *Hair*, sung by the Broadway cast and several New York choirs. The mass was released on an album called *Divine Hair/ Mass in F*.

Let the Sun Shine In

It's impossible to describe the experience of performing *Hair* to someone who hasn't done it. Many artists tell of how their lives were fundamentally changed by working on this show. From the choosing of the tribe name to the overwhelming rush of emotion in the show's finale, it is truly an experience unlike any other. It is not a musical; it is a happening. Its spontaneity and its authenticity are everything. Not only does the experience bond each member of the tribe to every other member (and this includes actors, director, designers, musicians), it bonds each tribe to all the other tribes around the world, past and present. It centers people, changes them, guides them toward balance in their lives, guides them back to paths in their lives they've forgotten or abandoned, guides them toward a deeper spirituality. Even the most cynical among us is transformed by *Hair*. It holds a mystical, primal power that is impossible to explain. Just as it is utterly unique in so many concrete ways, it is just as unique in all the unexplainable ways.

Despite *Hair*'s apparent vulgarity and simplicity and sexual frankness, it really does work magic on people. And maybe the transcendence of *Hair* can be partially explained this way. Humans seem to have an endless hunger for knowing the unknowable, understanding that which cannot be understood. Our hopelessly insufficient human language can never *begin* to express all that is eternal and infinite and sublime about existence. And that's what poetry is for, language that reaches beyond our normal capabilities, that expresses what can't be literally expressed, which must instead be penetrated and explored and experienced from within. And that's what *Hair* does. The human hunger for transcendence is no less today than it was in the 1960s. Perhaps it's even greater today. The experience of performing or watching *Hair* on stage works like the greatest of human poetry, like Eliot or Shakespeare, by taking language beyond its literal meaning, coupling it with music, that most ineffable, most abstract of all languages, and exploring those mysteries we all yearn to understand. Why are we here? Is there a God? What is death? What lies beyond this world? What do we leave behind?

Hair dares to go there. *Hair* dares to tell us that we don't need priests to explore those questions and we don't need the revealed word of human religion. We are divine ourselves and have every right to that exploration and to those answers. That was subversive in the 1960s and it's still subversive today.

Jesus Christ Superstar

We made him a type of Everyman. Judas did not think of himself as a traitor. He did what he did, not because he was basically evil, but because he was intelligent. He could see Christ becoming something he considered harmful to the Jews. Judas felt that they been persecuted enough. As far as what Christ was saying, general principles of how human beings should live together—Judas approved of this. What Judas was worried about was that as Christ got bigger and bigger and more popular, people began switching their attentions from what Christ was saying to Christ himself. They were saying that Jesus is God, here is the new Messiah, and Judas was terrified because, a.) he didn't agree with it—he thought Christ was getting out of control and it was affecting Him, and b.) Judas reckoned that if the movement got too big and people began worshipping Christ as a god, the Romans who were occupying Israel would come down and clobber them.

—Superstar *lyricist Tim Rice*

The play represents a confused and commercial portrait of Christ —a Christ that does not rise from the dead. Of course, the Christ the authors present would not have risen from the dead. They are not men of faith, and their statements only serve to undermine the scriptures. I have not seen the show, and my objections are based on what friends who have seen it tell me.

—Minister Dennis Miller, Calvary Baptist Church

Here's the truth: *Jesus Christ Superstar* is about politics, not religion, about a political activist, not the son of God. And it's about the 1960s, not the Roman Empire. If Tim Rice's searing, smartass lyrics and Tom O'Horgan's trippy original production weren't enough proof of that, just read the lyric of the title song—sung from the point of view of "today" and of "mass communication." Rice's story was a story about an authoritarian government and an institutionalized religion trying to snuff out the voice of enlightenment and of peace. In other words, the 1960s. And maybe also the early 2000s.

Tim Rice and Andrew Lloyd Webber's *Jesus Christ Superstar* set the world buzzing when it first appeared on vinyl in 1970 and on Broadway in 1971. The executives at MCA Records were terrified by it. In reaction to the single "Superstar," one MCA executive said, "A song like that will offend everyone." Another said, "If we put that record out, every churchman in the country will stone us." It made one secretary cry, who said, "It's sad when a company like Decca [owned by MCA] has to make money by making fun of Jesus!" Later on, the film's director, Norman Jewison, would say, "My hope is that audiences will take this for what it is—an opera, not history. These kids are trying to take Jesus off the stained-glass windows and get him down on the street. Some people are not going to like that." As author Robert Short put it, "It is a complete misunderstanding to view *Jesus Christ Superstar* as an expression of anyone's answer . . . Its purpose is, first, to put to Jesus the question we have today about the meaning of life, and second, to put this question in *our own way of putting it.*" Tim Rice did with this iconic story the same thing that clergy across America do every Sunday morning: remove it from its distant past and foreign culture and give it resonance and relevance to the issues and obstacles we face every day.

But today, *Jesus Christ Superstar* has been dumbed down, made palatable and comfortable, robbed of the rebellious, youthful arrogance that originally made music and theatre history. Surely more than forty years after its creation, it is time to return the piece to its rebel roots and allow Rice's aggressive text to offend, stun, shock, and disturb once again.

In setting the story of Judas's betrayal of Jesus for the modern stage, lyricist Tim Rice approached the story as political history instead of revealed scripture, and Jesus as a radical political activist (mirroring the times) rather than as the son of God (a label Jesus himself never used in the Bible to describe himself). After all, Jesus *was* a radical in the true sense of the word—"of or pertaining to the root or original; fundamental"—by cutting right to the root of every problem and every issue he addressed. Jesus knew, just like today's radicals, that many social and political problems boil down to poverty, inequality, and education, and until those root problems are solved, no other problems will be. This Jesus does not point the way to God as much as he points the way toward social justice and to living a moral, engaged life. And that's why politics takes center stage here instead of religion: we forget sometimes that politics is nothing more than the way humans decide questions of collective morality, how to live together in a community (of whatever size) and which values will be shared by that community.

Rice says he was first inspired by the lyric from Bob Dylan song "With God on Our Side," a song asking if Judas Iscariot had God on his side. Rice was quoted at the time saying, "We need to humanize Christ, because for me, I find Jesus as portrayed in the Gospels as a God as a very unrealistic figure . . . The same is true, on the other hand, for Judas, who is portrayed just as a sort of cardboard cut-out figure of evil." Strangely, the bulk of American and British critics complained repeatedly that this was not a proper retelling of the biblical story of Christ, and the respected British director Peter Hall said, "I think *Jesus Christ Superstar* says nothing about Christ and nothing for or against religion." Of course, they were exactly right, but they hadn't understood that this was the creators' intention. Rice and Lloyd Webber never intended to tell a Bible story but instead an alternative story of famous events; and what's more, they were telling the story of Judas, not Jesus. Rice even tells us all this in the second line of the show: "If you strip away the myth from the man, you will see where we all soon will be." He's talking to Jesus, but he's also talking to *us*.

Rice and Webber approached this story in somewhat the same way Thomas Jefferson had, as history instead of religion. In his book, *What Jesus Meant*, Garry Willis writes:

> The Jesus of the Gospels is scandalous, and one of those scandalized was Thomas Jefferson. He was so offended by the miracles and the curses, by the devils assailing and defeated, that he created his own more acceptable Jesus, excising all those parts of the Gospels that he considered unworthy of a wise man's story. The result, cleansed of all the supernatural hocus-pocus, is the tale of a good man, a very good man, perhaps the best of good men—therefore a man who would not pretend to work miracles, to wrestle with demons, or to have unique access to God the Father . . . He is a man of his time, or even ahead of his time, but not outside time.

With *Superstar* Rice and Lloyd Webber broke new ground in several ways. First, the idea of rock opera was still brand new; though the Who's *Tommy* had already been released, no rock opera had been staged. Second, the idea that rock and roll was an acceptable—even a *preferable*—language with which to tell this story was quite radical. And perhaps most important to us today, the choice to focus the show on Judas rather than on Jesus lifted the show out of the category of mere cultural rebellion and into the realm of legitimate intellectual and artistic endeavor. This was a show *not* about Jesus's teachings, his divinity, his suffering on the cross, or his resurrection. This was a story that asked a simple question: why did Judas feel he needed to betray Jesus? As the quote above shows us, Rice delved deep into all these characters, infusing them with personality, psychology, and ideology that the more simplistic storytelling style of the Bible never offered. Other dramatizations of this story fail because there's no tension, no surprises, nothing unknown—we all know this story too well. But Rice told us a *new* story and that choice gave us back the dramatic elements that make a good story. Rice's story also gave us an *active* Judas and Jesus, rather than the passive, inherently *un*dramatic characters the Bible gives us, unable to change fate, tossed around by the winds of divine providence. This show dramatized not just *what* happened, but *why* it happened. The show opened with Judas's warnings of disaster (in "Heaven on Their Minds") and ended with Judas's I-told-you-so song, "Superstar." This is Judas's story; he is the only central character who changes, who learns, who goes on a journey. Jesus is the same at the beginning of the story as he is at the end. He is not the protagonist.

The show's title song was released as a single before MCA recorded the whole opera (to see if it would be a commercial disaster), but no one knew when they first heard it that this was Judas speaking, and more specifically, that it was Judas *scolding* Jesus. They also didn't know that this lyric would become the central point of the entire show and the answer to the story's central question: Why did Judas betray Jesus? Like the single, the title of the opera is snide, sarcastic, angry. It reveals Judas's point of view, that Jesus had become a "superstar," a shallow, hyped personality worshipped merely for the hype, like so many pop stars of the '60s and '70s and today. All this baggage became more important than the central philosophical message Jesus wanted to convey, a message Judas believed in. To Judas, Jesus lost his stature as philosopher when he gained his status as superstar.

The show never suggested that Jesus wasn't divine, but neither did it reinforce the view that he was. This was not an entirely bizarre approach—though the canonical Christian Gospels stress Jesus's divinity, the Gnostic Gospels (including the Gospel of Thomas, the Gospel of Mary, the Gospel of Judas, and others) came from a different strand of early Christianity in which Christians believed fully in the wisdom and philosophy of Jesus but never even mentioned the idea that he was God. Likewise, in *Superstar* that issue was off the table, irrelevant to the story Rice was telling. Everyone already knows the story of Jesus as the son of God. This was the other, rarely examined side of the story of Jesus, an ordinary guy who became an unlikely star. After all, the name "Jesus" was one of the most common Jewish male names of that time and place; calling this man Jesus would be like a modern author calling a character Everyman, or, in Bible-speak, "the son of man."

It is that ordinariness that gives *Superstar* resonance and life but it also outraged Christians. Most people think of Jesus as a religious icon, but the people who lived and worked around him saw him as just a man. Despite what most of us think, Jesus was not a carpenter in the sense of a trained artisan—the Greek word used to describe him (and his father) in the Gospels is *tekton*, meaning anyone who makes things with his hands. The modern equivalent might be a construction worker or day laborer. Jesus's family had no land, putting them extremely low on the economic ladder. But *Superstar* was also the story of Jesus the social revolutionary, political insurgent, radical philosopher, apocalyptic prophet, a speaker of truth to power who terrified the religious and secular authorities. His ascendancy from such humble roots made him even more of a puzzle and therefore more dangerous to the priests. Today, most productions of *Jesus Christ Superstar* are far blander than Rice intended, comfortably reinforcing mainstream beliefs. But this show was meant to be a call to political action, a reminder that many of the great political and human rights movements in Western history found their roots in the very radical political agenda of Jesus and Judas.

Not surprisingly, this approach was considered blasphemous by mainstream Christians. Many of the show's critics believed that the story of Jesus should not be trivialized by rock music. But merely because an art form is popular doesn't mean it can't treat serious subjects; Bach's music was popular in its time, yet no one today would complain that Bach's Passions are irreverent. Unfortunately, many people today equate seriousness and import with antiquity. Another problem with the stand against *Superstar* is that Jesus himself was a major rebel of his time; he fought against the establishment, the high priests, the Pharisees, and the government. What better way to tell his story than with the musical language of rebellion? Keeping the story of Jesus and his views in antique forms takes the teeth out of his activism. There's no reason why people should not celebrate their beliefs using the language and music of their lives. Today, *Superstar* doesn't seem nearly as controversial because rock and roll is now the music of adults, and Christian rock has emerged; but imagine the uproar if the Catholic church began allowing rap music as part of the liturgy . . .

Another source of consternation for some Christians came during the Last Supper scene, when Jesus sings, "For all you care, this wine could be my blood. For all you care, this bread could be my body." This was an extremely radical new approach to these words, but not an entirely unsupported interpretation. The earliest copies of the Book of Luke describe the Last Supper very differently from what later, less authentic texts say and what most Bibles say today. In the original text of Luke, Jesus says "Take this and drink it among yourselves, for I say to you that I will not drink from the fruit of the vine from now on, until the kingdom of God comes." And after breaking the bread he says, "This is my body. But behold, the hand of the one who betrays me is with me at the table." There is *no mention* of his body or blood being sacrificed for the salvation of believers. That idea is nowhere to be found in the original Bible texts—not surprisingly, since it implied ritual vampirism and cannibalism, both of which were considered pagan rituals. Furthermore, the earliest texts of the Bible make it very clear that the sharing of the wine and bread were not special rituals, just standard dinner traditions. The meaning is in the sharing of the meal, not in grand, metaphysical metaphors. But that also means that, according to the earliest manuscripts, Jesus's death on the cross is *not* what provides salvation to believers. *Superstar* was making an entirely different point with these lines, that these men and women thought about what Jesus meant in their lives as little as they thought about what food or wine they put in their bodies—they weren't completely apathetic, but gave it only minimal consideration. Jesus was also implying that they were the ones killing him, by their apathy, their cowardice, their gluttony. This was an *accusation*, not a clue to eternal salvation.

The greatest objection from the religious critics was that the show did not include the resurrection. Rice told an interviewer that he did not believe Jesus was the son of God, but for him that made the story all the more amazing. Another bone of contention was the song "I Only Want to Say" that Jesus sings in the Garden of Gethsemane. Though Jesus has some doubt in the biblical version of the story, those doubts are articulated so completely and so intensely in the show that they sounded to some like more blasphemy. Critics also found the relationship between Jesus and Mary Magdalene uncomfortably sexual. They were right—her physical attraction to Jesus is strongly implied; after all, when the show was written, people still thought Mary Magdalene was a prostitute (we know now that's a misreading enshrined by Pope Gregory). Another complaint was over the periodic humor in the show, though it was minimal. The drunken apostles at the Last Supper and King Herod's frighteningly comic song and dance did not amuse some people. Rice and Lloyd Webber both felt the story of Christ, especially the crucifixion, had been much too romanticized into a beautiful, graceful event, instead of the brutal, savage act that it had been. To reopen our eyes to the horror and tragedy of the story, they decided they needed to shock the audience.

The Virgin Birth

In 1971, no one expected the next big Broadway musical would be based on the Bible. And they certainly didn't expect it to be based on a pop album about Judas and Jesus. After all, the youth movement of the '60s had been about newfound spirituality but *also* about a rejection of institutionalized religion. Young people's drug use was not just an escape; it was also a means to help them find the spirituality they believed their parents had lost in the meaningless hypocrisy of organized religion in the 1950s. In 1967, Father James Kavanaugh had published his book, *A Modern Priest Looks at His Outdated Church*. Looking at their parents and the rest of the "older generation," young people saw evidence that mainstream religions had reduced religious experience, the act of living through faith, to nothing more than symbols and metaphors, subverting and short-circuiting the religious experience itself. They believed that mainstream religious traditions and rituals got in the way of true faith and the search for ultimate truths. The language of the King James Bible was as remote from their lives as it could be, full of *thee*s and *thou*s, strange grammar and sentence structure; young people did not believe this dusty old relic related to their lives in the tumultuous late '60s and early '70s. Rice's intentionally slangy, often consciously unpoetic language in *Superstar* was a direct reaction to these feelings, to put blood and flesh back on these cardboard biblical characters (much like the musical *1776* did for America's Founders), to make them *accessible* to modern audiences.

The opening images of the 1973 film version of *Superstar* created stunning visual metaphors for this modern cultural tumult, panning across actual ruins in Israel, literally showing us the crumbling edifice of organized religion; and there in the middle of the ruins, the camera reveals modern-day scaffolding, the hint of a coming "reconstruction" of the philosophy of Jesus for modern times; and finally, the camera revels a busload of The Younger Generation coming toward us in the distance. And all this in one uninterrupted shot. Because more young Americans than ever before were attending college in the 1960s and '70s—and while there, studying other world religions—they were finding that the Christian creation/Genesis story, the sacrifice/crucifixion and resurrection of Jesus Christ, the miracles performed by Jesus, and most of the rest of the central stories of Christianity had shown up in other world religions long before the birth of Christianity. Though this did not automatically discount all of Christianity for them, it did throw its claims of absolute and unique truth into question. As a result, many young adults began exploring the older Eastern religions.

In the song "Superstar," Judas speaks for these young people as he grills Jesus. That, more than anything else, is why the single sold so well all over the world. Judas asks what so many people still ask today: How can so many different religions all claim to have the *only* truth? And why should we believe that the Bible's truth is necessarily more true than the other truths? Or, more pointedly, why should we believe in any religion at all?

John Lennon said in an interview with London's *Evening Standard*, "Christianity will go. It will vanish and shrink. I needn't argue about that; I'm right and will be proved right. We're more popular than Jesus right now. I don't know which will go first, rock 'n' roll or Christianity. Jesus was all right, but his disciples were thick and ordinary. It's them twisting it that ruins it for me." Rice, Lloyd Webber, and their various directors were trying to find new meaning in the rubble of Jesus's moral philosophy. Christianity was in crisis (as it remains today), and far from mocking it or capitalizing on its woes, *Jesus Christ Superstar* was a legitimate, thoughtful response to the crisis. In fact, the apostles in Rice and Lloyd Webber's story were like much of the Western world's youth in the early '70s, questioning, thirsting for a more substantial, less arbitrary, more participatory philosophy of life. Judas and his angry anthem became a rallying cry for youth all over America and Europe. On the jacket of the original single, "Superstar," the record company printed a quote from Martin Sullivan, the Dean of St. Paul's in London, "There are some people who may be shocked by this record. I ask them to listen to it and think again. It is a desperate cry. *Who are you, Jesus Christ?* is the urgent enquiry, and a very proper one at that. The record probes some answers and make some comparisons." When the single was released, many US radio stations played the record, then followed it with a discussion group.

In October 1970 MCA released the full-length, double-album rock opera, not the first of its kind—*Tommy* gets that distinction—but certainly a landmark. The studio cast included the cream of London rock and roll—Ian Gillan, of the heavy metal band Deep Purple, as Jesus; Mike d'Abo, of the band Manfred Mann, as Herod; Paul Raven, who would later become the glam rocker Gary Glitter, as one of the priests; Murray Head, who had recorded the single of the title song, still singing Judas; the Hawaiian folk singer Yvonne Elliman, who was singing in London folk clubs at the time, as Mary Magdalene; and Barry Dennen, who had appeared in the London staging of *Hair*, as Pilate.

By February, the single reached the top of the American charts. Some stations played the entire double album without commercial interruption. The Vatican's own radio station played the album, even though the official Vatican newspaper didn't approve. Ministers began using the lyric as a basis for their sermons. Unauthorized touring companies sprang up all over America, performing the show in concert, usually in churches. Thomas Willis wrote in the *Chicago Tribune*, "I am neither a theologian nor a rock critic but if *Jesus Christ Superstar* isn't the most important religious music of the year—and one of two or three significant recordings of the decade—I am sadly mistaken." Derek Jewell in London's *Sunday Times* called it "every bit as valid as (and to me, more moving than) Handel's *Messiah*. This is a work on a heroic scale, masterfully conceived, honestly done, and overflowing with splendid music and apt language."

Jesus on Broadway

The $700,000 show opened on Broadway at the Mark Hellinger Theatre on October 12, 1971, with an unprecedented advance of two million dollars, and under the flamboyant, over-the-top direction of *Hair*'s skipper, Tom O'Horgan. Sadly, O'Horgan's outrageous sensory-assaulting production wasn't what the young writers wanted. They and producer Robert Stigwood had wanted to stage the piece more simply, perhaps using projections and television screens to underline Tim Rice's themes of celebrity and stardom. Stigwood first hired Frank Corsaro, a veteran theatre director who been working in opera, who seemed perfect for the project. But Corsaro was in a severe auto accident and was unable to do the show. O'Horgan replaced him, and no one involved—Stigwood, Rice, or Lloyd Webber—was particularly happy with the way the show turned out. It started its run selling out every night, but the enthusiasm diminished quickly and the show never made it to its second birthday.

Clive Barnes wrote in the *New York Times*, "Nothing could convince me that any show that has sold two-and-one-half million copies of its album before the opening night is anything like all bad. But I must also confess to experiencing some disappointment when *Jesus Christ Superstar* opened last night. It all rather resembled one's first sight of the Empire State Building. Not at all uninteresting, but somewhat unsurprising and of minimal artistic value." He went on to criticize O'Horgan's production: "Once he startled us with small things, now he startles us with big things. This time, the things got too big. For me, the real disappointment came not in the music, but in the conception. There is a coyness in its contemporaneity, a sneaky pleasure in the boldness of its anachronisms, a special undefined air of smugness in its daring." In the *New York Daily News*, Robert Crane interviewed people after seeing *Superstar*, and one Catholic housewife from Queens said, "My heart is beating, I am moved more than I am by a sermon in church. It enlightens the scriptures for me."

As it often does, life imitated art with *Superstar*, with the leads and the writers thrust unexpectedly into superstar status themselves, actually living (in a small way) part of the struggle Jesus deals with in the show. Rice said in one interview, "It's all a bit incredible. It has all gotten a bit out of hand—the orgy, the *Superstar* buttons and pocket calendars, the pickets, the T-shirts, the pirated concert versions touring around purporting to be the real *Superstar* . . ." Yvonne Elliman (Mary Magdalene) tells a story in the book *Rock Opera* about a young girl who came backstage to ask "if I would come visit a friend of hers in the hospital. She just wanted me to go and touch her." Jeff Fenholt (Jesus) would get letters from women considering becoming nuns, wanting his advice, as well as letters asking for miracle cures, and letters from women asking him to find their lost husbands. He got one letter that said it was from "the real Judas."

Jesus Christ Superstar ran on Broadway for 720 performances. Ben Vereen, as Judas, was nominated for a Tony Award, and nominations were also received for Best Original Score, Best Scenic Design, Best Costume Design, and Best Lighting Design (all were lost to *Follies*). *Superstar* won nothing. The show did not receive nominations for Best Musical or Best Director, though three of the four nominees for Best Musical were rock shows (*Two Gentlemen of Verona*, *Grease*, and *Ain't Supposed to Die a*

Natural Death). In London, the show was staged more simply and more honestly by Jim Sharman, who would soon be helping to birth *The Rocky Horror Show*. It opened in London in 1972 and ran for eight years and 3,358 performances, breaking all West End records. Michael Coveney writes in *Cats on a Chandelier*:

> [W]hen Dmitri Shostakovich, arguably the greatest composer of the twentieth century, and certainly one of its greatest artistic spirits, came to London shortly before he died in 1975 to attend the British premiere of his Fifteenth Symphony, he asked to go and see a performance of *Jesus Christ Superstar*. He was so impressed by what he heard and saw that he went back the following night to see it again. Julian Lloyd Webber says that Shostakovich confessed that, but for Stalin, he might have tried to have written in such a way himself.

Soon the show was playing in Australia, Germany, France, Scandinavia, Japan, Brazil, Mexico, Spain, and other countries. In 1972, producer Robert Stigwood opened an outdoor production of the show in Hollywood starring the understudies from the Broadway production, Ted Neely and Carl Anderson—both of whom would go on to star in the film.

Poor Old Judas

Rice and Lloyd Webber began with the idea of writing a musical about Judas, in which Jesus was only a minor character. Though that's not what they ended up with, Judas still emerged as the protagonist, the most fully drawn character in the show, certainly more so than Jesus. Judas is passionate, fiery, impatient, smart, and a bit of a control freak. He clearly does *not* believe Jesus is the son of God and says so explicitly in the show's first song. Judas and Tim Rice both stake out their positions early on, to offer the audience a clear context and road map for the story they're about to see. It's important to remember that in these ancient times there were dozens of men constantly claiming to be the Messiah, each with his own devout followers who believed utterly in their teacher. Judas thinks his and Jesus's movement has accidentally evolved into one of those. He believes this turn of events is contrary to Jesus's intentions, but that's less clear to us; does Jesus believe he is the Messiah? We don't know what's in Jesus's head any better than Judas does. It leaves Jesus as a difficult character to define, but it makes the story infinitely richer, more complex, more human.

The dichotomy between Judas and Jesus is a fascinating one. Judas is the practical one, concerned with image, message, public opinion, money. Jesus is concerned only with the Message. Interestingly, the relationship between Judas and Jesus mirrors the relationship between the show's twin antagonists, Annas and Caiaphas. Like Judas, Annas is the practical one, trying to see the obstacles ahead, worrying about public opinion; while Caiaphas is utterly single-minded, just like Jesus.

That central relationship between Judas and Jesus shows us a mammoth tug-of-war. Each of them is missing what the other has. Judas finds himself constantly frustrated and confused by Jesus's refusal to look at the practical side of their situation, as verbalized in "Heaven on Their Minds," "Superstar," and the fragment of "Superstar" at the end of the Last Supper. They fight because they both care passionately about the cause and about each other. There are three main arguments that break out between them, during "Strange Thing Mystifying," "Everything's Alright," and at the Last Supper—the latter two set to the same music. Judas acts as a kind of business agent and PR man, concerned over the political message they're sending out, concerned about the perceived inconsistencies in Jesus's teachings and the money wasted on Mary Magdalene's ointments and oils. He believes in Jesus's philosophy, perhaps also in his ability to lead, but not in his methods and his choices.

The lyric to the chorus of the title song originally just repeated "Jesus Christ" every time the melody repeated. But before recording it, Tim Rice wanted to give the lyric some variety. The word *superstar* was just beginning to be widely used, mostly to refer to rock and pop stars. Rice changed the second repeat of the chorus to include the word *superstar* because that's what Christ was, a superstar of his time, widely popular, complete with his own groupies who cared more about his star status than about his message. He was thronged when he went out in public, and, like many rock stars today, he was considered dangerous and corrupting by the establishment. Jesus had a new message for the people, and they embraced it, for a while, at least. Despite his intentions to the contrary, he became a controversial political figure as well as a spiritual leader. The songs "Hosanna" and "Simon Zealotes" point out to Jesus the tens of thousands of followers who are hanging on his every word. Simon wants Jesus to use his power to bring about a rebellion against Rome; but Jesus doesn't want to be a political figure.

In the Bible, an important question is ignored: Why was Jesus so "big," so successful, so influential? According to scripture, the answer is that he was divine; but from a historical, sociological angle, there must be more to it. Like our country today, the people wanted a new message, a change, relief from the tyranny of Rome. Today, many Bible scholars believe the Book of Revelation isn't about the end of the world, but rather that it was a thinly disguised, coded promise to the Jews that Rome would soon fall and their persecution would end. Jesus came at the right time with the right message, just as the Religious Right did in America in 1994. As Jesus grew to adulthood, Galilee was in turmoil. The region had been conquered by Rome and Herod Antipas had been installed as a regional governor of sorts. But the Jews suffered under the weight of incredible taxation, both from Rome itself and also from Herod, who taxed the Jews heavily in order to build new cities. Meanwhile, the rich got richer while the poor got poorer. The Zealotes emerged as a secret group of vigilantes, insurgents, revolutionaries, guerilla warriors, never hesitating to use violence, rising up to protest their oppression by Rome and its surrogates. Like Americans today, most Jews of the early first century wanted an alternative to the violence, corruption, and economic stranglehold under which they were straining. Jesus's message was one of peace, of morality and fairness, but also a message of complete social upheaval.

Garry Willis writes in *What Jesus Meant*:

> Jesus knew all the talk about him, and summed it up himself: "The Son of Man has arrived eating and drinking and you say: 'This man is a glutton and drunkard, the associate of tax collectors and the unclean.' " (Luke 7:34) For Jesus to be called a glutton and a drunkard was not a light criticism. It was based on a matter of Levitical law. In Deuteronomy 21:20, that is the description of a son rebelling against the people's way, the basis of a charge before the elders of the tribe that leads to death by stoning. Jesus is so radical that he needs execution.

More and more, Jesus's subversive message was exactly what the people wanted. But it made him dangerous, and that endangered his followers.

And Co-Starring . . .

Other central characters in the story are never fully drawn in the Bible, but Rice thoroughly characterized them in the musical in order for us to understand them and their relationship to Jesus and Judas. Secondary characters get very little "dialogue" in the Bible, but in *Superstar* we see Mary Magdalene as a complete, complex person. She just wants to comfort Jesus and help him relax, and the only way she knows how to do that is by soothing him physically. She bathes him in ointments and oils, rubs his feet, massages his head and shoulders. There was a reason so many women traveled with Jesus that we don't always understand today. At that time, women had virtually no rights, were not allowed to interact with men in most situations, and they could not discuss the events of the day or offer opinions—women didn't matter. But Jesus is different from other men. He and his followers treated women as nearly full equals—they ate together, discussed politics together, his women disciples performed their poetry at feasts, and in the most radical departure from the norm the women were welcomed alongside men as serious students worthy of an education. No wonder so many women found themselves among Jesus's closest followers, and no wonder there were always several rich women around to finance the movement. This was a movement worth financing.

On a personal level, Jesus treats Mary Magdalene with real respect, with genuine love. He appreciates her efforts. As she sings in "I Don't Know How to Love Him," this throws her completely. How does she respond to his unusual treatment of her? Her first impulse is to return that affection physically, but she knows that's not appropriate. She doesn't know how to express love without physical forms of affection; she literally does not know how to love this man. Judas hates her because he sees Mary Magdalene and her relationship with Jesus as a PR liability. He also seems at times to be jealous of her. He is a man full of frustration, and one of the ways his anger manifests itself is in jealousy against the one other person to whom Jesus is very close. Mary Magdalene cares about the movement but she cares about Jesus more; in contrast, Judas cares very much about his friend Jesus, but he cares more about the movement. At least in the world of *Superstar*, Judas and Mary Magdalene dance a spiritual, emotional tug-of-war over Jesus throughout the entire story.

Pontius Pilate, the Roman governor, is a fascinating character, and is another person Rice and Lloyd Webber discussed writing a musical about, again with Jesus as a minor character. As the Roman prefect of Judea, Pilate commanded Roman military units, authorized construction projects, arranged for the collection of imperial taxes, and decided civil and criminal cases. According to the "Famous Trials" section of the University of Missouri–Kansas City Law School's website:

> During his ten years as prefect, Pilate's tenure was associated with "briberies, insults, robberies, outrages, wanton injustices, constantly repeated executions without trial, and ceaseless and grievous cruelty."
>
> Given what is known about Pilate's concern with crowd control, it is hard to imagine that he would not have willingly acceded to a request from high Jewish officials to deal harshly with anyone who proclaimed himself "King of the Jews." Pilate undoubtedly knew that past messianic claims had led to civil unrest. It seems likely that he would have been eager to end the potential threat to the existing order presented by the subversive theology of Jesus. The form of execution used—crucifixion—establishes that Jesus was condemned as a violator of Roman, not Jewish, law.

Like Judas, Pilate finds himself in a no-win situation in this story. The region is in turmoil. Several Jewish insurgencies have already been put down, thousands executed by the state. Jerusalem is straining under the weight of thousands of pilgrims who have come to the temple for Passover week. In the past, this had led to violent political uprisings. Pilate needs to keep a lid on the unrest this year. And then this Jesus thing is dropped in his lap . . .

The song "Pilate's Dream" paints a subtle portrait of Pilate as a politician trying desperately to avoid controversy, and, more than anything, responsibility. Here, he's not a bad person as much as he's a modern politician (at least, as Rice has written him)—amoral more than immoral, more interested in preserving his power than anything else, always looking to his own future and his climb up that political ladder. In his dream he sees all that will happen, and knows that despite his efforts to the contrary, he will end up being blamed for Jesus's death. He may even have an inkling that once Jesus dies, the whole thing will get even *bigger*. In the midst of the hassles of Passover week, he is told that the priests have convicted Jesus of blasphemy. And since they have no authority to put him to death as they would like, they send Jesus to Pilate for execution. Pilate tries to pass the buck by sending Jesus to Herod; since Jesus is a Jew, he falls under Herod's jurisdiction, but Herod sends him right back. Pilate doesn't really understand why Jesus is worth so much fuss; but the crowd has now turned on their leader and demands his crucifixion. Pilate even tries to convince the crowd that Jesus isn't worth their hatred. But there is legitimate reason for Pilate's fear—if the mob now demanding Jesus's death decides they're unhappy with Pilate's decision, there could be yet another uprising in the city.

And then there's Caiaphas and Annas. Again according to the UMKC website:

> Joseph Caiaphas was the high priest of Jerusalem and the chief religious authority in the land, with important responsibilities including controlling the temple treasury, managing the temple police and other personnel, performing religious rituals, and—central to the passion story—serving as president of the Sanhedrin, the Jewish council and court that considered the case of Jesus.
>
> Caiaphas was the son-in-law of Annas, high priest from 6–15 CE and head of a family that would control the high priesthood for most of the first century. It is possible that Annas, as a high priest emeritus, might have served at the side of Caiaphas in the Sanhedrin called to resolve the fate of Jesus.
>
> Although little is known of Caiaphas, historians infer from his eighteen years as high priest that he must have worked well with Roman authority. For ten years, Caiaphas served with Roman prefect Pontius Pilate and the two presumably had a close relationship. It is likely that Caiaphas and Pilate had standing arrangements for how to deal with subversive persons such as Jesus. High priests, including Caiaphas, were both respected and despised by the Jewish population. Many Jews suspected the high priests of taking bribes or practicing other forms of corruption. Unlike other temple priests, Caiaphas lived in Jerusalem's Upper City, a wealthy section inhabited by the city's powers-that-be.

As in many musicals, the community—sometimes slangily referred to as "the friendly villagers"—is a character in and of itself. In most musicals, the protagonist must either learn to assimilate into the community or be removed from it. In *Superstar*, Jesus can't assimilate, can't join the mainstream, so he must be removed, in this case, by capital punishment. Judas must be removed as well. But there are two sets of "friendly villagers" in this story—the apostles and the Jews at large. The apostles are a motley crew, uneducated, unskilled laborers (comparable to today's longshoremen or day laborers), so average of intelligence that Jesus had to create all those farming parables to communicate his complex ideas. These were common men and women. But the larger group of "friendly villagers," the Jewish mob, becomes one of the antagonists, actively demanding Jesus's death. The crowd begins the show as Jesus's followers (singing "Hosanna"), a group whose loyalty the priests don't want to lose. The crowd is in the middle of a tug-of-war between the priests and Jesus. They ask Jesus to be healed, to be cured, to be fed; yet once the priests have condemned him as a blasphemer, the crowd turns on Jesus and demands Pilate crucify him. As it still does today, public opinion can swing quickly and unexpectedly from one extreme to the other. The loyalties of the masses can change with the wind, and this phenomenon was just as dangerous and unpredictable then as it is now. The change of the crowd's position is seen through a series of songs: "Hosanna" and "Simon Zealotes" (all devout followers), "The Temple" (the moneylenders opposing him and the sick asking for healing), "The Arrest" (the people turning fickle, taunting him), "Pilate and Christ" (turning against him), and finally "Trial Before Pilate" (demanding his death).

Jesus Rocks

The music of *Superstar* is relatively conventional harmonically, but there is a richness of melody there, with obvious roots in Puccini, Bill Haley, Richard Rodgers, even some Leonard Bernstein; and there's also the cockiness of youth in both the music and lyrics. Rice and Lloyd Webber could not have written this show when they were forty. This material had to have the tang of youthful arrogance and rebellion to give voice to the radical, young activists Jesus and Judas. There is nothing in the music that's overly complicated, nothing that requires much of the listener, but the music holds our interest nonetheless. Lloyd Webber doesn't use literal reprises—repeated songs with the same or similar lyrics—except for a couple of fragments in Act II. Instead, he reuses music with entirely new lyrics, a device known as *contrafactum*. This works in much the same way as reprises, connecting characters or events by giving them the same music. He doesn't really develop musical themes or motifs, choosing instead to repeat them exactly or almost exactly. Though the music is not as sophisticated as a lot of other theatre scores—or even Lloyd Webber and Rice's own *Evita*—his use of contrafactum is interesting, and in most cases dramatically motivated. This would not be the case with any of his scores after *Evita*.

The show's overture is packed with musical hints of what's to come. It starts with melodies that we will later hear in "This Jesus Must Die," "Trial Before Pilate," and other pieces sung by the priests and Pilate—it's always the music of the antagonists—including music that will later accompany both the crowd of zealots singing "Hosanna" and also Caiaphas's words, "We need him crucified." In fact, every melody in the overture will later be heard during the trial before Pilate, with two exceptions; in addition to the antagonists' music, there is also Judas's "doom" vamp, which will begin "Heaven on Their Minds," and a quote from "Superstar," in which Judas will later confirm his predictions of doom and death. Today, for audiences who come into the theatre already knowing this famous score, this overture sets exactly the right mood, with a focus on Judas, Pilate, and the great tragedy about to unfold. The overture ends with music that will end the first act by commenting on Judas's betrayal, and that will also show up in Act II commenting on Judas' suicide. Every tragedy in the show is mapped out first in the overture—all their intermingled fates are sealed before the story even begins.

The first eight songs in the show introduce eight melodies that will be used again and again throughout the score. The show starts with "Heaven on Their Minds," introducing Judas, his relationship with Jesus, his doubts about Jesus's approach, and even some information about Jesus's growing ministry. The song establishes Judas as the central character, dramatically, an intelligent and perceptive man whose concerns are legitimate ones. The repeated ostinato vamp in the bass will later accompany the thirty-nine lashes and we will see that Judas was right all along about the dangers ahead. The next song, "What's the Buzz?," introduces the apostles and their collective character—curious, questioning, impatient, and basically ineffectual; they want to know what's up only because they want to be a part of the movement. Quite noticeably, they don't ask *why* things are happening or why their movement matters. They're far more interested in itinerary than in philosophy.

Jesus sings for the first time here, treating the apostles more like children than adult students of his teachings. In effect, he's teaching them to be more Zen-like, to focus on where they are, not where they may be down the road. The next song in the scene, "Strange Thing Mystifying," dramatizes Jesus and Judas's first confrontation, in which Judas directly challenges Jesus's actions, specifically with regard to Mary Magdalene. Jesus fooling around with an unmarried woman is not the public face Judas wants to put on this movement. And since Judas is already worried about being arrested, he'd rather not give the authorities any more reasons to do so. To Judas, this is a modern-day political campaign. To Jesus, he's nothing more than a philosopher who honestly believes his ideas can help people live better lives. These two friends are not working toward the same goals. But there seems to be even more here. This argument between these two devoted friends over this woman hints at deeper issues. When Jesus sings to Judas, "Leave her, leave her, she's with me now," it almost sounds like Mary Magdalene had been with Judas before. There is some biblical evidence to suggest that the real Mary Magdalene may have had money, and therefore real independence, and that may have financed much of the movement. And her established—even *favored*—place in Jesus's movement leaves open the possibility, if she's been around for a while, that Judas may have been with her. This is only the first of several fights the two friends will have. Mary Magdalene sings her first song, "Everything's Alright," clearly defining her character, the balance and calm she brings to this combative group of friends, as well as her relationship with both Jesus and Judas. Also, recent biblical scholarship adds a new wrinkle to Mary's lyric because we now know that the Jewish people of that time used an extract of cannabis (the marijuana plant) in their anointing oils and in their religious incense to help them achieve inner peace and to encourage religious visions. The oil Mary anoints Jesus with may well contain THC.

And then Jesus and Judas fight again—over Mary Magdalene. Again. Judas's argument is petty and everyone knows it. He's picking a fight now, and we sense—and perhaps they do, too—that this friendship has passed the point of no return. The tragedy can't be avoided now. And all to the happiest song in the score. The rest of them sing contentedly that "everything's all right," and yet that couldn't be further from the truth. Nothing will ever be all right again. Like the best theatre writers, Rice has introduced an irony into the situation that marks only the best storytellers.

The scene changes and we meet the bad guys, the high priests Caiaphas and Annas, as they sing "This Jesus Must Die," establishing the secondary conflict of the show (Jesus versus the authorities) and confirming for us Judas's worst fears. They see the situation as a serious crisis; to them, it boils down to Jesus's life or their own. They acknowledge that Jesus is now more popular even than John the Baptist, Jesus's famous and politically controversial cousin, "when John did his baptism thing." They decide Jesus must be murdered "for the sake of the nation." The music to this song is the same music they will sing in almost every scene in which they appear. The "friendly villagers" are introduced with "Hosanna," showing their blind enthusiasm for Jesus and his ministry. But this number is more complicated than it might seem at first. This song is political theatre, a kind of guerilla street theatre that parodies the way the Roman Emperor was received when he entered a conquered city. Here Jesus and his followers are creating a public event that implies ironically (even comically?) that Jesus and his cohorts are entering the city as conquering heroes. All this also brings the story into modern politics, showing us the birth of a political movement and its public tactics, much like the grassroots political movements we see in America today. The public is now behind Jesus. And he's never been more dangerous to those in power.

In the next song, "Simon Zealotes," Simon and the crowd offer Jesus their loyalty if he wants to seize political power as well. This is a shallow, freaky, vaguely disturbing lyric. Simon and his friends aren't devoting themselves to Jesus's message or philosophy; they're fans. They're groupies. These are the followers of rock stars. The lyric sounds more like teenage girls in the '60s screaming for the Beatles or the Beach Boys, not the robed apostles we read about in the Bible. These fanatics even suggest that they'd be willing to topple the government if Jesus asked them to. Like some modern-day religious leaders, Simon suggests that "hate" would be an energizing message for Jesus's followers. He obviously does not understand Jesus's philosophy at all. Jesus doesn't want power and he certainly won't use hate as a tool. The song ends with Jesus singing "Poor Jerusalem," realizing that among his followers only Judas really understands the message.

But Judas doesn't agree with his methods.

At this point, with all but one of the main characters and conflicts introduced, Lloyd Webber begins to reuse music for dramatic purposes (just like classical opera does), and the pace at which he does this increases as the show progresses. The music of "Poor Jerusalem" becomes an introductory verse to "Pilate's Dream." And this musical connection underlines a character connection as well. These twin pieces show us the anguish, apprehension, and ambiguity of both Jesus's and Pilate's situations, and joining them melodically also provides a strong segue between scenes. After spending time with Jesus, we delve into his inner thoughts, then cross-fade into the related inner thoughts of one of Jesus's antagonists. It's a remarkably skillful moment, succeeding in terms of character, theme, psychology, and musical structure, all at the same time. In the main body of this song, we see for the first time the inescapable grip of fate, a major theme of the show; because we already know this story, we know that Pilate's dream will come true, no matter how hard he tries to avoid it. And it also dramatizes for us the banality of what people see as "evil." Pilate is just a politician, a power broker. He is what Judas fears Jesus will become. Pilate is trapped to a large extent by what the People want, just as Jesus seems to be with "Simon Zealotes." But this time, the trap will (perhaps unfairly) etch Pilate's name onto the history of the world as a villain of biblical proportions.

The next scene, "The Temple," uses mostly new music, including a short fragment of "I Only Want to Say," which we'll hear in its full form later. It's interesting to note in this sequence that the music the moneylenders sing as they try to sell their wares is the same music the sick and crippled sing asking Jesus to heal them; is Lloyd Webber equating the two groups? Are the sick and crippled just as greedy and demanding as the moneylenders? Are they as upsetting to Jesus? Is capitalism a sickness? And it forces us today to ask ourselves about the alliance between the Republicans, the party of capitalism and Big Business, and Evangelical Christians. Jesus talked about serving the poor, compassion for the weak, peacemaking, and this scene, as potent now as it was in 1970, reveals the hypocrisy at the heart of modern mainstream religion.

The next song is Mary Magdalene's big number, "I Don't Know How to Love Him," in which her character's deepest conflict is expressed. This is new music except for the fragment of "Everything's Alright" that opens the song. She knows that she will soon lose him to the movement, either by merely losing his time as he gets busier and busier, or because he'll be arrested. When she wonders if she should "bring him down," the phrase is loaded with layers of meanings: Should she load the baggage of her feelings on him at this pivotal moment and tell him exactly how she feels? Should she demand a place at his side no matter how busy he gets? Should she try to get him to pull back from the movement so that she can spend more time with him and so that he'll be safer? Then again, she wonders, what would she do if he said he loved her back? To live up to that love might be more than she's capable of.

Judas's "Damned for All Time" is also new music, as Judas realizes the consequences of the actions he feels compelled to take. And he curses his self-knowledge, his ability to see the terrible consequences coming at them all like a freight train. But are his intentions entirely practical ones? Is it only about the movement getting out of control? We've only seen Judas and Jesus really angry at each other thus far in the show. Did that color this decision? Did Judas's jealousy of Mary Magdalene coming between the two friends have anything to do with it? Judas seems not to be sure himself, as he keeps begging Annas and Caiaphas to promise him he's doing the right thing. The priests oblige him and reassure him that he's chosen the right path in "Blood Money," set to the same music as "This Jesus Must Die." The fact that the priests have only one piece of music shows us that they have only one thing on their minds—Jesus's annihilation. But it also sneaks in some subtle character work—here and throughout the second act, whenever Judas bares his soul (as in "Damned for All Time"), Annas always responds with the mocking, condescending music first established in "This Jesus Must Die." This trivial-sounding, "fun" music undercuts any drama, any angst, any tragedy it comes up against, trivializing Judas's gut-wrenching emotional moments, perhaps suggesting that they aren't entirely genuine or that they are unworthy of the priests' serious consideration. It's a subtle trick that may not register consciously with all listeners, but it works anyway, refusing to let the "tragic" music rule any scene.

As the first act ends, Rice has thrown every main character into crisis. Jesus and Judas are at odds and both of them see the danger ahead. Judas is now ridden with guilt over his decision to help the authorities arrest Jesus. Mary Magdalene is in love with Jesus and can't decide whether or not to tell him. Caiaphas and Annas are terrified of Jesus's growing power and need to eliminate him as soon as possible. Pilate sees some bad stuff coming over the horizon and knows he's gonna be waist-deep in it all soon.

The Trials and Tribulations

As Act II begins, the drunken "Last Supper" is mostly new music, again portraying the apostles as relatively uneducated, shallow men who are more interested in fame, book deals, success, and avoiding a hangover. But the scene also borrows musical fragments from other songs. Jesus and Judas argue again, to the same music they argued to in "Everything's Alright," even though the subject of their dispute has changed. This time, Judas is angry because things would have still been okay if Jesus had just listened to him! And he feels Jesus forcing him to betrayal. Judas is disgusted with Jesus and his naiveté (and he's probably drunk). This friendship is over. The end of this argument uses a short fragment from "Superstar," which will return as the last song in the show.

Jesus then sings a short section, "Will no one stay awake with me?" that introduces a new melody that will be used again later as a musical betrayal motif. He goes out into the Garden of Gethsemane to sing "I Only Want to Say," his song of despair and doubt over the coming events. Though the song is mostly new music, a small fragment of the melody was used in the temple scene earlier. It's fascinating to note that in this sequence Jesus goes through the five stages of death, as codified by psychologists in the 1960s, stages that everyone apparently goes through. As "I Only Want to Say" begins, Jesus goes through the first stage, denial ("Take this cup away from me"); then on to the second stage, anger, as the music turns into harder rock and Jesus makes demands of God; then on to the third stage, bargaining ("Can you show me now that I would not be killed in vain?"); then the fourth stage, depression ("Then I was inspired; now I'm sad and tired"); and finally the fifth stage, acceptance ("I will drink your cup of poison."). The song ends with one phrase of the betrayal motif, last set to "Will no one stay awake with me," this time as Jesus asks Judas why he has betrayed him. Jesus knows now that he can't count on anyone but himself; he is utterly alone.

The Roman soldiers arrest him. As the drunken apostles wake, they sing "What's the Buzz?" The crowd that gathers uses the melody from the moneylenders in the temple as they taunt Jesus and demand he be taken to Caiaphas, who questions him and declares him guilty. The song ends with the crowd telling Caiaphas to take Jesus to Pilate for execution, singing the music from "Strange Thing Mystifying," in which Jesus accused the apostles of not caring if he lived or died. Apparently, he was right. Someone stops Peter on the street after the arrest and accuses him of being one of Jesus's apostles; Peter denies Jesus three times, as Jesus predicted. His melody is the main theme from "Strange Thing Mystifying," which originally accompanied Judas's criticism of Jesus's relationship with Mary Magdalene—thereby connecting Peter musically with Judas, both of them now betrayers of Jesus. Mary Magdalene points out that Peter did as Jesus said he would, and she sings this to the betrayal motif from the Last Supper, further underscoring Peter's betrayal.

Jesus is taken to Pilate for a scene that employs three musical themes. The first is new, a creepy but majestic theme showing us both Pilate's power and the danger of that power. Pilate dodges the issue for the moment by arguing that since Jesus is a Jew, King Herod (who was more a mid-level, local politician than what we think of today as an actual king) has jurisdiction. Herod is also the man who had beheaded Jesus's cousin, John the Baptist. Pilate is technically correct about the jurisdiction question, but it's clearly a dodge. Pilate takes over Caiaphas's main theme from "Hosanna," followed by the crowd reusing their music from the same song, this time expressing the exact opposite sentiment from the first time they sang this melody; this time they want him dead. Once again, Rice and Lloyd Webber use irony to dramatic effect.

The next song, "King Herod's Song," is among the most interesting, for both good and bad reasons. First, Herod is arguably like many modern Christians, always *asking* God for something, always making deals, always begging for miracles, always flocking to far-flung places to witness the latest fake miracle sighting. Herod here plays the role of the Pharisees in the Bible, goading Jesus, tempting him to *prove* he has God on his side. But Jesus sees how shallow and inconsequential Herod is, and he knows that no matter what he says, his situation isn't getting any better. This song is Lloyd Webber's only obvious use of pastiche, a kind of raucous, blackly comic, British music hall song and dance number, presumably chosen to trivialize Herod, to show us how insignificant he is. Still, though it's clear that Lloyd Webber wanted to paint Herod as a grotesque man playing at being king, the use of such different music is a questionable choice. The song doesn't belong with the rest of the show stylistically, and certainly Herod isn't the only villain in the story; so why aren't the others portrayed with equally bizarre, non-rock music? As unexpected as it is, introducing this kind of musical anomaly so far into the evening leaves the audience feeling disoriented, and sometimes more hostile toward Rice and Lloyd Webber than toward Herod. Merely using more rock sound in the instrumentation would have helped the number immeasurably, but as it stands it just doesn't belong. British audiences, who are more familiar with the tradition of the British music hall (their version of vaudeville), probably found this music less jarring than Americans did, but it still seems weaker than the rest of the score.

In the 1994 recording *Jesus Christ Superstar—A Resurrection*, "King Herod's Song" is re-imagined as a 1950s rock and roll number; not only is it stronger dramatically, it also fits into the score better. Many modern productions now nudge the music into something closer to rock, to satisfy audiences that are now used to fully integrated pop opera scores like *Les Misérables* and *Rent*.

Herod's number is played as silly, comic relief in most productions, inexplicably making Herod *gay*! (Apparently, for some folks, Herod's decadence in the Bible is easily expressed by homosexuality because we all know how decadent those gays are!) But the truth is that there is far more substance in this material than is usually apparent. For this great philosopher and political leader to be treated so disrespectfully, so grotesquely, should be deeply upsetting, particularly with the extra baggage of two thousand years of Christian culture we have. "King's Herod's Song" should be ridiculous—Rice once wrote, "King Herod was a bit of a debauched bloke, who sat around smoking and drinking all the time with a lot of women around him"—but he should also be scary, dangerous, disturbing. He must be a legitimate threat to Jesus, not just a punch line.

The next song, Peter and Mary Magdalene's "Could We Start Again Please," was not on the original concept album but was written for the Broadway production, and its musical material is completely new. Peter and Mary Magdalene express their desperation and confusion; they don't understand how things got so out of hand; and they don't understand why Jesus has taken things to such an extreme. Mary Magdalene says they've been both *living* to see him and also *dying* to see him, that they've been hopeful but also now pessimistic. Like Jesus himself, like his movement, this moment is rife with emotional and intellectual contradictions. Peter and Mary Magdalene even echo Judas's opinion that Jesus has gone too far, the two of them begging Jesus to stop all this—just as Judas had. Even Mary Magdalene no longer believes that Jesus is on the right path—could it be because he's *not?* But the song also tells us that Mary Magdalene finally realizes that she has lost forever her chance to express her love to Jesus. She was scared and now she's lost him.

Judas decides to commit suicide, angry at Jesus for using him for his martyrdom (whether or not that position is justified). Just as Jesus has his breakdown in the Garden of Gethsemane, now Judas has a parallel breakdown, the show still connecting these two friends who will forever stay connected, even after death. All the music in this sequence is from earlier songs; as Judas prepares to die his life flashes before him musically, looking back over the events that have led Judas to this point. The music includes a fragment of "Damned for All Time," "This Jesus Must Die," an ironic and sad version of "I Don't Know to Love Him," the vamp from "Heaven on Their Minds," and finally the choral tag from "Blood Money." Only this time, the lyric "good old Judas" becomes "poor old Judas," and he hangs himself. The use of the music for "I Don't Know How to Love Him" is especially poignant, because in the beginning, everything Judas did was out of love and respect for Jesus, and now he has (probably) become the instrument of his death. It is literally true that he doesn't know how to love Jesus.

Judas is dead and soon Jesus will be too. The "Trial Before Pilate" begins with the intro from "This Jesus Must Die," Pilate again appropriating the priests' music—the music of authority. New music accompanies Pilate's pleas with the crowd to forget about Jesus, but they want him crucified, and he gives in to them. The thirty-nine lashes are administered to the vamp that opens "Heaven on Their Minds," the song in which Judas predicted that Jesus's actions would lead to disaster and death—a "doom" motif—and here that motif returns as Judas's prediction comes true. Pilate's music after the lashes is related to the melody of "Everything's Alright," but appropriately it's now in minor, with the same rhythm and a somewhat similar melody line.

As Jesus slips in and out consciousness from the brutal beating he has received, he sees the dead Judas appearing to him from beyond the grave to sing "Superstar," a fragment of which was quoted at the Last Supper. But is this Judas as an angel, as a hallucination, a ghost, a demon sent by Satan? Jesus is beaten half to death by now, so a hallucination is certainly possible. And since the show studiously avoids any position on divinity, seeing Judas as an angel or ghost or demon may seem logical on the surface considering the show's topic, but it would be at odds with the world the rest of the show has established. It would be the only supernatural moment in the show. If we see Judas as a hallucination, then Judas's criticisms of Jesus come from Jesus himself. Then we could conclude that Jesus finally sees what Judas wanted him to see, although it's too late now.

The one piece of textual evidence for seeing the song this way is the appearance in "The Last Supper" of a fragment—a kind of preview—of this title song. Jesus hears this fragment and later that fragment expands in Jesus's mind into a full song, a more thorough condemnation of all he's done, exactly the way real dreams or hallucinations work, taking a fragment of real life and expanding and revising it in the unconscious.

This last song sums up Judas's confusion and frustration throughout the entire show; but it also places Judas as a surrogate for audiences who (today as much as in the late '60s) "only want to know." Judas—like the rest of us—is just looking for straightforward answers to the most perplexing issues people of faith face in the modern world: Is Jesus God? What sense are we to make of other religions and worldviews? Why did Jesus have to die if God's the one making the rules? And most confusing of all, how did a failed political movement spawn a religion that's still going strong two thousand years later?

Even from the "other side," Judas still can't understand Jesus's blindness to the dangers ahead. Judas only understands reason and logic, while Jesus is a philosopher. Both see truth, but two different kinds of truth. Just as Judas said he would, Jesus has sabotaged himself. The battle between faith and reason has no easy resolution; both men's strategies lead to their deaths. By the end of this story, *everyone* has mocked Jesus: the priests, Herod, Pilate, the Jews themselves, and worst of all, Judas. In fact, according to early texts even God is mocking him! Several ancient Greek texts don't have Jesus saying on the cross, "My God, my God, why have you forsaken me?" Instead these early texts have him saying, "Why have you mocked me?" That's quite a difference. Still other early texts have him saying "My power, O power, why have you left me?" Since none of the original texts of the Bible have survived, we'll never know which text is authentic. But whichever one is, the fact remains that Jesus died alone. And in *Jesus Christ Superstar*, if we believe the title song is a hallucination, then all this condemnation comes from Jesus himself—*Jesus* is the one questioning his own methods and, interestingly, trying to see into the future to see if his movement will have any real impact. Yet at this moment, in his deepest despair, Jesus concludes that he has failed; he will die thinking nothing he's done will matter, making his death even *more* tragic. In this version of the story, Jesus can't really see into the future, perhaps because the issue of his divinity is taken off the table.

The crucifixion is set to strange, atonal vocal clusters, a kind of 1970s experimental rock, not unlike the music Brian Wilson was working on with his 1969 experimental album "Smile," which was only finished and released many years later. The final moments of the show, an instrumental piece titled "John Nineteen Forty-One," are underscored by the music from "Gethsemane"—Jesus has finally accepted his fate. Though well-meaning directors often insert a resurrection scene at the end, it is not in the script. A few misguided directors even move the title song after the crucifixion, so the audience goes out "happy," oblivious to the song's caustic, abusive lyric . . .

Superstar is produced all the time all over the world, but it doesn't always work as theatre. Because the show was recorded in the studio before it was staged, it was originally written for the ears, not the eyes, and some of the score is very difficult to stage adequately—repeating the same lyric multiple times on a recording works, but justifying that on stage is tough—especially for audiences used to the skillful storytelling of modern pop operas like *Les Misérables*, *Rent*, and others. Too many directors stage the show as if it were a glorified rock concert, a pageant, instead of a theatre narrative. The structure of *Superstar* can feel disjointed, almost like a series of music videos rather than one coherent narrative; but this problem can be overcome by smart and careful direction focusing on story. The writers didn't write a stage spectacle; they wrote a very personal, very emotional story. Spectacle only distances audiences from that emotion. Walter Kerr wrote of the original Broadway production in the *New York Times*, "All that had to be done with it was to put it on a stage baldly—baldness is very much of its essence—and, after establishing a few simple traffic directions, let it sing for itself. Instead, O'Horgan has adorned it. Oh, my God, has he adorned it." Instead of just trying to tell a great story as clearly as possible, too many productions try to dazzle audiences. And it's just not that kind of story.

This is a story of deep and profound human emotion, passion, betrayal, death—*that's* the stuff of which great drama is made, not stage fog or lighting effects. This is a story about politics and betrayal, not about theatrical wizardry. The audience should not be *impressed* by the crucifixion of Christ; they should be *upset* by it, *disturbed* by it, even *horrified*. Too many productions make the gruesome, brutal practice of crucifixion into cheap but thrilling theatre, destroying the dramatic and tragic impact of this powerful story.

If the choice is made to set the show in the present, as the authors intended, so many possibilities open up. Must Jesus be crucified on a cross? It's important to remember that although the cross has become the symbol of Christianity over time, it wasn't really the *form* of Jesus's execution that was meaningful—common criminals were crucified back then—it was the *reason* for his execution, that he was executed for his political activity. One of the points of the story in the Bible was specifically that Jesus's execution was ordinary, that he was treated no better than a petty thief, a very conscious choice on the part of the authorities to prove to his followers that he was not, in fact, a superstar. The show isn't about Jesus's suffering on the cross, after all. That's a religious issue and this show does not deal in religious issues.

This is a story about politics.

The Rocky Horror Show

The Rocky Horror Show, that unlikely cult phenomenon with music and lyrics by Richard O'Brien, and a script by O'Brien and (uncredited) director Jim Sharman and the original cast, hit the London stage in 1973, and it was certainly an animal like no other. At its core it tells a tale we've heard many times before, back even before Shakespeare, of braving a wilderness, of surviving lost innocence, of sexual awakening, about accepting differences, about birth and death, forgiveness and redemption, about the fall from grace of a transgressive god. And yet there is something different here, born as it was in the midst of the alternative theatre movement and at the dawn of the punk rock era. Of its first production in London, Jack Tinker wrote in the *Daily Mail*, "Richard O'Brien's spangled piece of erotic fantasy is so funny, so fast, so sexy, and so unexpectedly well realised that one is in danger of merely applauding it without assessing it. That would be a pity. Because I believe Mr. O'Brien has something quite nifty to say."

Rocky Horror explores American sexual hang-ups, the cultural chaos of the sexual revolution, and the sometimes cruel myth of the American Dream. It uses as its vocabulary a heady mix of cultural icons like Charles Atlas and muscle magazines, Frederick's of Hollywood, old science fiction B-movies with scantily clad women, horror movies with barely sublimated sexual fantasies, and punk and glam rock with their blurring of gender lines, collectively representing a long history of Americans hiding sex behind other things, of pretending to be sexless. And far from being an irrelevant museum piece today, *Rocky Horror* holds lessons for us even now about how Americans arguably overreact to nearly everything that comes along, and about how much happier we'd all be if we'd just stop doing that.

Because the show was created entirely by British artists, it has the advantage of an outsider's objectivity in its exploration and satire of these mostly American phenomena. But its parentage also allows us to see its cross-dressing not as a subversive transgression, but instead as just one more example in a long tradition of cross-dressing, from boys playing girls in Shakespeare's original productions, to men playing women in British pantomime, to the later androgyny of British glam rockers like David Bowie, Elton John, Freddie Mercury, Bryan Ferry, Boy George, and others. For the British, the cross-dressing in *Rocky Horror* was perhaps the *least* subversive element when it opened in London.

The *Rocky Horror* score is often dismissed as simplistic bubble-gum pop, but a closer examination shows sophisticated storytelling through the music, delineating character and showing us the relative intensities of sexual awareness and openness among the characters. In this score, sexuality is expressed through the beat of rock and roll. Notice that Brad and Janet sing the softest pop ("Dammit Janet," "Once in a While"), the servants sing rock with a harder beat ("The Time Warp," "The Sword of Damocles"), and Frank gets the hardest beat, complete with electric guitar distortion ("Sweet Transvestite," "The Charles Atlas Song"). Eddie sings late 1950s rock and roll ("Whatever Happened to Saturday Night?"), a form already in the past, showing us that he and his innocent view of sexuality are no longer part of this world. When Brad and Janet become sexually awakened, they are able to sing the harder rock of "Rose Tint My World" and "Wild and Untamed Thing." We can watch Brad's transformation, from the innocence of "Dammit Janet" to the self-awareness of "Once in a While" to the frightening sexual awakening of the floor show to the despairing but perceptive poetry of "Super Heroes." You can trace the musical journeys of Janet and Frank the same way. Whether O'Brien did all this consciously or not, it's all there and it tells us musically who these people are and how they change, just like all the greatest works of musical theatre do. Though many people might laugh at the notion, *Rocky Horror* is in many ways a serious musical and a serious social document.

Interestingly, many of the artists involved with the original productions of *Rocky Horror* have said in interviews that they believe the subsequent American productions in Los Angeles and New York and the film version lost much of what's important about the show—its grit, its rawness, its confrontational directness, its relationship with its audience, a relationship that's quite different than the one the film has with its audience. The original *Rocky Horror* confronted and challenged its audience. Like *Hair*, *Rocky Horror* was born out of the alternative theatre experiments of the 1960s. When it was mainstreamed (to the extent that *Rocky Horror* can be mainstreamed), when it was made slick and expensive, when the sets got better, when the score was more fully orchestrated, some believe it lost its soul, its politics, its pre-punk sound, its edge. One listen to the original London cast album from 1973 reveals a *very* different show from what many of us know today. Those who know only the film may not really understand what *Rocky Horror* was like in an upstairs, sixty-seat theatre.

And this may explain why it is that the original production in London got such positive reviews and all subsequent productions and the film have gotten such negative reviews. The material was not changed in any substantial way, but its presentation was changed greatly. Perhaps the reason *Rocky Horror* has not been embraced by the critical community since 1973 is that they haven't seen *Rocky Horror* as it was meant to be.

It Was Great When It All Began

The Rocky Horror Show began its life as a show called *It Came from Denton High* (in an homage to the 1953 sci-fi film *It Came from Outer Space*), then later *The Rocky Hor-*ROAR *Show*. Richard O'Brien said in a *New York Times* interview in 2000 that he had wanted "to write a rock 'n' roll show that combined the unintentional humor of B-movies with the portentous dialogue of schlock horror." With just the narrator's dialogue and a few songs finished (none written down), O'Brien took the project to director Jim Sharman, who immediately decided to produce the show in the experimental theatre upstairs at the Royal Court Theatre in London, where artistic director George Devine believed totally in his motto, "Here we give you the right to fail."

The Royal Court was the center of new work and experimental theatre in London, playing home to up-and-coming "bad boy" playwrights like John Osborne and Joe Orton. *Rocky Horror* was born out of the experimental theatre going on in London in the late '60s and early '70s, street theatre, guerilla theatre, political theatre, confrontational, rule-breaking alternative theatre. Many of the show's creators had worked on both *Jesus Christ Superstar* and *Hair*. O'Brien had been in *Hair* and had understudied Herod in *Superstar*. With music director Richard Hartley's help, the *Rocky* score took shape and was arranged for a four-piece rock band. With the help of Jim Sharman and the assembled cast, the script was developed, almost as a group creation. The role of Columbia was created specifically for "Little Nell" Campbell, a street performer, and "The Time Warp" was written both to give the servants something more to do, but more than that, to give Campbell a tap solo in the midst of this crazy revisionist rock musical. Originally the show used a framing device of a kid watching sci-fi movies on TV, but that was scrapped early on.

Sharman took the cast to see the 1970 camp classic film *Beyond the Valley of the Dolls*—which was playing in London at midnight as a cult hit—and told them that was to be their stylistic inspiration. On the other hand, Sharman made it very clear that the characters should be played completely sincerely, that the stakes had to be high, that it was a fight of good versus evil. Like the later musicals *Little Shop of Horrors* and *Bat Boy*, *Rocky Horror* only works when it's played sincerely, despite its inherent craziness. In David Evans and Scott Michaels' collection of interviews, *Rocky Horror: From Concept to Cult*, Barry Bostwick, the film's Brad, says of the acting style, "There was a slight over-the-top acting that was required, yet it had to be grounded in reality and very real. Sort of fifteen percent hyperness that had to be added on top of every character's reality." Playing the story for laughs killed it.

The show's original three-week run was extended to five weeks, then it was transferred to an old movie theatre destined for demolition. After the cinema was demolished, it moved to the King's Road Theatre. It was named Best Musical of 1973 in the *London Evening Standard*'s annual poll of drama critics and ran 2,960 performances. Critic Irving Wardle wrote, "This is theatre made out of the rawest and crudest ingredients, and forming a charge strong enough to obliterate anything standing in its tracks." Michael Billington wrote in the *Guardian*, "This show won me over entirely. It achieves the rare feat of being witty and erotic at the same time." Naseem Khan wrote in the *Evening Standard*, "O'Brien has created a satirical and affectionate send-up that, unlike Rocky, remains well within control." The *New Statesman* wrote, "The intention of course is to celebrate such freaks of pop culture as Hammer films, Alice Cooper, and the sci-fi of Michael Moorcook; and the result has tremendous invention, energy, and glee, right up to the final paean to bisexuality." The show has since been translated into over a dozen languages and played more than twenty countries.

According to some accounts, *Rocky Horror* created the punk movement in London; according to other accounts, *Rocky Horror* helped fertilize the very earliest seeds of the movement. But putting aside the chicken-egg debate, the punk sound and the *Rocky Horror* sound shared much, both returning to the simplicity and directness of the song, rejecting complexity and sophistication for directness and honesty. Just as the earliest rock and roll did, punk rebelled against ornament and ambition. The punks wanted to express simple (though not simplistic), honest emotions in the most direct way possible. The same could be said for the *Rocky Horror* score.

Likewise, whether *Rocky Horror* inspired the punks or vice-versa, *Rocky Horror* was there at the beginning, and its faded-glamour, sadomasochistic look was the look of a new London subculture that would change the look and sound of rock and roll, and later all of pop culture. Sue Blane, the original costume designer, says in *Rocky Horror: From Concept to Cult*, "I wouldn't dream of taking credit for inventing punk! *The Rocky Horror Show* was definitely a big part of that build-up. It was happening at a time when the King's Road [the bohemian section of London] was boiling up to something. I think certain elements of punk—for instance, ripped fishnet tights and glitter, and the funny-coloured hair—a lot of those aspects of it were directly attributed to *Rocky*." She would go on to costume the stylish 1950s teen rock-fable film *Absolute Beginners*. The biggest surprise for Blane, O'Brien, Tim Curry, and others was the reaction women had to Curry's corseted, fish-netted Frank N. Furter. No one would have ever guessed in 1973 that women would consider a man in a corset, platform heels, and ripped fishnet stockings to be sexy. Maybe it was the times. Or maybe it was that our overly delineated boundaries between "male" and "female" weren't—and still aren't—as normal or as natural as we'd like to think.

Cards for Sorrow, Cards for Pain

After unprecedented success in London, the show was brought to the Roxy Theatre in Los Angeles, but it wasn't the same there—flashier, slicker, less sincere, less innocent—yet it still ran for a year and received some positive reviews. After the L.A. run, the artistic staff and much of the cast returned to England to shoot the film for 20th Century Fox. They made the film on a modest budget and a tight schedule, then flew back to the States to open the show on Broadway. Inexplicably, the theatre in New York was set up with the audience sitting cabaret-style at small tables. The New York critics hated it; the show was universally panned and was a dismal flop, lasting only forty-five performances. It received one Tony Award nomination for lighting design but lost.

Patricia Quinn, the original Magenta, says of the American productions, "The show lost a lot of its naiveté. It lost its gritty appeal. These people improvised and made it glitzy." Clive Barnes wrote in the *New York Times*, "It was unexpected, unpretentious, and the cinema itself [in the original London production], from the peeling walls to the grubby seats, provided it with the perfect ambiance. It now looks flashy, expensive, and over-produced. Why did not someone understand—before the Los Angeles paint job—that the entire point of *The Rocky Horror Show* in London was that it was tacky?" But those who did not know the original stage version could not see the show's strengths beyond its over-produced spectacle in New York. Martin Gottfried wrote in the *New York Post*, "*The Rocky Horror Show* is simple-minded, however beautifully it has been produced." Once the show's creative staff lifted *Rocky Horror* up out of the realm of low-budget, minimalist, fringe theatre, they betrayed the low-budget B-movies that were *Rocky Horror*'s source material, and many argued they also lost *Rocky Horror*'s soul.

Some critics were still fighting the idea of rock musicals themselves. In the previous six months, two ill-conceived rock musicals had crashed and burned, *Sgt. Pepper's Lonely Hearts Club Band*, based on the songs of the Beatles, and *The Night That Made America Famous*, based on the songs of Harry Chapin, reinforcing that prejudice. One of the anti-rock brigade, James Spina, wrote in *Women's Wear Daily*, "Rock is an approved forbidden fruit, the required final course for those theatre majors already well-graded in transvestitism, bisexuality, and gore." He found the show "tacky, boring, and highly forgettable."

The film version was a big flop too. Until enterprising movie theatres started running the film at midnight. Some say it first happened in Austin, Texas, others say it was at the Waverly Theatre in New York (immortalized in *Hair*'s song "Frank Mills"). Within a few months, a cult hit had been born. Stage and screen director Jim Sharman and designer Brian Thompson based the style of *The Rocky Horror Picture Show* (the film version added the word *Picture* to the title) on another small film they'd made in 1972, *Shirley Thompson Versus the Aliens*. They consciously changed *Rocky Horror*'s look for the screen, making the film more gothic, less punk than the stage version had been.

The show was revived in London in 1999 and on Broadway in 2000. Of the New York production, Ben Brantley wrote in the *New York Times*, "For eight or nine times the price of a movie, in other words, you can relive in simulation a film you have already seen and, if you're a cultist, seen many, many times." Clive Barnes wrote in the *New York Post*, "The show, which has book, music and lyrics by O'Brien, started in 1973 at London's Royal Court Theater, moving after a few months, to a wonderfully sleazy and dilapidated cinema in King's Road, where I first saw it. It was then bizarre, sweet and oddly charming. Arriving on Broadway two years later in an ill-advised and pointless cabaret setting, it looked weird, preposterous and distinctly charmless, and went belly-up after 45 performances. The current over-produced Broadway offering, directed by Christopher Ashley, clearly believes that nothing succeeds like excess and has piled encrustation upon ornamentation." Barnes reviewed it again later with several cast replacements and wrote, "What do you say in the second place about a show you didn't much care for in the first place? I have nothing against *The Rocky Horror Show*, even Christopher Ashley's souped-up, over-staged and glossily vulgarized version at the Circle in the Square." The *Journal News* said, "It wasn't exactly revolutionary in 1975, of course, but there was a freshness about it that is entirely gone now. Some very young audiences may get some kind of frisson out of it, but it all seems eminently safe, proper and self-conscious."

The revival made the mistake of trying to emulate the film, most notably by encouraging audience participation and even selling ten-dollar "prop" kits, but most reports suggest that the show wasn't very successful in that respect. Most of the eighty-dollar seats were filled with older theatre patrons who either did not know the film (and therefore the jokes) or with folks who couldn't afford the extra ten bucks for the prop kit on top of the high Broadway ticket price. *Variety* wrote, "This new production isn't so much a revival of the original stage show—a huge hit in London that flopped quickly on Broadway—as a theatrical transcription of the 1975 screen version . . . Energetic participation is all but demanded." But the question arises: Why just do the movie on stage when the movie already exists and can be viewed on home video for far less than eighty dollars a pop? Apparently, only a few audience members participated at any given performance, and unwilling audience members were often pestered by chorus members at certain points in the show until they submitted. So director Christopher Ashley reportedly paid actors to sit out in the audience and be the participatory audience the real audience would not be.

But it's fair to ask why the show's producers thought the audience participation from the film would work with the stage version, which has a fairly different script, different lyrics, and, most important, timing that changes from night to night, unlike the leisurely pacing of the film, which *real* interactive audiences can count on to make room for the same jokes every night. More than that, O'Brien didn't write the show to incorporate audience participation. And the film's audience participation happened spontaneously, so any attempt to force it with a stage production was probably doomed from the start. Certainly, if the director had to pay actors to do the audience participation, something had been lost. Audience expectations walking into a Broadway theatre with an eighty-dollar ticket in hand are very different from expectations while seeing a midnight show at a seedy movie theatre with sticky floors.

The results of the revival's misguided attempts were that critics blamed the misfires on the material, rather than the approach—material, don't forget, that was universally praised in London when done with respect and the right aesthetic sensibility. *Entertainment Weekly* wrote, "Why would anyone want to stage a Broadway revival of *The Rocky Horror Show*, an artifact as mired in the 1970s as a pet rock? It surely can't be because it's a good play." New York's *Daily News* wrote, "Ashley, rightly, doesn't even pretend that the original musical can stand alone." Production designer David Rockwell was praised for capturing the "contemporary zeitgeist" with his *Rocky Horror* design, but apparently no one noticed that *Rocky* isn't about 2000; it's about 1973. In a chilling example of all that was wrong with the revival, director Ashley said in an interview with *Time Out New York*, "I decided to take the '70s out of it." And, just as when Walter Bobbie took the 1920s out of his Broadway revival of *Chicago*, the show collapsed. Just as *Chicago*'s central themes and its wicked social satire rest entirely on the time period in which it's set, so too are *Rocky Horror*'s social insights and satire inextricably linked to the '70s. As the saying goes, "the more specific the details, the more universal the connection."

Rocky Horror is satirizing the 1970s. We may see resonance there for our own times, but the more specifically the show lives in the '70s, the easier it can serve as a metaphor for today, allowing us to stand back from our own times and see them objectively. Frank is presented as a glam-rock star because that was the only period of rock and roll during which gender became both fluid and irrelevant (the same reason Hedwig, of *The Angry Inch* fame, finds her home in that subgenre). The dissolution of gender roles was one of the things straight America feared the most. Frank's lack of clear gender is his real monstrosity, which is why it's always a mistake for productions to re-imagine Frank as anything other than a glam rocker.

To take the '70s and its issues out of *Rocky Horror* both emasculates it and short-circuits its social satire. No one in 2000 seemed to noticed that the leather and S&M themes in the revival costumes went exactly opposite to O'Brien's original intentions of innocent, campy, goofy sexuality. *Rocky Horror* is not soft porn—it's a satiric cartoon of sexuality at a particular time and place in American history. But director Ashley and his designers didn't understand that. Only the *Wall Street Journal* could still see *Rocky Horror*'s smarts behind all the distractions, and its reviewer Amy Gamerman, wrote, "The carnival atmosphere of *The Rocky Horror Show* is so enveloping that it takes awhile before you notice how clever the show itself is—a smartly calibrated blend of salty, sweet and sarcastic, with its pierced tongue lodged firmly in its cheek."

Partici . . . pation!

These days, the film *The Rocky Horror Picture Show* has eclipsed the stage version, with its wildly transgressive, vocal audiences. One commentator, Simon Fanshawe, wrote of the film, "The mantra of *The Rocky Horror Picture Show* was 'Don't dream it, be it,' and it hit the G-spot of the sexually omnivorous and opportunistic 1970s. Glam met rock, cross-dressed it, slept with it, and taught the audience all the tunes." But what most of the film's fans didn't know was that famous mantra came from vintage Frederick's of Hollywood magazine ads, originally nothing more than a manipulative cashing-in on the desperate, sexual dreams of isolated suburban housewives. On stage, for the stage show's original audience, the dark irony would have been obvious. The famous phrase was one of many cultural devices that helped the people with power and money tell those without what sex should be. It represented the establishment as it cynically commercialized sexual pleasure. Could it be that *Rocky Horror* as a film worked on young Americans in the '70s and '80s exactly the same way the magazine ads once worked on those housewives? *Rocky Horror* was (perhaps unintentionally) promising them sexual freedom and deviation, even though that promise would probably never be fulfilled.

But the film offered something else that may be more important. The majority of *Rocky Horror* fans consider themselves misfits and outcasts in the real world. The communal ritual of *Rocky Horror* screenings both welcomes them without judgment and also allows them an opportunity to actually *choose* their differentness, to be finally in control of the reasons why they live outside the mainstream, to *choose* outsider status. In this world where weird is no longer weird, everything is normal except normality. Here, Brad and Janet are the weirdos.

Perhaps the film took on its life of audience participation precisely because *Rocky Horror* is and must be an inherently shared, live experience. But many of those involved with the original stage versions lament the loss of the material's meaning and impact through the shouted responses of the film audiences. But maybe the magic on stage could only be replicated on screen with an analogous live component. Of course, much about the *Rocky Horror* film experience was not new. The Palace Theatre in San Francisco had been showing midnight films for years, with audiences dressing in costume, dancing in the aisles, even staging live shows alongside the films.

Sue Blane, *Rocky Horror*'s original costumer, says of the audience participation, "It is funny, but on the other hand, it doesn't allow you to see what a damn good piece of theatre it is. The script is really tight, very funny. The music is sensationally good. You will never witness the original again because of the audience participation." Of course, that's not true; theatres all over the world produce the stage show more or less in its original form. Most of them do not encourage audience participation, and the script and style of the stage show are different enough from the film that many of the traditional shout-outs don't make sense. Susan Sarandon, the film's Janet, says of seeing the film, "You couldn't understand what anyone was saying. It was just obscenity. Chaos. So it had lost what it had before, what made it clever. Though it may not be true of the stage show, the film no longer belongs to its creators; it belongs to the audience. It's their show now."

Several *Rocky Horror* stage cast members over the years have gone on to stardom. In addition to Tim Curry and Meat Loaf, Russell Crowe appeared as Eddie, Dr. Scott, and the Frank N. Furter understudy in Australia in 1987, Tracey Ullman played Janet in London in 1980, and Jerry Springer played the narrator in Cincinnati in the early 1980s. And the film cult continues. On July 11, 2001, over 2,500 people attended Red Rocks Amphitheater in Denver, Colorado, to watch the film in the biggest *Rocky Horror* gathering on record.

Rocky Horror is not just about sex and rock and roll. It's not just mindless entertainment. *Rocky Horror* is about something bigger, issues that need discussing, questions that need answering, maybe more now in our cyber-age than ever before. Richard O'Brien once said, "We have a contract with life: the more intelligent you are, the more responsible you are. The more intelligence that's given to you as a gift, the more you have to give back to society, the more your responsibility to make change, to improve things, is incumbent upon you. That's the deal."

David Evans, co-author of *Rocky Horror: From Concept to Cult*, writes, "I remember how I felt, coming out into Sloane Square on that first night in

June 1973. I felt such surging joy, such euphoric elation. I know I must have been grinning from ear to ear for hours. I felt empowered, validated, and no longer alone."

Give Yourself Over to Absolute Pleasure

In 1948, Alfred Kinsey published his world-shattering *Sexual Behavior in the Human Male*, which declared that more than 90 percent of American men had masturbated, more than half had had affairs, 69 percent had visited prostitutes, and 39 percent had reached an orgasm with another man. Not surprisingly, his book was an overnight bestseller. Kinsey hadn't *changed* sex in America; he had just told us what we were all doing, especially the things no one talked about. Suddenly, almost overnight, Americans were talking about sex—in detail—over their kitchen tables. Politicians immediately denounced all this as immoral and shocking and announced that it would mean the end of the Family—just as religious extremists in the 1980s and 1990s declared that gay marriage would destroy that same Family. Needless to say, none of these folks were happy when Kinsey published his next book in 1953, *Sexual Behavior in the Human Female*. This study revealed that 33 percent of American women were not virgins when they married, 13 percent had had sex with more than six partners, and 69 percent of unmarried women who'd had premarital sex had no regrets about it.

Inspired by this new sexual honesty in America and in response to the reinforced efforts at sexual repression and demonization, Hugh Hefner published the first issue of *Playboy* in 1953, with a then unknown Marilyn Monroe on the cover and naked inside. In 1962, *Harper's Bazaar* published a full-page color ad featuring the famous model Christina Palozzi, completely nude. Perhaps the Powers That Be could have tamped all this down a bit had it not been for the explosion of rock and roll that took America by storm in 1954 and the years following. But the times, they were a-changin', and in 1957, in response to a pornography case, the US Supreme Court finally officially acknowledged that sex "is one of the vital problems of human interest and public concern," finally dispelling the notion that sex equaled pornography. Standards were loosening.

Teenagers became more promiscuous than ever but had not learned enough about birth control. Twenty percent of teenage girls who had sex were getting pregnant. But in 1960, the world changed forever with the invention of the Pill, the first oral contraceptive. For the first time, women had control over when they got pregnant, which allowed them to enjoy sexual experimentation outside of marriage with no dire consequences. Though condoms and diaphragms already existed, the Pill was much easier, safer, and more convenient, and it changed the way women had sex. Within its first six years on the market, five million women began taking the Pill. In 1962, Helen Gurley Brown wrote her great subversive sex manifesto, *Sex and the Single Girl*, also a bestseller, which said it was okay to have sex outside of marriage and, even more subversive, that it was okay never to get married at all. In *Rocky Horror*, Janet's famous mantra in "Toucha, Toucha, Touch Me" represented a generation of woman desperate to explore and celebrate all the things their mothers had condemned as dirty and disgusting, as improper and unladylike. The conventional wisdom on sex and the female body was being called into question in big ways. And at the same time, Betty Friedan's 1963 book *The Feminine Mystique* persuasively and controversially attacked the myth of the "happy homemaker." In 1966, William Masters and Virginia Johnson, two sex researchers, published *Human Sexual Response*. Until then, many people honestly did not know what the clitoris did; so Masters and Johnson told them, most notably in a 1969 *Playboy* interview. By the end of the '60s, many states had struck down their adultery and sodomy laws, and eight million women were taking the Pill.

In the early 1970s, the hardcore pornography industry exploded in America, cranking out more porn films than ever before, including several that attracted curious, mainstream audiences—*Deep Throat*, *Behind the Green Door*, and *The Devil in Miss Jones*. The surprise hit *Deep Throat* was made for $25,000 and grossed more than $10 million, just from theatre exhibition, not counting later profits from video. This wasn't a complete surprise since mainstream films like *Midnight Cowboy*, *Carnal Knowledge*, *Bob and Ted and Carol and Alice*, and *Last Tango in Paris* had already been quite sexually explicit. Porn films were interesting because they were a kind of postmodern, metacinematic form; the actor and character could no longer be separated because when the character was having sex, so was the actor, and everybody knew it. Porn became not only a threat to "polite society," but in a strange way an entirely new art form.

But it also essentially ended the sexual revolution, transforming it from a movement into a business. With the incredible commercial success of *Deep Throat* and other films, sexuality was now a commodity, more so than it had ever been before. And that ended the idealism about sex that the 1960s had embodied.

Whatever Happened to Saturday Night?

Puritans weren't the only ones who thought the sexual revolution was a bad thing. Others disliked it because they felt this new movement took all the mystery and magic—and, most important, the romance—out of sex. In *Rocky Horror*, Eddie's song "Whatever Happened to Saturday Night?" (also called "Hot Patootie") addresses this issue of how the hippie movement and the sexual revolution ruined everything. There's even a reference to the change (for the worse, in Eddie's opinion) in American pop culture and music, away from the romance of 1950s rock and roll, and toward the politics and disenfranchisement and nihilism of 1960s acid rock, embodied in the image of rock icon Buddy Holly's premature death. Far from the pointless interruption of the show that someone people accuse it of being, Eddie's song is a pointed commentary on the way the sexual revolution (in the person of Frank) was ruining romance in America (in the person of Columbia), a last metaphorical stab at stopping the tide of the sexual revolution, and a final warning as the show's first half comes to a close that Brad and Janct's world is gone. Frank and the sexual revolution are too strong, and they silence forever the simplicity and purity of '50s rock and romance through Frank's act of murdering Eddie, in effect also shutting the door forever on Brad and Janet's old-fashioned world of sexual innocence.

This is also a theme addressed, though more subtly, in the show's opening, "Science Fiction Double Feature." A close reading of this lyric shows a real longing for the innocence of the 1950s, when sex was all subtext and metaphor. The song starts by taking us back to that idealized time when movies told Americans what was good and bad, right and wrong, acceptable and "deviant." And they told us all this very carefully and indirectly. But subtextual sexuality couldn't stay hidden forever. Rock and roll would emerge, alongside drive-in movies, and these forces would change sex forever. This opening song sets up the central conflict of the show, though like the movies it celebrates, it does so subtly. It positions open, overt sexuality as not just a threat, but also a despoiler of the innocent, sweet, teen sexuality of the 1950s, a kind of innocence that existed more on the screen than in the back row of the local movie house.

O'Brien is talking about the very center of the culture of the '50s: the nexus of sex, drive-ins, and rock and roll. And a big part of the drive-in experience was low-budget science fiction, often in double features. "Science Fiction Double Feature" is O'Brien's prologue, his statement of purpose. This will be a story about the (false) moral perfection of the 1950s as it slams up against the sexual revolution, here rendered in the back row.

I've Been Making a Man with Blond Hair and a Tan

But even though no one was supposed to talk about sex in the 1950s, America had other sexual outlets during that time, including one that takes comic center stage in *The Rocky Horror Show*. Bodybuilding and its accompanying muscle magazines became in the 1950s not only an innocent way for gay men to ogle beautiful, mostly naked men, but also the birthplace of gay soft porn. Richard O'Brien takes all the innocent sexual metaphors of the past, all the ways of talking about sex without talking about sex, and makes them all explicit in *Rocky Horror*, showing how silly they always were, not the least of which are Charles Atlas muscle ads and "fitness" magazines.

The first muscle magazine to acknowledge (though subtly) the connection between bodybuilding and sex was Joe Weider's *Your Physique*, which debuted in 1938. Many magazines followed, and even today's muscle magazines make no secret of the muscle-sex connection. Damion Matthews wrote in 2000 for Salon.com:

> Available at most any newsstand, muscle magazines are homoerotic pornography for the masses. Their appeal seems to cross sexual orientations. Straight, gay and bisexual men have been known to enjoy them. In their pages, they eroticize both the flesh and the culture of men. To read them is to be sexually seduced into a fraternity to which all men are invited. They unite their readers in a kind of sexually charged adulation of masculinity. To the cult of testosterone in America, they have an almost biblical authority.

Though the appreciation of male strength and muscle goes back as far as Samson and Hercules, and though the modern bodybuilding culture began in America in the early 1900s, today's popular muscle culture wouldn't exist if not for a very few pioneers like Jack LaLanne, Vic Tanney, and most notably Charles Atlas. Atlas established a mail-order business at the beginning of the twentieth century but had little success. It wasn't until 1929, when Charles Roman joined him, that business took off because Roman suggested advertising their products in comic books. The

Charles Atlas "Dynamic Tension" program (mentioned in *Rocky Horror*) sold millions of copies, becoming the most successful mail-order business in history, and is still advertised in comic books. The ads declared, "In just seven days I can make you a man!" Surprisingly, Atlas's plan did not include weightlifting, but instead consisted of stretching, calisthenics, isometrics, and daily affirmations. It made a lot of weight trainers angry, but no single man did more to popularize bodybuilding in America. He earned the title (though how and from whom is still unclear) "The World's Most Perfectly Developed Man." According to the CharlesAtlas .com website, Atlas's measurements are "on file" (who knows where) as the "ideal male specimen for twentieth-century man"—and the obvious choice as a model for Frank N. Furter's experiment. Interestingly, *Rocky Horror* flirts in "The Charles Atlas Song" with the popular sci-fi theme of "science run amok" when Frank suggests that Charles Atlas's plan is a waste of time, that Frank can make the perfect man more quickly and with far less effort. As so many sci-fi movies implied, anything that doesn't take good old-fashioned hard work is suspect and probably the sign of science run amok. After all, just look at the eventual results of Frank's attempt at playing God.

The other bodybuilder mentioned in *Rocky Horror*, the very handsome Steve Reeves, brought muscle mania to the silver screen, most notably in the not very good but very popular *Hercules* (1957), a film not even intended for US release until its producer saw Reeves's star power and changed his plan. Originally filmed in Italian, it was redubbed in English and released in America. Reeves quickly became a gay icon. Interestingly, Charles Atlas always claimed a statue of Hercules in the Brooklyn Museum of Art is what inspired him to begin his own bodybuilding. So, of course, Frank N. Furter's blond creation, Rocky Horror, is the pop cultural offspring of both Reeves and Atlas.

Transsexual Transylvania

Rocky Horror's roots lie in both science fiction and horror films. The horror genre, in books and films, has always been one way humans deal with their greatest fears, primarily death, science, "other people," and sex. *Dracula* was about the fear of unbridled sexuality (both in its original novel and in film versions). *The Fly* and *Frankenstein* were about the fear of science gone too far (which some still fear today). *Invasion of the Body Snatchers* was about the fear of Communists infiltrating America. *The Day the Earth Stood Still* was about the fear of nuclear war. *Forbidden*

Planet was about the fear of teenage sexuality and the classic sin of man playing God.

Rocky Horror's opening number pays tribute to and frankly acknowledges the contributions of many horror and science fiction B-movies. It's interesting to note that while the song references several movies from the 1950s, two from the 1930s, and one from the 1960s, there is nothing there from the 1940s. Sci-fi films were virtually non-existent during World War II, replaced by war movies and stories of "traditional" families being happy and hyperpatriotic. Also, most of the movies cited in "Science Fiction Double Feature" are shorter films, generally running only about eighty minutes. True to the song's title, most of these films were intended to run as part of a double feature, and the theater owners wanted to get two of them in, along with a cartoon and a newsreel, in under three hours.

Horror films have always represented our current cultural fears. In the 1930s, horror films dealt with our fear of our more primitive, animal side. In the 1950s, they dealt with our fear of science after America's use of the atom bomb. In the 1970s, they dealt with our fear of *ourselves*, the excesses of the '60s and '70s, the loosened moral code (which is why the most sexually active characters are the most likely to die in these films). All three of these subjects can be found in *Rocky Horror*. And the most sexually active characters in *Rocky Horror* are the ones who must die.

The movies references in "Science Fiction Double Feature" include *The Day the Earth Stood Still* (1951), the *Flash Gordon* serials (1936–1940), *The Invisible Man* (1933), *King Kong* (1933), *It Came from Outer Space* (1953), *Doctor X* (1932), *Forbidden Planet* (1956), *Tarantula* (1955), *The Day of the Triffids* (1962), *Curse of the Demon* (1957), *When Worlds Collide* (1951), and *The Bride of Frankenstein* (1935). The song also mentions George Pal, the special-effects pioneer and director who helmed *War of the Worlds* (1953), a film with parallels to the story of *Rocky Horror*.

Rocky Horror references *When Worlds Collide* through both an older male character in a wheelchair—Mr. Stanton in *When Worlds Collide* and Dr. Scott in *Rocky Horror*—and the promise of a trip to another planet in a rocket ship. Dr. Scott also has a parallel character in Professor Deemer in *Tarantula*. The theme of science gone too far, a central theme in *Rocky Horror* and a common theme in 1950s sci-fi, shows up in *Tarantula*, *The Invisible Man*, and *Frankenstein*. *Rocky Horror* shares several parallels with *Doctor X*—a strange, murderous scientist doing experiments in his lab, a doctor in a wheelchair, a maid and butler (in tails, no less), and a prominent shot of a grandfather clock striking midnight. And of course *Doctor*

X owes a lot to *Frankenstein* (which was released one year earlier), the clearest model for *Rocky Horror*, though surprisingly it's not mentioned in "Science Fiction Double Feature."

One of the less obvious references in that first song is to the unfairly forgotten classic horror flick *Curse of the Demon*. In the film, psychologist Dana Andrews is investigating the mysterious death of a colleague. Over the course of his investigation a curse is placed on him by a dangerous cult leader, and it turns out the method of placing the curse is to pass into the victim's possession a piece of parchment covered with ancient runes—but it must be done without the victim's knowledge, which explains why passing those runes used lots of skills. The last part of the film is filled with the surprisingly effective suspense of whether Dana Andrews will be able to pass the runes—and the curse—back to the villain.

One tribute most people don't notice is that part of *Rocky Horror*'s narrative exposition closely mirrors *The Werewolf vs. the Vampire Women*, a trashy but surprisingly entertaining 1971 drive-in movie. *Werewolf* contains two young people—both women—driving through the woods and getting lost, a breakdown, a rainstorm, an old gothic mansion, a weird '70s sexual vibe, and a sexy lesbian vampire queen. A car accident in a rainstorm also shows up in the classic 1934 film *The Black Cat* (which weirdly combines elements of *Dracula* and *Sweeney Todd*), as a young couple is taken to the castle of a satanic priest who performs a bizarre ritualistic ceremony. Another possible inspiration can be found in *The Manipulator* in 1970 (with Mickey Rooney!), complete with a madman who kidnaps women and forces them to co-star in imaginary movies with him. Well into the mid-1970s, the "drive-in" genre still had plenty of room for lots of sexy, gory horror films for horny teenagers, though most would be quickly forgotten.

Rocky Horror also follows in the footsteps of Bram Stoker's *Dracula*, using its metaphors to express our anxieties about our culture and our sexuality. In *Rocky Horror*, even the aliens' home planet, traditionally the metaphor for the roots of whatever evil was coming at us, is called Transsexual. And like *Dracula*, *Rocky Horror* deals with issues of alternative expressions of sexuality (including scenes of group sex in both), advances in science, women's independence, and foreigners. In *Dracula*, Stoker was thinking about the changes in women's roles in Victorian England, their changes in clothing and social independence, as well as widespread fear of the implications of Darwin's new theory of evolution, the greatly increased influx of foreigners into England, and perhaps even his own (suspected) homosexual relationship with actor Henry Irving. All those things scared Stoker and his readers, and he gave them an outlet for those fears in his mysterious count. In *Rocky Horror*, O'Brien was thinking about the sexual revolution and how it was changing Western society, the women's liberation movement, nuclear proliferation and the paranoiac fear of Communism, growing drug use among mainstream society, and again, his own very fluid sexuality.

Rocky Horror's roots can also be found elsewhere. Richard O'Brien says Frank N. Furter is based on Eisenstein's *Ivan the Terrible, Part I* and on Disney's Cruella De Vil. The "Time Warp" dance was inspired by Jean-Luc Godard's film *Bande à part* (1964). The words "love" and "hate" written on Eddie's knuckles were taken from *Night of the Hunter* (1955). The scene in the film in which Rocky emerges from the water tank is taken directly from Hammer Films' *The Curse of Frankenstein* (1957), apparently even using the same prop tank. Dr. Scott is at least partly based on Peter Sellers' masterful comic character Dr. Strangelove, the wheelchair-bound German scientist in the film *Dr. Strangelove or How I Learned to Stop Worrying and Love the Bomb* (1964). Also, interestingly (and in a break from its sci-fi roots), *Rocky Horror* parallels *Mutiny on the Bounty* (1935, 1962), with Frank as the crazy, abusive, power-mad Captain Bligh and Riff Raff as the kinder, saner Fletcher Christian. Frank/Bligh mistreats those under his command until Riff Raff/Christian can't take it anymore and commits mutiny. Parallels range from the fact that both sets of characters are on long journeys to the fact that both captains are sadists who whip their underlings. There's even a little taste in *Rocky Horror* of the 1930s "scare" film *Reefer Madness*, which tried to convince audiences that just one puff on a marijuana cigarette turns the user into a sex-crazed, homicidal maniac; certainly a possible target of O'Brien's satire, when one whiff of Frank's LSD-like spray (in the stage version) turns Brad, Janet, Rocky, and Columbia into sex-crazed glam-rock performers.

In a less obvious tribute, *Rocky Horror* also pays homage to the early television "horror hosts," to "shock television," and to the live "spook shows" that often accompanied showings of horror movies in theatres. Touring magicians provided shocking, scary, sometimes very gory magic shows called "spook shows" before screenings of late-night horror movies. That tradition morphed during television's early days into the "horror hosts" like Vampira, A. Ghastlee Ghoul, Baron Daemon, Chilly Billy, Crematia Mortem, Svengoolie, and later Elvira, among many others (the documentary *American Scary* explores all this). These local TV hosts emceed late-night, usually low-quality horror films—"shock theatre"—that local TV stations bought in inexpensive packages to fill up late-night programming hours. In many cases, the films they were introducing were so bad, the hosts became the real reason viewers tuned in, returning every fifteen minutes or so throughout the films for jokes, sarcastic commentary, even sketch comedy. Some hosts were costumed as horror movie monsters themselves, others were not. The narrator in the stage version of *Rocky Horror* is likely modeled on these characters.

Great Scott!

Usually sci-fi films of the '30s expressed through metaphors (either explicit or not) the American public's anxieties about advances in science and technology, and sci-fi films of the '50s expressed the American public's anxieties about Communism and the atomic bomb. It was in the 1920s, after World War I, that the first science fiction feature films appeared, films like *Metropolis* (1926), cautionary tales about the excesses of science. In fact, we can see parallels between *Metropolis*'s mad scientist and the beautiful, seductive robot he creates, and *Rocky Horror*'s Frank and Rocky. The parallel is even more striking today because in 1984 this classic silent film was rereleased with a hard rock score. Frank N. Furter and his fellow aliens victimizing the poor, dumb humans find their earliest ancestors in the many space/alien movies of the 1930s and 1950s, like *The Things from Another World*, *War of the Worlds*, *Invasion of the Body Snatchers*, *This Island Earth*, and others. Aliens were often metaphors for those un-American, godless Communists. But there were also alien films that took the opposite point of view. In *The Day the Earth Stood Still*, the alien was a peaceful visitor with an anti-nuclear war message. There were also sci-fi films throughout the 1950s that warned of the dangers of man playing God, of science going too far, inspired primarily by panic over advances in nuclear science. Films in this genre included *The Beast from 20,000 Fathoms*, *Them!*, *It Came from Beneath the Sea*, *Tarantula*, *The Incredible Shrinking Man*, and *These Are the Damned*.

But there are also explicit biblical references in the show. Rocky is the result of a virgin birth, after all. In "The Charles Atlas Song," Frank promises, "In just seven days I can make you a man," echoing the actual promises of Charles Atlas's comic book ads, but also making a clear God reference, and, in doing so, also referencing *Frankenstein*. And Frank plays the role of serpent in the Garden of Eden ("innocent" pre-sexual revolution America), suggesting to Janet's Eve that she taste from the "tree of knowledge," and Janet in turn corrupts Rocky as an innocent Adam figure. (This interpretation is supported by the album cover of the original London cast album, which pictures a serpent winding around Frank's body.) Later, after "the fall," Brad begs Frank to take this dream away, in parallel to Christ's plea to "take this cup away."

Rocky Horror followed in the footsteps of many sci-fi films, which sometimes contained biblical references, like *The Day the Earth Stood Still*, in which peace-loving alien Klaatu has come to Earth to bring a message of love and peace, takes the name "Mr. Carpenter," and then dies and is resurrected.

Where There's a Will . . .

Rocky also has surprising parallels to Shakespeare's plays in general, and *The Tempest* specifically. Perhaps this shouldn't be a surprise since the show was created by a classically trained British director and group of actors. And if anyone thinks it's sacrilege to compare *Rocky Horror* to the Bard, let him not forget that Shakespeare's plays were full of dirty jokes, improbable plots, supernatural events, and lots of drag.

Rocky Horror employs the Shakespearean theme of innocent young lovers going off into the woods (or an exotic island) where rules don't apply, where sex and gender roles are fluid, where characters are changed, as in *A Midsummer Night's Dream*, *As You Like It*, and *Twelfth Night*. It's all about *transgression*, crossing lines that normally cannot be crossed, but doing it all away from polite society, out in the woods. And as in many Shakespearean comedies, *Rocky Horror* uses the devices of gender-bending, surprises at the end, arrogance deflated, and the idea of servants becoming masters. Like Shakespeare's comedies, *Rocky Horror* blurs the line between sanity and insanity, good and bad, love and lust. There are even similarities, most notably, between Brad Majors and the earnest but not too bright Orlando in *As You Like It*. And the LSD-spray that Frank has Riff Raff spray on nearly everyone in the lab before the floor show has its parallels in the drops that Oberon has Puck drip onto the eyelids of the four lovers in *A Midsummer Night's Dream*—a drug to make them lose their inhibitions and arouse their desires. And when *As You Like It* and *Twelfth Night* were first performed, in each play a boy actor played a girl pretending to be a boy. Sounds a bit like *Rocky Horror*, doesn't it?

The classic science fiction film *Forbidden Planet* frankly acknowledged its debt to Shakespeare's *The Tempest* and the parallels extend to *Rocky Horror* as well. The themes shared among all three pieces include the opposition of reality and illusion, untamed nature versus civilization, and ideas about performance of gender and identity. Specific parallels between *Rocky Horror* and *Tempest* abound. *The Tempest* starts with a shipwreck amid thunder and lightning, while *Rocky Horror* begins with a car breaking down amid thunder and lightning. Frank N. Furter and Prospero both act as magical ringmasters manipulating everyone around them. Caliban and Rocky serve as the untamed, primitive creatures controlled by Frank/Prospero; and Caliban's attempted rape of Miranda is reflected in Janet's seduction by Rocky. Prospero also puts on a small performance, the Masque of the Goddesses, in parallel to Frank's floor show. Jan Frans van Dijkhuizen, in his article "Prospero's Dream: *The Tempest* and the Court Masque Inverted," writes:

> The court masque played a crucial role in the way Renaissance monarchs chose to think about themselves. Masques served essentially as images of the order, peace and harmony brought about by the monarch's mere presence, and expressed didactic truths about the monarchy. Lavishly spectacular and visual, designed to enchant the eye, they formed a genre fundamentally different from the drama performed on the public stage.

Sounds a lot like Frank and his floor show. Shakespeare used a play-within-a-play in many of his shows. The *Rocky Horror* floorshow also owes a debt to the play in *Hamlet*, in that both are staged in order to reveal hidden truths.

Both Prospero and Frank make plans to return home at the end, though only Prospero makes this decision of his own will, and Prospero must give up his powers in order to return, just as Frank's power is taken from him. Frank and Prospero both even indulge in metaphors about death. Prospero says, "We are such stuff / As dreams are made on; and our little life / Is rounded with a sleep." Frank sings about going home, an unwitting prediction of his own imminent death, when he will return metaphorically to the earth. It's also noteworthy that *The Tempest* has more songs than any other Shakespeare play (even though it's fairly short), as well as references to instrumental music. If any of Shakespeare's plays were ripe for making into a musical, this one was it. And as luck would have it, Bob Carlton did turn *The Tempest* into the rowdy rock musical *Return to the Forbidden Planet* in the early 1990s.

Erotic Nightmares and Sensual Daydreams

Here in the upside-down world of *Rocky Horror*, Brad and Janet, two people who would be considered normal under almost any other circumstances, are the weirdos, the outsiders, the unusual ones. The yardstick for what is and isn't normal is shattered, just as the same thing was happening in America. What was normal in the 1950s—Ozzie and Harriet and the like—was no longer the norm. As the 1970s began, the hippies of the '60s were having children and starting families. Now parents were smoking pot. Adults were having wife-swapping parties. Normal wasn't normal anymore. And what was even more frightening to certain people—the idea of normal wasn't just changing, it was falling apart entirely in some parts of the culture.

Brad and Janet come to Frank's castle as two entirely different people and they will have two entirely different experiences, Janet's ultimately positive (in some ways), Brad's clearly negative. It's clear that both are looking for something as the story begins, both hoping for something they can't quite name. The narrator's second monologue describes metaphorically what is to come:

> It seemed that fortune had smiled on Brad and Janet and that they had found the assistance that their plight required—or had they? There was certainly something about this house . . . that made the both of them uneasy. But if they were to reach their destination that night, they would have to ignore such feelings and take advantage of whatever help was offered.

Though this paragraph seems straightforward enough on its surface, it's easy to see below the surface. What is Brad and Janet's *inner* plight and what is their *inner* destination? What feelings will they have to ignore? And what kind of "help" will be offered? Janet will find Frank's assistance a lot more helpful than Brad will.

As early as "Over at the Frankenstein Place," Janet is prepared to some degree for what's to come, for her sexual "coming out." Though she may or may not know it consciously, she's using sexualized language—*velvet* and *burning*—and we might wonder if she's been listening to the hippies more than Brad has, as she trusts that life will take her where she's meant to go.

Brad's verse (left out of the film) tells us that he's hoping for something as well, but though Janet is sure she has a guiding star, Brad only *hopes*, maybe even tries to convince himself, that good things are ahead. Brad clearly references the two of them as a couple, but Janet does not. Janet is ready for an individual journey, while Brad is hoping for a dual journey. Janet is ready for sexual experiences, and she clearly revels in the experience she has with Rocky during "Toucha, Toucha, Touch Me."

Later, in the floor show, Janet declares her new life, while Brad can only be terrified. There's a role reversal in the floor show; Janet and Brad have traded places. Whereas Janet was the "weak" woman who needs protection at the beginning of the story, now she is the strong one. She has gotten power from expressing her sexuality so freely. She's in charge of her life now (although she's still presumably under the influence of LSD drug spray used on her in the previous scene). And just as Janet has gained power, Brad has lost all his. He has gone from being the dominant hunter-gatherer protector to calling for his mommy. He is lost in this world, the same world in which Janet is finally finding her way. Just as real American women did during and after World War II and into the 1960s, Janet has discovered there's more to life than being a housewife, and she can never again go back to the way things were before.

Of course, that reversal of traditional gender roles is most obvious in the cross-dressing of Frank and other characters, but its real import is felt in Brad and Janet's relationship. What is "naughty" and transgressive in one context brings about the disintegration of an engaged couple in another context. What is funny and ridiculous in the form of a transgendered alien is sad and tragic when Brad and Janet sing "Super Heroes" and we see that their lives have been devastated. *Rocky Horror* could see ahead to the crumbling of the sexual revolution. In 1980, *Cosmopolitan* magazine reported, "So many readers wrote negatively about the sexual revolution—expressing longings for vanished intimacy and the now elusive joys of romance and commitment—that we began to sense there might be a sexual, counter-revolution under way in America." Brad and Janet have been through the sexual revolution and found it not just unsatisfying but destructive.

Brad's lyrics in his big ballad, "Once in a While" (unfortunately and carelessly cut from the movie), reveal more about him than any other moment in the show. He believes in love just as innocently, just as passionately, just as fully as Frank believes in physical pleasure. Brad tells us that Janet's infidelities have broken his heart and ended their relationship. And yet, despite the fact that Janet's behavior goes against every moral precept in which Brad believes, still his love for her is stronger, and he knows that if she just apologizes, if she still loves him, they can be all right again. He'll take her back, apparently no questions asked. We have to understand just how huge that is for this very straitlaced guy who sees the world entirely in moral black and white. Perhaps it's his own transgression (passive though it was) that has mellowed him, humbled him, taught him the world isn't as black and white as it once seemed. Unfortunately, Brad seems to think that once the apology is made, once forgiveness is granted, he and Janet can go back to the way things were before all this happened. Of course, they can't. They'll never be the same again. They've lived in blissful ignorance—metaphorical darkness—all this time, blind to the dark side of life, of sexuality, of lust, of betrayal, but that light "Over at the Frankenstein Place" has been turned on in their lives, and once they've seen this side of themselves and each other, they can't hide in the dark anymore.

So what *will* Brad and Janet be like when they get home? Will they stay together? Will they get married? Brad seems to be destroyed by his experience, but Janet is empowered by hers. Is this telling us that we can choose how we react to the excesses of our culture, that the culture itself is not dangerous, but merely how we interact with it?

Their last words, in the song "Super Heroes," tell us a lot about what they've gone through and offer some insight into where they go from here. Brad has tried to live the life he was expected to live, tried to find the right wife, get the right job, plan the right future. Like most Americans, he believed that some deceit was justified in the climb up the social and corporate ladder. But even though he's done everything he was supposed to do, his life has now taken an unexpected turn and nothing he was taught prepared him for this. Polite adults just didn't talk about homosexuality, about drugs, about "experimentation," so he has come to this adventure completely ill prepared.

Janet regrets her actions to some extent, but she will not deny her feelings. Her sexual appetite can no longer be set aside, ignored, denied in favor of living a "decent" life. Janet has been sexualized and she will not refuse these new feelings, even though they scare her, even though they go against most of what she was taught about "proper young ladies." Her innocence has been taken by the "super heroes" who have come to feast on her flesh, the icons of pop culture: movie stars, rock stars, and self-constructed cultural icons like Timothy Leary, Andy Warhol, Goldie

Hawn, Hugh Hefner, and others, who present their overly sexualized personas as the only real alternative for the hip cultural elite and those who aspire to that hipness.

The Rest of the Family

Unlike Rocky in the film version, the stage Rocky actually speaks, and is a very different character. Rayner Bourton, the original Rocky from the first London production, hated the film presentation of his character. He says, "Rocky is the noble savage, the feeling beast. The beast within everyone. Rocky is the character whom we all either want to be or take care of or advise or have as our best friend. Something untamable." Bourton sees Rocky as a Pinocchio figure, a good boy who is tested. He doesn't like that Rocky was reduced to a nonverbal "thing" in the film, rather than the fully formed character he was on stage. Bourton says, "My Rocky had an incredible amount of truth, and an immense amount of naiveté."

Considering *Rocky Horror*'s obvious parallels to *The Tempest*, Rocky is a strange mixture of Caliban the savage and Miranda, Prospero's innocent daughter. But Caliban can also be seen as the unwilling slave, just as Rocky is slave to Frank. Caliban's attempted rape of Miranda is often interpreted as a brutal act, but it can also be seen as his innate—and yes, primitive—desire to "be fruitful and multiply," to people this island that belonged to him long before Prospero showed up, just as God intended, some might say. We can see Rocky's attraction to Janet in somewhat the same way. He is Natural Man (despite his unnatural origins), propelled entirely by primitive drives not yet civilized out of him.

If Brad represents a too-repressive reaction to the sexual revolution and Janet is a too-permissive reaction, then Rocky represents the simple, natural state of sexuality. Maybe Rocky is what sex is *supposed* to be, a completely natural human impulse, free of baggage—not a sociological movement, not a political issue, not a source of guilt or sin, just an innate part of being human. With Rocky, sex is not a reaction to anything. There is no agenda. There is no ulterior motive. Rocky feels an attraction to Janet and he wants to have sex with her. Rocky represents a return to the Garden of Eden. Rocky—made by science, not born of a human mother—stands *outside* the fall of man, unstained by original sin, unfettered by human hang-ups and the labyrinth of Bible-based sexual dos and don'ts. Rocky represents human sexuality free from the insanity of 1970s America.

Also basically innocent, Columbia is a rock groupie, the kind of young girl who follows rock bands around, sleeps with the musicians, and worships them from far or near. Frank "collected" her at some point in the past just like he did with Eddie, Brad, and Janet, just one more toy, one more playmate (or is it "play*thing*"?) in Frank's collection. Unfortunately for her, she fell in love with Frank, as groupies often do. She loved him and he grew bored with her (as he does with all his playthings), and moved on to Eddie. Then, when Frank tosses Eddie aside in favor of Rocky, Columbia tells us that she *very nearly* loved Eddie, in one of the show's saddest lines. Very *nearly*. Maybe if she had actually loved him, the two of them could have left the castle together. But as much as she *wanted* to love him, she didn't. She only *nearly* loved him. It's interesting how much we know about Columbia and Eddie, despite how few words are said about or by either of them. We know Columbia tried to rescue Eddie—at least emotionally. In the midst of the craziness of this freakish commune of aliens and humans, Columbia tried to keep Eddie from falling apart. Apparently, it didn't work. Of course, we don't know if she tried before or after Frank removed half of Eddie's brain.

If we see Frank as the sexual revolution, if Brad is the part of America that freaked out and tried to retreat into greater puritanism, if Janet is the part of America that went crazy with sexual abandon, if Rocky is sexuality in its natural state, then Columbia represents those who tried free love and found it unfulfilling, those who followed the craziness of the sexual revolution but discovered sex without love wasn't right for them. Columbia can't separate her heart from her loins. She couldn't enjoy the sexual circus that is Frank's world because she fell in love with Frank, and maybe that's why Frank discarded her when the fun became serious for her. Like the title character in *Pippin*, written just one year earlier, Columbia tries sex without rules and it leaves her feeling empty and hollow, just as many of the sexual revolutionaries did in the late 1960s and early '70s.

The Floor Show

The floor show is not only the culmination of all the themes in the show, it's also a little capsule history of the sexual revolution in America. Is it a comment that "free sex" is unnatural and can only be maintained when participants dress up in costume and play a role? In other words, was the sexual revolution really just a performance of this new freedom, in contradiction to the deeper human connection, intimacy, and trust that people wanted? Or is the floor show a stripping away of the rules of polite society that reveals humans in their most natural, unencumbered sexual selves? In *The Century of Sex*, Petersen writes, "Porn offered one form of public sex. Couples learned that sexual energy was a movable feast, that watching sex was a turn-on. For some, the cinematic version wasn't enough. They wanted to break the fourth wall, to participate. The seventies unleashed an unprecedented wave of exhibitionism, of public sex, of shared sex."

Now as masked performers in Frank's freaky sex show, Brad and Janet more explicitly explain their responses to the events of the night, once again mirroring the two halves of America at that time. Brad's feelings of sexuality are overwhelming to him, uncontrollable, and decidedly mysterious and unwelcome. He doesn't want to feel this way, but he can't turn back this tide. Once he has become sexually active (and, more to the point, *bi*sexually active), he can never go back to being a virgin again. This has been Brad's rite of passage into adulthood, however unconventional, and no matter how loudly he cries for his mother, he cannot go back to being a boy again. He can never undo the sex he has had with Frank, just as America could not undo and/or forget the sexual revolution once AIDS hit and it came time to pay the price for the freedom we had enjoyed. On the other side of the equation, Janet is reveling in her newfound sexuality, and even offers a prayer to the stripper Lili St. Cyr. Janet is a long way from Denton, and like Brad, she can really never go back to her old life. The difference is, she doesn't want to.

So what is the message of *Rocky Horror*? Is there a statement beyond its satire of America's sexual insanity? What about the kids who devote their lives to the film, hanging on desperately to the words, "Don't dream it, be it." Are they missing the dark underbelly of those words? Do they just ignore the three deaths only minutes after those words are sung? Or is the lesson of the story that freedom is good and sex is healthy, but mindless gluttony, of whatever sort, is dangerous? Both Brad and Janet experience sexual freedom and they both survive, though it's unclear in what state. Maybe if we knew how their story ended, we'd know better what *Rocky Horror* is saying. Maybe Richard O'Brien's proposed sequel will give us some clues, although it's interesting that in several interviews he has admitted that he has no idea what happens to Brad and Janet after this story ends.

In O'Brien's sort-of sequel, *Shock Treatment*, we do meet Brad and Janet again, sometime after their nightmare in the castle. They're married now, the sexual revolution is over, and they're living a basically normal life, but they both bear the scars of their adventure. Brad is damaged, weak, passive, while Janet has become dominant, powerful, active. Though the narrative doesn't directly follow *Rocky Horror*, these two characters have a clear through-line connecting back logically to the horrific events of *The Rocky Horror Show*.

If *Rocky Horror* asks all these questions, can there be any doubt that it's far more than the silly, oversexed rock musical that too many people assume it to be? This is smart, insightful satire that asks us to think about our culture, our appetites, our relationships, and the way we live our lives. It ranks comfortably with the best social-issue musicals: *Company*, *Assassins*, *Cabaret*, *Chicago*, *Rent*, *Urinetown*, *Hedwig and the Angry Inch*. *The Rocky Horror Show* is about sex and death. And what could be more important, or more central to the human experience, than that?

Richard O'Brien has been working on a stage sequel, tentatively titled *Rocky Horror: The Second Coming* (continuing *Rocky Horror*'s religious imagery), in which Frank N. Furter comes back from the dead, with a song called "Frankie Phoenix." O'Brien also wrote a film sequel called *The Revenge of the Old Queen* (the title refers to Frank's mother, Queen of the Planet Transsexual), which was never produced.

Part of the reason *The Best Little Whorehouse in Texas* works so well as a musical—the reason it *had* to be a musical—is that it deals with people and events for which emotions cannot be openly expressed. And because music is an abstract language, it can convey emotion much more fully and effectively than the more earthbound language of spoken words can.

These were not ordinary musical comedy characters, even though they found themselves in a musical comedy. The proprietress of the Chicken Ranch, Miss Mona, would never tell anyone the depth of her regret over the choices she's made or the profundity of loss she feels in closing the house, but her song "The Bus from Amarillo" can get at that depth of emotion through its wistful, melancholy music. Sheriff Dodd would never say out loud that he loves Mona, so the simple, gentle, country waltz of "Good Ol' Girl" does it for him. Doatsey Mae would never have the right words to describe her secret desires and regrets, but when blended with the sweet, sad music box sound of her song "Doatsey Mae," those hidden feelings find a voice and take on a level of legitimacy and dignity that is very moving. The sad simplicity of her lament about her Frederick's of Hollywood dreams reveals the lie behind Frederick's famous slogan, "Don't Dream It. Be It." Doatsey Mae will always only dream it.

The Best Little Whorehouse in Texas, the serious little musical comedy that surprised them all (much as *Grease* did a few years earlier), tells the true story of the high-profile closing of a 130-year-old brothel outside the small town of La Grange, Texas in 1973. But *Whorehouse* isn't really about sex any more than *Fiddler on the Roof* is about violins. At its core, *Whorehouse* is about how putting life on TV changes it, how it changes people, how the TV camera leaves its heavy footprint on that which it records. It's a story about the power of the media left unchecked, about privacy, about journalism itself, about America's never-ending parade of moral and sexual hypocrisy. The Chicken Ranch, the whorehouse of the show's title, had been in business since 1844. Everybody knew it, and nobody cared. But put it on the TV and suddenly it's a scandal, it's an outrage, denounced by all the politicians who had frequented the place themselves. This felt like a folksy, naughty country musical, but it was a really a smart, penetrating piece of social commentary.

After the Chicken Ranch had been closed, Sheriff J. T. "Jim" Flournoy was quoted in the *Austin American-Statesman*: "It's been there all my life and all my daddy's life and never caused anybody any trouble. Every large city in Texas has things 1,000 times worse." The editor of the *La Grange Journal* wrote in an editorial, "I think it's alright. There's no organized crime attached to it. I've never seen anything bad come from it and I've lived here all my life. The girls buy all their clothes here, their eats. It brings in business for the community. They pay taxes same as everybody else. It keeps down rape, venereal disease. I think most of the people here are in favor of it." So why was it shut down?

Because Americans are moral and sexual hypocrites, many of us. Many Americans are terrified of sex. We don't want to talk about it, don't want to know about it, don't want to *think* about it. At the same time, we're obsessed with it; we're constantly talking about it, thinking about it, writing about it. Not surprisingly, pornography is one of America's biggest industries. People claim they would never buy or even look at it, but *somebody's* buying it. A lot of it. If it's not you, it's probably the guy who works next to you. Americans arguably have a distinctly unhealthy and often genuinely comic relationship with sexuality, both their own and that of others.

The Birth of the Singing Whores

Texan Larry L. King (no relation to the talk-show host) tells the story of the show's genesis in his very entertaining memoir *The Whorehouse Papers*. King had written an article for *Playboy* in April 1974 called "The Best Little Whorehouse in Texas." Actor Peter Masterson saw the article in early 1976 while acting in *That Championship Season* on Broadway, and the way he tells it, "It hit me: *Goddamn, this is a musical!*" Masterson brought it to songwriter and fellow Texan Carol Hall. In spring 1976, Hall called King.

But King didn't like the idea. As he tells it, he said, "Look, my ignorance of the subject is absolutely awesome. I've only seen three musicals in my life and didn't care for any of them. I saw a number of dramas, but I quit musicals after three. Not my cup of whiskey." He went on, "As a writer it irritates me when the story comes to a screeching halt so a bunch of bank clerks in candy-striped suits and carrying matching umbrellas can break into a silly tap dance while singing about the sidewalks of New

York." Hall and Masterson promised King this would be a different kind of musical. So eventually King gave in, and the three formed a tight but often cantankerous team to write a musical based on King's article and on the true story of the Chicken Ranch. None of them had ever written a Broadway show before. In October 1976, they brought some friends together and did an informal reading of an early draft in Carol Hall's living room. King wrote about hearing the opening number for the first time and thinking, *My God, that's beautiful! This fucking thing may work!* That night, Masterson announced a workshop production at the Actors Studio in New York.

Masterson was a member of the prestigious Actors Studio and so the Studio agreed to a small workshop production in the fall of 1977, for twelve performances. Along the way, the three collaborators fought like cats and dogs. Hall and Masterson wanted a love song for Mona and the sheriff. King wouldn't hear of it. The two argued that the sheriff was too central a character to walk through the entire show without a song. King bellowed at them, "I can't see a cussing lawman and a woman who peddles pussy for a living yowling love songs at each other like Nelson Eddy and Jeanette MacDonald. That'd be goddamn ridiculous!"

Despite the problems and massive rewrites, the show went on. A representative from Universal Pictures happened to see a performance and immediately made an offer, not just for film rights but for stage rights as well. Universal wanted to produce it off Broadway, and maybe even on Broadway.

In preparation for the off Broadway production, Tommy Tune, the up-and-coming young choreographer and director, was hired to rechoreograph the show and co-direct with Masterson. Again, rewrites continued and songs were added and cut. They cut a big, oversexed production number called "Two Blocks from the Capitol Building" illustrating the far more salacious goings-on in Houston while Melvin P. Thorpe was "exposing" the Chicken Ranch scandal in La Grange. The number portrayed flashers, bestiality, and other perversions. Other songs cut included "The Memory Song," the girls' "Doin' It and Sayin' It Are Two Different Things," the sheriff's "Goddamn Everthang," and the Aggies' big song, "Pussy." (No kidding.) And "The Bus from Amarillo" was reassigned during previews, taken away from the character of Angel and given to Miss Mona, at the end of Act I. It would eventually be moved to the end of Act II. Also cut was a tender dialogue scene between Shy and Leroy Sliney (forever after called only "Young Cowboy" in the script). Briefly, a new opening number, Mona's "You Tell Me Your Dream" was added before "20 Fans," but it was eventually cut. The show was worked on more, yet so many problems persisted—most notably, they couldn't get the Act I ending right—that the off Broadway opening had to be postponed twice.

To the team's great surprise, three of the seven television stations in New York City refused to use the show's title on the air, so commercials were created that never once mentioned the title. Some stations agreed that the word *whorehouse* could air as a graphic but it could not be spoken. At first, none of the New York papers would run ads with the title. Eventually, a couple independent papers relented, and then the other papers caved—except the *New York Times.* It wasn't until ten days before the off Broadway opening that the *Times* finally accepted an ad with the show's title, after it was pointed out to them that they had run ads for a production of the classic play *'Tis Pity She's a Whore.* Later on, when the show toured, newspapers across the country refused to print the title and so ads were run that sold tickets to "The Best Little Chicken Ranch in Texas," "The Best Little Bawdy House in Texas," "The Best Little Blank in Texas" (no kidding again), and, most vague of all, "The Best Little House in Texas." The hysteria seemed never ending. As late as 1997, a student production of *Whorehouse* at Wentworth Institute of Technology outside Boston was cancelled by faculty, who deemed the title "dangerous for students."

The show finally opened off Broadway at the Entermedia Theatre on April 17, 1978, where it ran eighty-five performances. Most of the critics liked it. Clive Barnes, in the *New York Post*, wrote, "Considering the subject matter, the show is beautifully clear-eyed and totally free of the gooey sentimentality you might have feared. It calls a spade a spade with a frankness that is exhilaratingly delicate." Douglas Watt, of the *New York Daily News*, predicted the show would run *Annie* and *A Chorus Line* out of town, calling it "a lively, genial, unassuming musical." *Variety* said, "For sheer entertainment, *Whorehouse* is one of the most enjoyable musicals of the current season." *Time* magazine said, "This is the best new musical of the season." The Associated Press called the show "an arousing, and rousing, musical with a great deal to boast about." Pia Lindstrom on NBC said, "This is a comedy that has all the look of a show that is Broadway bound." Virginia Woodruff, of the local Channel Ten, said, "The Lone Star State got the treatment in a livewire, sassy, classy, full-of-spirit, fun musical."

The show was a hit, and the producers moved it to the Forty-Sixth Street Theatre on Broadway, a theatre just vacated, conveniently enough, by the flop musical *Working*, which had run only three weeks. *Whorehouse* opened on June 19, 1979, where it stayed happily for 1,584 performances. *Women's Wear Daily* called the show "more fun than a beer-totin' hayride at a Mardi Gras," and said the whorehouse was "actually located in that vast desert between respectability and profanity." Edna Milton, the real-life model for the show's Miss Mona, was given two small non-speaking roles in the show, although she drove everyone involved crazy. And Marvin Zindler, the model for Melvin P. Thorpe, was flown up to see the show, which he loved. The following January, Henderson Forsythe, who played the sheriff, was due for a two-week vacation, so, despite profound misgivings and paralyzing stage fright, author Larry L. King went on as the sheriff for two weeks (a role he had played at the Actors Studio).

The Broadway production received seven Tony Award nominations, for Best Musical, Best Book, Best Director, Best Choreographer, Best Featured Actor (Forsythe), and two Best Actress nominations for Carlin Glynn as Mona and Joan Ellis as Shy. The show won two Tonys, for Forsythe and Glynn, though the Tony telecast butchered through bleeping the performance of "The Aggie Song." The equally unlikely *Sweeney Todd* won Best Musical.

Alexis Smith headed the first national tour, and Fannie Flagg took over as Miss Mona on Broadway when Carlin Glynn left. For the tour, a new song was added for Melvin P. Thorpe in Act II, called "Lonely at the Top." Both Glynn and Forsythe returned to their roles to open the show in London in 1981. The show also opened productions in South Africa (where it was heavily censored) and Australia.

In 1982 the producers got into a fight with the musicians union, and they shut the show down, moving it to Boston for a while. Eventually, they moved it back to New York to the Eugene O'Neill Theatre, with most of the original leads, where it ran another sixty-three performances. If not for the union problems and the subsequent loss of momentum, insiders think the show might well have run longer. Still it was one of the longest-running musicals of the 1970s and at one point had three national companies touring at once. *Women's Wear Daily*, one of the top magazines of the clothing industry, credits *Whorehouse* for the Western-wear fashion trend that gripped America in the early 1980s.

A movie version was made in 1982 with Dolly Parton, Burt Reynolds, and Dom DeLuise. King had wanted Shirley MacLaine and Willie Nelson to play the leads, casting which would have instantly made the film far more faithful to the stage show. Masterson and Tune were originally slated to direct the film, but those duties went instead to Colin Higgins, who had just directed *Nine to Five*. The movie watered down the content, completely rewrote the ending (despite the fact that it was a true story), and did only moderately well at the box office. Burt Reynolds insisted on major plot changes, character changes, and other rewrites, plus reducing the sheriff's age considerably. Dolly Parton insisted on writing some new songs, which were well crafted but not as organic to the score as the original songs were. The movie's climactic song "I Will Always Love You" later became a monster pop hit as recorded by Whitney Houston. But in 1982, the era of movie musicals was over (temporarily) and *Whorehouse* in its watered down state had little that was fresh or exciting to offer. All that had been taken out.

A terrible stage sequel was attempted by most of the same creative team in 1994, called *The Best Little Whorehouse Goes Public*. It ran fifteen performances and Universal Studios lost about seven million dollars on it. The original *Whorehouse* was revived in 2001 for a national tour starring Ann-Margret and Gary Sandy, but minus the bite and grit of the original.

It Was the Nicest Little Whorehouse Y'Ever Saw

Perhaps the most surprising thing about the musical is that almost the whole story as told in the musical is actually true. Like any dramatization, some events are consolidated or reordered, some characters are combined, but almost none of the story is completely fiction.

The whorehouse now known the world over as the Chicken Ranch first opened its door for business in 1844 in what is now La Grange, Texas. Over the years, a succession of women managed the house as it moved from location to location, and a succession of sheriffs looked the other way. One could look askance at that fact or realize that every time elections for sheriff came up, the citizenry of Fayette County had the option of electing a sheriff who would shut the Chicken Ranch down. Even though prostitution was illegal in Texas, the voters of Fayette County never did that.

The first proprietress of the place was a woman known in the history books only as Mrs. Swine, so called for her personal appearance and odor. In those days, customers did not take off their clothes, but merely undid what required undoing. Most of the girls who worked there came from extreme poverty and ignorance, many heavily pockmarked, some severely retarded or with other profound disabilities. Many came from families in which incest was a way of life. And though most of them would have loved to escape "the life" through marriage, it was a rare man who would find them attractive. Still, it did happen, especially in the 1800s when women frequently died during childbirth and men sometimes went through three or four wives in their lifetimes. Mrs. Swine may have lost an employee or two in those situations, but she also made a tidy profit in her role as paid matchmaker.

Jessie Williams (born Faye Stewart) took over the house in 1905, coming from Waco, where she had already been a successful "working girl." She had started in Waco at age fourteen as a maid and serving girl, but she studied the ways of her rich employers and learned how to act like a proper young woman. Eventually she went to work in Waco's most popular brothel and rose to the top. Within a few years, she had bought her own place and employed three girls. Soon after, she moved to La Grange and took over what would soon become the Chicken Ranch. One of the town's periodic "clean-up crusades" might have threatened Miss Jessie's success if she hadn't made such good friends with local law enforcement, and if they hadn't been such good and regular customers. With a comfortable amount of advance warning, Miss Jessie sold her land in Waco and bought eleven acres and a house just outside the city limits, and just a couple blocks off the interstate. Miss Jessie made a deal with the sheriff that she and her girls would get suspicious-looking strangers to open up to them and then pass along any pertinent info to the sheriff, aiding him tremendously in cutting down crime and establishing an outstanding law-enforcement record.

During the Great Depression, business was just as bad for the Chicken Ranch as it was for all other businesses. A "regular date" (no perversions or improvisations of any kind were permitted) cost $1.50, but it wasn't always easy for a boy to come up with that kind of cash during the Depression. So Miss Jessie soon made a compromise—"one chicken for one screw." A chicken was easier to come by than $1.50, although it seemed that chicken stealing increased during the period. Soon the house had been nicknamed the Chicken Ranch. When President Roosevelt's Works Progress Administration set up a Civilian Conservation Corps camp right near the Chicken Ranch, things started looking rosy again.

By World War II, the girls were giving their all for the war effort again. And things had changed for whorehouses. As one book puts it, "The quality of the average whore was upgraded considerably when self-reliant young women entered the profession by choice, free of guilt and a fear of ostracism." During this period, lots of female students at the University of Texas paid their tuition by working at the Chicken Ranch during the summers. (They say that one young woman who did this earned her MFA in piano performance while working her summers at the Ranch, and became one of the top classical pianists in America.) It was during the 1940s that the boys at Texas A&M University discovered the Chicken Ranch and began making regular trips. Soon, wealthy alumni would treat the football team to a night at the Ranch if they won the big game against Texas University. Edna Milton, who would later be fictionalized as Miss Mona, took over the place in 1961. Not only did high-profile politicians frequent the Chicken Ranch, so did a wide assortment of clergy. Miss Edna delicately put it this way: "We had Catholic priests come to my place late at night, and since they'd took a vow not to screw they'd ask to eat us and jack off and stuff." *Tell the truth, can you imagine Dolly Parton saying that?*

A former Texas Ranger and the inheritor of a long family tradition of lawmen, Sheriff Flournoy was the real-life model for *Whorehouse*'s Sheriff Ed Earl Dodd. He had been elected sheriff of Fayette County in 1946 at the age of forty-six and was seventy-three at the time of the Chicken Ranch scandal. There are lots of monuments in Fayette County, mostly for war heroes, but there's one there now for Sheriff Flournoy. An estimated four thousand to five thousand criminals were arrested and imprisoned on Flournoy's watch, giving him one of the best records in the state. He was the first sheriff to install a direct phone line from the Chicken Ranch to his office in the courthouse building, to keep track of any trouble out at the Ranch and to more easily get any information the girls had collected from customers each night.

KTRK-TV's consumer affairs reporter Marvin Zindler and reporter Larry Connors (later a longtime news anchor in St. Louis) always claimed that they began their 1973 exposé after receiving an anonymous tip about the Chicken Ranch and another less famous brothel. Why Zindler needed a call to tell him about the already legendary Chicken Ranch was never explained. At the time, many speculated that they chose the Chicken Ranch at that particular time as nothing more than a ratings grab. After all, Zindler had only been at KTRK for six months, after being fired for his excessive zeal as a Harris County deputy sheriff in charge of consumer fraud. Years later, Zindler changed his story about the anonymous tip, now claiming that Texas Attorney General John Hill called him and asked him to do a story because Sheriff Flournoy wouldn't close the place down. Larry Connors is quoted on KTRK's website:

> [Cameraman Frank] Ambrose stayed in the van as a third member of our party and I went inside. I was carrying a small scope camera in my coat pocket. I was getting what pictures I could inside, while Ambrose filmed customers. Nearly three dozen came and went in a little over an hour. At one point, one of the girls spotted my camera. I was sent outside, but told I could return without the camera. I kept asking if I could buy pictures of the girls, but my request was denied.

Zindler interviewed District Attorney Oliver Kitzman. Zindler asked, "Are you aware of the operations of two bawdy houses that are operating both in Sealy and La Grange?" Kitzman said, "I think most knowledgeable people in this community have heard about those places." Zindler asked, "As District Attorney have you ever tried to close these places down, either in a civil injunction or by a criminal raid of any kind?" He replied, "No, sir, frankly we have never had any indication by anyone that these places are a problem to law enforcement or otherwise." Zindler pursued the story.

Soon it had gotten big enough that Johnny Carson was making nightly jokes about it on national television. After the scandal broke, Flournoy circulated a petition to keep the Chicken Ranch open and collected several thousand signatures, but when the dirt threatened to get on more politicians, the governor ordered Flournoy to shut it down. The Chicken Ranch was closed down permanently in 1973. A year later, Zindler returned to La Grange for a report on how the Chicken Ranch's closing had affected the town's economy. The sheriff forcibly ejected him and Zindler sued. Zindler won the suit but Flournoy bragged, "You know, my people here in this town raised the money to pay him down to the penny. He never got one goddamn nickel out of my pocket, by God!"

Jim Flournoy finally retired as Fayette County sheriff in 1980 and died in 1982 at the age of eighty-two. After his death, he was honored by the governor for having solved every murder and bank robbery committed in Fayette County during his thirty-four years as sheriff. Significantly, some of the information that led to those arrests came from the girls at the Chicken Ranch.

Today, one of the country's few legal brothels, right outside Las Vegas, is now named the Chicken Ranch, in honor of the original, and it contains some furnishings from the original house, including some lamps and paintings. The house itself was partially dismantled and moved and turned into a restaurant. Only part of the original structure remains.

Sex and the Single Chicken

One resident of La Grange was quoted in King's original *Playboy* article saying, "That place paid good taxes, friend. It was clean. The girls had good manners. The prices didn't hold you up. Friend, they never so much as gave a *hot check* out there! I had a buddy, he was overseas during the Hitler war, and one of the girls out there, she mailed him cookies. Regular." A successful Texas lawyer said, "I went over there back in my law school days, and it was so goddamned proper I felt out of place. It was just too goddamned *wholesome* for somebody with a hard pecker hunting raunchy sin and eager to whip up his old Baptist guilts."

The apparent truth of the matter—and one of the primary conceits of the show—is that the Chicken Ranch was a *home*. The girls were safe there, with a warm bed and three square meals a day. They were protected, not only by Miss Edna (Miss Mona in the show), but also by the sheriff. Many of the girls felt safer and more at home there than they had at any other time in their lives. Miss Edna had a long list of very strict Victorian rules that kept the place more respectable than anyone might expect. It was a homey place where the men didn't feel dirty or sinful, and that no doubt contributed enormously to its longevity and success. The title of the song "Lil' Ole Bitty Pissant Country Place" is probably a reference to fellow Texan Lyndon Johnson who infamously called Vietnam 'a little bitty pissant country."

But despite the Chicken Ranch's reported wholesomeness, prostitution is prostitution, after all, and many women today can't even for a moment consider the sex industry in objective terms. In the early 1970s, when the women's movement was campaigning against the exploitation of women and their bodies, against pornography and prostitution, some women sitting in the audience no doubt had a problem with the way the business of selling sex was portrayed in *Whorehouse*. The scene and song "Girl, You're a Woman," in which the other girls fix up Shy for her first day of work, conjured up a real conflict of emotions for many women in the audience. After all, Shy is surrounded by a big supportive family of women, putting on a nice dress, putting on makeup, getting her hair fixed, things that usually have fun, pleasant connotations for many women, and yet she's doing it all in order to sell herself to strange men.

And that's the very complicated point. What too many people then and now missed about the show is that *Whorehouse* is neither pro-prostitution nor anti-prostitution. It's just telling a story that illustrates a larger truth about our culture. And that misunderstanding has led to many shallow, creepy productions of the show.

Big picture-wise, there has always been prostitution. The Chicken Ranch was just one blip in a long history of humans selling sex to each other. The *Whorehouse* story just happened at a very unique time in American cultural history, smack dab in the middle of the sexual revolution of the 1960s and '70s, a weird, wild, confusing time for many people, a time of open homosexuality for the first time in modern Western culture (or the second time if you count the Roaring Twenties), a time of free love, wife-swapping and swinging, and a kind of sexual openness America had never explored to this degree, an openness upon which the door would shut just a few years later in 1981 when AIDS appeared.

Filthy, Dark Details and Carnal Lust

The Best Little Whorehouse in Texas is a reversal of the norm. In the stage show (unlike the film), the women are not objectified, even though that seems that's what a show like *Whorehouse* would do. The women are rarely seen in any state of undress. Instead, the women are the ones who have an objective, relatively rational (though some might argue not entirely healthy) perspective on sex, and the men are the ones who are wildly oversexed and a little bit crazy. It's the men who *need* sex, who can't stop thinking about sex. And when the locker room scene is done with partial nudity, as many productions have done, that also underlines *Whorehouse*'s reverse perspective, by sexualizing and objectifying the men in a way usually reserved for women. In contemporary movies, female nudity has gotten relatively commonplace but male nudity is still somehow shocking. With a nude locker room scene in *Whorehouse*, the reverse is true. The women now are in the position of sexual control, and the men are being objectified.

And the satiric point at the heart of the character Melvin P. Thorpe points out the obvious but usually overlooked point that the moralists and religious extremists often seem to be the ones who are constantly thinking about sex. It makes us wonder why Pat Robertson and Jerry Falwell care what gay couples do in the privacy of their own homes, and why private gay sexual practices have such a place of prominence in their work. When the heterosexual porn industry is far larger than its gay counterpart, when the heterosexual prostitution industry is so much larger, why do Robertson, Falwell, and their ilk focus so strongly on the gay stuff? Why are they thinking about it so much? And similarly in *Whorehouse*, why is Melvin P. Thorpe so obsessed with the sexual goings-on in a quiet little whorehouse sixty miles from his TV station? While Zindler was spending all his time and energy on "exposing" the Chicken Ranch, the torture and murder of twenty-seven young boys was taking place in Houston, Zindler's backyard. And still Zindler went after the Chicken Ranch.

And that's what *The Best Little Whorehouse in Texas* is about. Not sex itself, but the terror, the hypocrisy, and the insanity always swirling around sex in America. The Chicken Ranch had been operating with the full knowledge of most of the inhabitants of Texas for over a hundred years. But putting real life on TV always changes it, and once Marvin Zindler broadcast his exaggerations and misrepresentations over the public airwaves, everything changed. Rational men became raving idiots. After a century and a half of quiet anonymity, the Chicken Ranch became a very public and very "dangerous" problem that needed action taken against it. Along the way to purification, people's lives were ruined. The reason *Whorehouse* works so well as compelling theatre is that it pushes its social and political satire to the background, and focuses on the real people whose lives were greatly complicated and in some cases destroyed.

The Language of Lust

One of the most fun parts of *Whorehouse* is its language, even beyond the adventure of trying to advertise a show with that title. Since every major creator of the show was from Texas, and since Larry L. King was a professional writer specializing in work about Texas, the language of the show creates a world foreign to most audiences but rich in detail and local color. The sheriff cusses more than any other character in a musical, with the possible exception of the characters in *Hair*, but fewer obscenities would have made him less real, less authentic. And in this 1973 world, before cable and satellite TV, before HBO and Showtime, cussing on television was unthinkable. But elected officials hadn't learned to deal with television yet. Murders and other crimes did not require daily news briefings, broadcast live. Sheriff Dodd is ill equipped to deal with the power and mysterious rules of being on TV. Interestingly, the sheriff finally learns the lesson that cussing on TV is a bad idea, but too late. And even at the end of the story, he still doesn't understand what's really going on. He thinks all the problems could have been avoided if only he hadn't cussed on television. He doesn't understand the very powerful moral hypocrisy and political opportunism behind what has happened. The sheriff is too straightforward to comprehend the duplicity of Senator Wingwoah, the governor, and Thorpe.

King had originally gone ever farther, writing one line for the sheriff with the word *nigger* in it, but Henderson Forsythe, who played the sheriff, refused to say it. King argued that it was authentic. Forsythe argued—rightly—that once that word was spoken the audience would be lost, if not for the rest of the show, at least for the rest of the scene. Still, another line remains that refers to Mexicans as "little greasers."

Melvin P. Thorpe, on the other hand, knows how to use the medium. He knows how to talk about "dirty" topics without offending viewers. He knows how to be salacious without using four-letter words. In fact, the content of what Melvin says on camera is far more obscene than what the sheriff says; it's just that Melvin knows better which words to use. And the ridiculous song-and-dance TV show Melvin hosts (the musical's biggest departure from reality) is a prescient social satire of America's gradual move toward news as entertainment. The phenomenon wasn't nearly as prevalent then as it is now, when it's often very difficult to tell news and entertainment apart. That was just beginning in 1973. Today it's an epidemic.

Language is also an issue for Mona. When Angel and Shy arrive, Mona lays down her rules. One of the rules is that the girls aren't allowed to use words like *Johns*, *pussy*, *ass*, and others. Mona prefers delicate language when talking about sex. In her own way, she's much like Melvin in understanding that offending people isn't about content; it's about vocabulary. As many women did at the time, Mona even refuses to talk explicitly about a woman having her period. Mona—and all her girls—calls it *the curse*. Oral sex is called *French*. The list goes on and on. But is this an example of Mona being just as hypocritical as some of the other characters, trying to whitewash human sexuality, trying to pretend that it's something other than it is? Is she caving in to the hypocrisy of the rest of the world? Or might we see her language choices as merely a business decision, an acknowledgement that her customers are uncomfortable with honest talk about sex? And what about the way she renames all her girls? Is that another form of verbal hypocrisy or deception? Is it a way to make the girls appear other than they really are, like renaming Nancy Jean Drury "Angel"? Or is that a form of protection for the girls?

The lyric of the opening song raises issues of language in a different way. The real Chicken Ranch was just a plain box house at the end of a dirt road, ugly in most ways, with additions added on over the years in haphazard fashion. But in the memories of those who love it, in the lyrics that open the show, it had a beautiful garden, pine trees, a painted barn, a picket fence, and other aesthetic pleasures. This is a romanticized time and place, rich with romantic images, with alliteration and rhyme, and as often happens memory has made it beautiful in ways that it never was.

She's a Good Ol' Girl

As Jan Huston writes about the real-life model for Miss Mona in her book, *The Chicken Ranch*, "Edna Milton's early biography reads like a saga of the Depression. Born to a dirt-poor Oklahoma farm couple, Edna and her sisters picked cotton like any other Okies lucky enough to have a crop during the dust-bowl years. But Edna found some time to sow some wild oats when she was not picking cotton. At sixteen she was pregnant. Her family turned against her with proverbial 'don't darken my door' rhetoric and Edna left the furrowed Oklahoma farm for the seamy side of Oklahoma City. The baby died."

Edna moved up in her chosen profession of prostitution but soon got married and bought a house in Austin, Texas. In 1952, she moved to La Grange and into the Chicken Ranch. In 1961, at age thirty-two, Edna's boss, Miss Jessie, died and Edna bought the Chicken Ranch from Jessie's heirs. Soon after taking over the Chicken Ranch, she married her second husband, Johnny Luke, but the marriage only lasted a few years. As far as we can tell, Edna and Sheriff Flournoy never had a relationship, though it's not entirely clear, and Flournoy was happily married. That part of the *Whorehouse* story is probably fictional, added in one of the few concessions to traditional musicals.

Interestingly, one of Miss Edna's rules was that no black or Hispanic customers were allowed in the house, and it was often her black maid's job to turn away minority customers. When the Chicken Ranch was closed down, it was making very good money. The girls turned over between fifty and seventy-five percent of their earnings to Edna, who provided them with room and board, all meals, clothes, and other necessaries. It is estimated by some that Edna was grossing about $500,000 a year, mostly accumulated through fifteen-dollar, fifteen-minute customers. Of course, this meant the girls were making somewhere in the neighborhood of $1,200 a month, not a bad income in the early 1970s. After the closing, Edna tried opening a new house in Nevada but gave up on it. Edna married again and moved to Gladewater, a small town in east Texas. All in all, she was married four times and divorced three.

The lyric for the song "The Bus from Amarillo" is one of the show's most poignant and most truthful moments. It asks a question the show could not avoid: How does a girl get to be a prostitute? Miss Mona got on that bus with a one-way ticket, with no intention of ever returning home. She wanted opportunity. She wanted possibility. But when it was presented to her, it was too scary and she gave it up. Now at the end of the show, she wishes she had it again. She knows her fear kept her from pursuing her dreams. Now her future lies open before her again, but more than half her life is gone.

The song is about making choices, and it mirrors Mona's earlier song, "Girl, You're a Woman," which she sings to Shy. Mona understands all too well the consequences of choices. She knows her life might have turned out differently had she stayed on the bus. She knows that Shy's life might turn out differently, too, and Mona tries to persuade Shy to leave, to take a job at the local diner. But Mona also knows that she offers a safe place, and if Shy is determined to enter this life, she might as well do it here.

"Girl, You're a Woman" is a song of pride, of support, but also of sadness about the road Shy has put herself on. It's about being an adult and taking responsibility for choices. It's about how Shy is making a choice she can never unmake, and how she must understand and accept the repercussions of that choice. Every girl singing the song has been there, and they all remember that moment when they made the choice that got them where they are now. Once Shy goes upstairs with her first customer, she can never go back. When the girls sing that after they fix Shy up, she'll be pretty and she'll look a lot like the rest of them, the song again takes on a double edge. It's funny that the girls say she'll be pretty *and* look like them, implying of course that *they* are all pretty. But they're also saying that she'll just be another whore, another girl who wandered in off the street to sell her body—just like each of them.

This song is not a happy one. And it's characteristic of the whole show. It does not extol the virtues of prostitution or take pride in that life; the exact opposite is true. This lyric is all about dealing with hard choices and past mistakes and horrors, about accepting the indignities of life with a stiff upper lip, about not showing weakness or regret, about hiding the real feelings of loneliness and disconnection, about handling heartache and despair. It's a very sad song. Nowhere does the song glamorize prostitution.

Likewise, Mona's maid and confidant Jewel's big showstopper, "24 Hours of Lovin'," is more than just a showstopper. It's strategically placed right after the girls talk about how much they hate the annual Thanksgiving party for the college boys, how annoying the boys are, how difficult the party always is. They hate it, but they know it's part of the job—they have to have sex with annoying, rowdy, boorish college boys because their alumni association is paying good money for it. When Jewel enters to sing of the fun she's going to have with her boyfriend during her twenty-four hours off, the girls are reminded (yet again) of the joy of sex that they've given up. Sex is a business for them now; for Jewel it's still fun, still exciting, still thrilling, still an act of love. Not so for the girls.

And to underline all this, the authors chose to interrupt this song, refusing to let it end neatly, by having a customer show up at the door wanting sex. Even this lighthearted bonding, this display of empathy, must take backseat to the demands of the customers. Prostitution, the authors are reminding us, is a business, with no room for sentimentality.

"The Bus from Amarillo" was first written for Angel (then named April), but the authors felt it was too strong a statement and too central to the themes of the show to give it to anyone but Mona. Since Mona had been a working girl as well, the song fits her fine, and when she sings it, she speaks for everyone in the house. It tries to get at the mindset that allows a woman to make the choice to enter this life. It reminds us that the issues surrounding prostitution, its morality, its causes and effects, its impact on society, are complicated and messy, and that there are no easy answers. Like other shows of the time—*Company*, *Follies*, and others—this is theatre that asks questions without offering answers. Great plays had been doing that for centuries, but musicals were doing it too now.

And as Mona sings "The Bus from Amarillo," there's additional subtext there. Maybe Mona didn't ever realize her dreams, but she did land in a safe place at the Chicken Ranch, and she found a surrogate mother in Miss Wulla Jean. And in the years since, Mona has offered the same haven for other girls. Girls like Shy, running away from other horrors, have found a relatively safe place in this house. And as Mona sings this last song, she realizes that she has allowed that safe place to be taken away. It was entrusted to her by generations past, to continue to "save" girls like her, and now she has lost it. Now those girls who get off that bus from Amarillo won't have a safe place to land. When this song was originally placed at the end of Act I, it didn't have that additional resonance. At the end of Act II, that additional tragedy is palpable.

The Celebrated Cussin' Sheriff of Lanvill County

The sheriff, more than any other character in the show, feels great emotion but cannot ever bring himself to express it. In the last moments of the show, Mona asks him if he remembers their first time alone together, their first taste of genuine intimacy, on the night of John F. Kennedy's inauguration. And though he does remember it, every detail, he doesn't do emotion. It's been drilled into him since childhood by his family, Texas Rangers one and all, that emotion is for sissies, so he pretends not to remember. It's often difficult for men and women to communicate fully and easily, but it was even more so in Texas in the 1970s, with the baggage of old-fashioned Southern machismo still in the mix.

The sheriff doesn't handle any kind of real emotion very well, so he stalls at Mona's question. He riffs on the topic of Kennedy, rambling away, saying anything to avoid the topic of that night that he and Mona fell in love. It's a filibuster. But the show goes further and deeper here than this single personal moment. The sheriff isn't just talking about anything; he's talking about Kennedy, the man who, for Americans of that generation, meant hope, safety, possibility. The Kennedy era represents for Mona and the sheriff an idealized, half-remembered youth, a time when choices and circumstances had not trammeled all the other possibilities. When the sheriff goes on to talk about Kennedy's death, it represents, here at the end of *Whorehouse*, the death of hope and possibility, the end of a kind of innocence.

This scene is about role-playing, about the rules changing and the sheriff being unable to play a new role. The sheriff is realizing his impotence, his inability to protect the woman he loves. It's strange and painful and humiliating for him, and he just can't deal with it openly. And the scene also subtly ties the Chicken Ranch, one piece of Texas history, to the Kennedy assassination, another piece of Texas history. But it's also about television—the power of Oswald's live killing at the hands of Jack Ruby beaming across American televisions. The sheriff doesn't realize it, but he knew television's power even back then; he just didn't recognize it for what it was.

The sheriff's one song, "Good Ol' Girl," tells us even more. He never goes so far as to say he loves Mona. We know he does but he won't say it.

And the things he remembers about her (he's already talking about their relationship in the past tense) tell us volumes, her lack of demands, her refusal to demand romance and displays of affection from him, the way she never demanded conversation from him. She understands him and what he can't offer her, and she accepts all that. But even these words of indirect affection he offers the audience in the song are too much to say to Mona. The second verse of the song is given to the male chorus as the sheriff calls Mona to tell her the Chicken Ranch must be shut down. We see this phone call in mime, accompanied by the chorus. It's an unusual but highly dramatic choice for the show's creators to make, one that reinforces for us the sheriff's inability to talk to Mona the way he would like. Here his words of love, as indirect as they are, must be given instead to a nameless chorus while he delivers the worst news possible to the woman he loves.

In the last scene in the show between the sheriff and Mona, he finally faces his one big failure. No matter how many criminals he apprehends, no matter how many crimes he solves, no matter how big the statue of him will be someday, he has failed her. It's unbearable for him and he jumps at the chance to demonstrate a success. He brags about how he's kept the media roped off around the property so that Mona and Jewel can leave in peace, conveniently ignoring the fact that he's partly to blame for them being there in the first place. He tells a story of arresting Mexican kids for stealing a goat, as if that success can make up for this failure, as if that success will redeem him in Mona's eyes. What he doesn't understand is that he doesn't need redemption from Mona. She forgives him. She understands better than he does the powerful forces that had lined up against them.

The audience longs for a Great Revelation for the sheriff at the end of the show, but they don't get it. One of the central points of *Whorehouse*, one of the story's great tragedies, is that the sheriff never learns anything from all that has happened. He almost gets it; he senses that the murder of Oswald grew in its power because it was broadcast live, that television gave it mythic proportions, but this is all too big for him to get his mind around. At the end, he still thinks the Chicken Ranch issue blew up just because he cussed on TV, when that's not even half the story. He doesn't understand that, like killing, sex takes on much greater size and power when linked to the cathode ray tube. Melvin P. Thorpe's images of Texas's beloved Aggie boys half-naked and freshly deflowered being beamed into living rooms across the state gave the Chicken Ranch and its "dangers" mythic proportions that could no longer be dismissed. Talking about it was one thing, seeing it in your living room was quite another.

Exactly like it had been with the Vietnam War.

Also, it apparently doesn't occur to the sheriff that if Mona had heeded his early warnings, if she had not continued with the Thanksgiving Day festivities, Melvin never would have caught the college boys in the whorehouse in the first place. The sheriff senses from his first dialogue scene that Melvin's exposé is potentially dangerous. He begs Mona to take it seriously. She shares in the blame for what has happened, but at the end he takes it all on his own shoulders. He believes he should have protected her, just as he always has, but the truth is he *tried*. There's an argument to be made that Melvin merely talking about the whorehouse on TV might not have stirred up as much furor as he hoped. But images of (presumably) clean-cut nineteen-year-old boys running around a whorehouse naked was more than most folks—and most politicians—could handle watching on TV. Melvin knows his audience and knows that when the "loveless copulation" involves kids, an entirely different kind of outrage arises in many people.

As the show ends, the sheriff is so close to understanding all these things, but he never makes the final connections. He has a simplistic worldview, and before now he never needed a more sophisticated one, still stuck as he is in the 1950s in many ways. He's too simple and direct a man to understand the complexities of what has happened. He doesn't belong in this new world of television and photogenic politicians.

Then we'd be free, sexually free,
Free to let each urge
We suppress freely surge
And our inhibitions melt;
Free, sexually free,
Free to cast our seed
On a stone if the need
For a stone should be felt.
Free, sexually free,
Free to follow love,
Though it lead to above
Or below thy neighbor's belt.
See what it is to be
Satisfied and unfrustrated,
Free and at liberty
To be loved and stimulated.
Be unashamedly
Sexually liberated . . .
—"Sexually Free" from I Love My Wife

I Love My Wife completes an unofficial trilogy of musicals about America's sexual revolution. This is a show about the mainstream rejection of the sexual revolution in the late 1970s, which in turn jumpstarted the "Culture War" waged by the Moral Majority, Christian Coalition, and others, which we're still fighting today. *Hair* introduced the revolution and its free love philosophy, and hinted at its darker side in 1968. In 1973, *The Rocky Horror Show* exposed the revolution's dark underbelly, the dangers of unthinking excess. And in 1977, *I Love My Wife* completed the trilogy as it showed us the end of the revolution, going out not with a bang but with a whimper, and its eventual irrelevance to much of America. (You could add to this group *Company*, *The Robber Bridegroom*, and *The Best Little Whorehouse in Texas*, as well.)

Strangely enough, *I Love My Wife* was not the first musical on Broadway about wife-swapping. That honor goes to the 1916 musical comedy *So Long, Letty*, in which two wives decide they'd be happier with each other's husbands. Of course, after a week, they see the error of their ways and they switch back. *I*

Love My Wife, on the other hand, knowingly captured the cultural zeitgeist of 1977 and the disillusionment the country felt over just about everything, and it expanded just a bit what was possible in a mainstream Broadway musical.

In 1982, *New York* magazine published an article called, "Is Sex Dead?" *Esquire* published "The End of Sex," which said, "As it has turned out, the Sexual Revolution, in slaying some loathsome old dragons, has created some formidable new ones." The divorce rate increased forty-two percent between 1970 and 1977, when *I Love My Wife* was written and when it's set.

I Love My Wife tells a very funny, truthful story about ordinary people who are out of sync with their culture, back in a time when all mainstream culture came through a very narrow filter, a time when the culture often led the public rather than the other way around, a time of *Deep Throat* and "porno chic," wife-swapping, key parties, swingers' clubs, and lots more. A time as chaotic and baffling as the times we live in today. In Manhattan, right across the Hudson River from the 1977 suburban New Jersey homes of the characters in *I Love My Wife*, was the famous swingers' club Plato's Retreat, at its peak at exactly that same moment. Two totally different worlds, right next to each other, both trying to figure out human sexuality. The absurdity of all this messy, cultural confusion is summed up in one of the most insightful lines in the show: "Then the four of them are pairing up and having a threesome."

Several reviews of later productions have criticized the show for being too tame for a sex farce, for stopping short of fully exploring the topic. And they're sort of right—the show does stop short and that's its point. It's not a sex farce; it's a serious comedy about American culture. Just as the show stops short of "going all the way," likewise, these four central characters also stop short of fully exploring their "multiple love experience." There's a line in the Act II opener, "Hey There, Good Times," which claims that even though this is a show about sex, it's also family-friendly. It's a sly joke, but it's almost true. After all, the show only contains a single "dirty" word (*titties*), and not one *shit* or *fuck*. Ultimately, this story isn't really about sex or the sexual revolution—it's about the world outside the sexual revolution, a world of mainstream normalcy in which most people would never be sexually adventurous. Many Americans, it can be argued, are terrified of sex. It's easy to see why—it's the most primal, the most fundamentally "animal" act a human can commit. If we acknowledge that even one part of us is animal, then we are animal, and the Bible forbids animal urges. Particularly in America, we're supposed to be civilized and decent, not primal. *The Rocky Horror Show* is about sex; *I Love My Wife* is about how, for most people, life isn't about sex.

Usually when sex is the topic of a show or film, everyone assumes that sexual/moral transgression is the agenda. Often it is. But here is that rare story in which the characters *try* to make sex the point but realize that's a mistake. The opening song, the show's statement of purpose, has literally nothing at all to do with sex, and the finale only marginally has to do with sex. Because it's not a show about sex. This script tells us this outright, when Alvin and Cleo are arguing about whether to get a man or a woman to join them in their proposed threesome, and Alvin yells, "Sex has nothing to do with it!" Again, it's a joke, but it's also true. The show tells us explicitly that, whatever you might assume, this is a show not about sexual intercourse, but about relationships being tested by massive cultural change—almost exactly the central theme of *Fiddler on the Roof*.

Falling in Love

Michael Stewart had already written the books for *Bye Bye Birdie* (which won him a Tony his first time out); *Carnival*; *Hello, Dolly!*; *George M!*; *Mack and Mabel*; and *The Grand Tour*. Later on he would write *42nd Street* (with Mark Bramble) and the book and lyrics for *Barnum*. But *I Love My Wife* was the first time Stewart wrote both book and lyrics. The inspiration for the show came from a French play Stewart had seen, *Viens Chez-moi, J'Habite Chez une Copine* (*Come to My Place, I Live with My Girlfriend*), by Luis Regio and Didier Kaminka, in which the actors stepped out of the dialogue scenes to lip-synch songs that commented on the scenes. Minus the lip-synching, this was a device musical theatre had explored before, first in Bertolt Brecht and Kurt Weill's *The Threepenny Opera* (1933, 1955), but also in more recent, commercial shows like *Company* (1970). But by the time the script and score of *I Love My Wife* was finished, its content held very little resemblance to that French play and appeared to be based more directly—though still loosely—on the iconic 1969 film *Bob and Carol and Ted and Alice*. Still, structurally and stylistically, the show owed a lot to both the French play and Stephen Sondheim, George Furth, and Hal Prince's landmark concept musical, *Company*.

Pop composer Cy Coleman had already written many hit songs and a battery of successful musicals (several of them built on jazz scores), including *Wildcat* (1960); *Little Me* (1962); *Sweet Charity* (1966); *Seesaw* (1973); and later, after *I Love My Wife*, also *On the Twentieth Century* (1978); *Barnum* (1980); *City of Angels* (1990); *The Will Rogers Follies* (1991); *The Life* (1997); and *Grace, The Musical* (2001).

I Love My Wife had a rough start. Investors backed out right before rehearsals started, producers came and went, director Joe Layton hurt himself very badly and had to be replaced by Gene Saks (who had initially turned the project down), and the reviews out of town were horrible. So they did major work on the material and moved the show's New York opening earlier, so that it would open ahead of *Annie* and *Side by Side by Sondheim*, thereby escaping comparisons with a probable commercial hit and the high art of Sondheim.

After the tryout in Philadelphia, *I Love My Wife* opened on Broadway in April 1977, starring Lenny Baker, James Naughton, Joanna Gleason, and Ilene Graff, and it ran an impressive 872 performances, closing in May 1979. During the run, the Smothers Brothers stepped into the male leads and gave the show an extended life. Later in the run, the producers installed an African American cast (much as *Hello, Dolly!* had done) featuring Lawrence Hilton-Jacobs and Hattie Winston, which boosted sales again. The show opened in London in October 1977 and ran 401 performances.

The New York reviewers really liked the show. In the *New York Times,* Clive Barnes wrote, "*I Love My Wife* is bright, inventive, amusing, and breezy. But it is a different kind of musical. It is something of a musical play." In the *New York Post*, Martin Gottfried called it "a thoroughly disarming entertainment" and said, "I can't see the harm in a healthy, well-adjusted, sentimental and cheerful musical about sex and marriage . . . It is friendly and charming, beautifully directed and engagingly performed."

I Love My Wife was nominated for six Tony Awards, including Best Musical, Best Book, and Best Score, but only director Gene Saks and actor Lenny Baker took home Tonys. The show was also nominated for eight Drama Desk Awards and won six of them. But *I Love My Wife* has never had much of a life post-Broadway. Perhaps it's the very adult content that makes it an unlikely candidate for regional and community theatres—and impossible for high schools to produce. Perhaps it's the show's overt sexism. But there's an argument to be made that the show has transitioned from being dated to being a period piece, exactly as it happened with *Hair* and *Rocky Horror*.

What the New York critics couldn't see—maybe because they were too close to it—is that *I Love My Wife* is more than a charming comedy about two somewhat uptight suburban couples. It's a well-crafted, insightful, cultural snapshot of America in 1977, of the wrenching changes the country was going through, the tentative openness about sex, the morphing of gender roles that had been solidly in place since the creation of the suburbs in the postwar years. Like *Hair* and *Rocky Horror*, this is a concept musical about America itself, and it uses these two couples as stand-ins. Among these four characters—Alvin and Cleo, and Wally and Monica—we see the whole spectrum of Americans' comfort with sexuality at this pivotal point in our cultural history. Wally is the most open, the most adventurous (the Hugh Hefner of the story), although we have to wonder if he's all talk; Alvin is scared but still wants to be "with it." Cleo doesn't much want to be adventurous, but is afraid of being left out; and Monica is horrified at the adventure laid out before her and its obvious implications.

At its emotional core, this is a story about searching for meaningful human connection amid massive cultural change. When America was mostly small towns and self-contained urban neighborhoods, before there was universally accessible mass media, it was easy to connect to the people of your small community. But by the '70s, mass media has turned the whole country into a single community in many ways, and genuinely connecting to that proved impossible. Along with being more spread out geographically than ever before, the isolation of the suburbs left people feeling more alone than ever before.

I'm Almost Sure

There's a difference between the action of a story and its point. For instance, *Fiddler on the Roof* isn't about Jews losing their homes in czarist Russia—that's just what happens in the story. What that show is *about* is the difficulty of hanging on to beloved traditions in a fast-changing world. Likewise, *Cabaret* isn't about people's lives falling apart in Weimar Germany; it's about the profound price of doing nothing in the face of evil. *The Wild Party* is about how if all you care about is winning, you'll end up alone and lost. *High Fidelity* is about how you have to grow up before you can have an adult relationship.

In any well-crafted show, the opening number announces the central theme of the show and the closing number summarizes it. (Think about the opening and closing numbers in *Company*, *Sweeney Todd*, *Chicago*,

Cabaret, *Man of La Mancha*, *Hair*, *Best Little Whorehouse*, etc.) Sometimes, this is very subtle, very subtextual; sometimes it's right there on the surface. The central theme of *I Love My Wife* is about the intersection between the sexual revolution and these longstanding friendships. This story shows us two couples surviving the rough cultural terrain of the 1970s, because they have these strong friendships that are based on lots of shared experience. They have found real human *connection* (something that Bobby in *Company* struggled to find in 1970). The show's opening number, "We're Still Friends," is all about how different these people are (both the couples and their Greek chorus friends, Harvey, Quentin, Stanley, and Norman), and how unlikely it is that they would all end up being friends, but that they've had all these shared experiences, in college and in the years since then, which have bound them to each other inextricably. They are *connected*. This song tells us that shared experience, that connection, is what defines friendship. That's what the opening—and the whole show—is about.

We know that, in the end, these friendships will survive this experience because they're just that strong. That's not to say the show's final little mini-scenes aren't full of tension and unease and regret, but both the women and the men make plans for tomorrow. No matter how unsettling this has been, no matter how strained things may seem for a while now, these people will remain friends—which is why Stanley and Quentin sing a quote from the opening number during the finale. In fact, the title of the opening number tells us how our story will end: "We're Still Friends."

The Act II opener, "Hey There, Good Times," is a more generalized version of this same idea. The two couples have the shared experience of their sexual adventure, but the Greek chorus guys have the less specific shared experience of just living through the crazy '70s—the energy crisis, recession, cultural upheaval—and they will survive it because they have these solid friendships. These guys' shared experience provides the context for the two couples' shared experience. Every song in the show is about shared experience and human connection, in one way or another.

Like the songs in *Company*, all the songs in *I Love My Wife* operate as commentary on the cultural and political zeitgeist as much as commentary on the story. The songs sometimes relate to the action in the book scenes, but they never grow out of the dialogue organically, like songs in most musicals do. They rarely move the plot forward. They explore ideas. They step *out* of the story. Like *Company*, you could remove all the songs from *I Love My Wife* without losing any of the story. That's unusual for a modern musical. Several songs in the show function strictly as cultural context, revealing the show's central idea of profound cultural change as the catalyst for the events in the story. "By Threes," "A Mover's Life," "Everybody Today Is Turning On," "Love Revolution," and "Married Couple Seeks Married Couple" all point toward that theme. Bertolt Brecht wrote that the most striking innovation of his theory of epic theatre "lay in the strict separation of the music from all the other elements of entertainment offered . . . [Songs] were not organic consequences of the whole, but stood in contradiction to it; they broke up the flow of the play and its incidents, they prevented empathy, they acted as a cold douche for those whose sympathies were becoming involved . . . The play had a double nature. Instruction and entertainment conflict openly."

The song "Monica"—essentially set to stripper music—is about sexism, about men objectifying women. This was the first time in American history when that wasn't okay. Wally's song, "By Threes," helps to move the plot along, but it also gives authentic voice to the pro-sex forces in America who preached the gospel of sexual liberation. Their rallying cry was, "If it feels good, do it." Sex often replaced emotion as a means of connection. It's no accident that Wally works in public relations, still a trendy, new industry at that time that forced connections.

The song "A Mover's Life" doesn't immediately suggest its direct relevance to the story, but it does give us cultural context. It describes what America had become in the '70s—nomadic, rootless, disconnected, a nation of people grasping for connection, not yet culturally evolved enough to match (and master) our social and technological evolution. It's a song about change—disorienting, tectonic change—and impermanence. Experts tell us that moving is one of the most stressful events in a person's life, and yet by the 1970s Americans were moving more often and further away than ever before, often disconnecting from family (and this is before airplane flight was as common as it is now). "A Mover's Life" is about how sad and apprehensive all this anthropomorphized furniture is, standing in for us disconnected humans, but these movers gently bring all of it to some new place that's warm and safe. That's also what these guys do structurally in the show, as a Greek chorus, for the couples and for the audience. They move us through this treacherous adventure, step by step—and of course, they also move the set pieces.

But this is also a character song in disguise. We can boil the point of this song down to five words, which also describe the entire plot of the show: "Change is hard and scary." Alvin is trying to change his entire worldview over the course of the show—and change his wife's at the same time—in order to become something he doesn't even really want to be, but he feels he has to, to keep up with the times. When he sings "A Mover's Life," Alvin is talking about furniture, but he's also talking about himself. He doesn't want to be left behind by his culture. Alvin's lyric describes in metaphor the chess game that Wally is playing with their lives. And though Alvin promises over and over to protect the vulnerable, this adventure of theirs might just be the wrecker's ball that ends one of these marriages.

The song "Love Revolution" is Cleo's moment to try and convince herself to go on this adventure. But it also characterizes many Americans at that time. They didn't necessarily believe in what they were being told about the sexual revolution, but they didn't want to be left out either. Since the invention of the suburbs, keeping up with the Joneses had become an important social duty. If everyone else was doing it, no one wanted to be the only person who wasn't. In this song, Cleo examines her lonely, empty suburban life and, when she compares it to the adventure being offered to her, her life seems even emptier. Until now, she didn't know she was missing anything. *Maybe she wasn't.*

In "Someone Wonderful I Missed," we see the two women questioning lifelong monogamy, a question that was part and parcel of the sexual revolution: Was it natural to be monogamous? All the rules were in question. In the Act I finale, "Sexually Free," they sing the praises of sexual freedom . . . except the entire lyric is phrased in terms of "if." *If* they could do this, *if* they could think this way, *if* they could just forget about that, *then* they'd be sexually free. The trouble is, most people can't get through all those *if*s. Here at the end of Act I, book writer and lyricist Michael Stewart is already telling us how the story is going to end.

Hey There, Good Times . . . ?

The second act opens with another song that doesn't immediately seem like it belongs in the show, "Hey There, Good Times." But when you really listen to the lyric, you hear that these guys are *begging* good times to show up, so they can no longer be "out there where the bad times blow." This song is a funnier, brighter companion piece to the very dark "Let the Sun Shine In" from *Hair*. Both songs have the same basic agenda, to end the bad times and bring on the good times. But while "Let the Sun Shine In" is asking the audience to end the darkness of war and death and hatred, “Hey There, Good Times” is talking about tough economic times and cultural confusion. The ’70s was a tough decade and these guys are trying to fight the malaise that was bringing the country down. There was a dissatisfaction, a disillusionment, a restlessness. Like “A Mover’s Life,” this song is part of a larger snapshot of America, and at the same time it also describes the emotional state that has led these four characters to this crossroads. (Listen closely and you’ll hear that during the vocal bridge, the band plays the verse again in counterpoint to the voices—just one of the many fun surprises Cy Coleman peppers throughout the score.)

“Lovers on Christmas Eve” is an important song in the score. Two-thirds of the way through the show, this is the first song about romance. And the realization of that makes the events of Act I even more unsettling. This is one of the few character songs in the show, but its point is very subtle. Right before this song, Wally and Monica have exchanged Christmas gifts, and Monica says, “I always loved Christmas when I was a kid, but now that we’re together, just the two of us, it’s the most wonderful holiday of all!” *Just the two of us.* And then she proceeds to sing about how much she loves Christmas, especially here with Wally, *exactly the way things are.* All her images are of romance and magic and love, though she admits to us that she realizes she may be naïve about such things. And then the more cynical Wally steps up and sings about how he finds everything about Christmas annoying. We see in this song that Wally and Monica are in two different, conflicting places emotionally, and that conflict may just erupt soon. In fact, we get a hint here that maybe Wally and Monica are not right for each other.

But this song also contributes to the big picture. As people in the ’70s felt less and less comfortable with the sexual revolution, many couples revolved 180 degrees and decided to tune out all the cultural chaos, focusing instead on having a loving, nurturing relationship, something the culture around them made very hard. Self-help books for couples flooded the market. Like the opening number, this song suggests that Wally and Monica are very different, even seemingly incompatible, but they are connected.

The song “Scream” describes both the ’70s zeitgeist *and* these two couples—jumpy, confused, anxious, frustrated, scared. This song is interesting partly because the music does what the lyrics describe, plowing through the weirdest chord changes, the jumpiest melody line, and literal primal screams at the end. Likewise, “Everybody Today Is Turning On” shows the bafflement more conventional Americans felt over marijuana and other now more socially acceptable drugs, along with the nostalgia they felt for simpler times. But the times, they were a-changin'. Up until this time, drugs were for hippies. But now the hippies had grown up, and for the first time, lots of adults were smoking pot. For those who weren't, this was a very disturbing development. All their lives they were told how deadly marijuana was; now suddenly their next-door neighbor is smoking every night. *What do they make of that?*

"Married Couple Seeks Married Couple" is a funny commentary on the mainstreaming of personal ads for sex. But it's not the adventure Wally pretends it is. He has to specify in his imaginary ad that calls are only welcome on weekdays after six o'clock or on Sunday evenings—there are other obligations in life, after all. All of them admit to being nervous, but as they sing, we see they're doing all this not out of adventurousness but out of boredom, or even worse, some kind of obligation to the peer pressure of the times. Then, as now, our high-energy, sense-assaulting, high-speed culture creates citizens who need constant stimulation. (Within a few years after this, MTV would make that even worse with its manic editing and its embrace of the short attention span.) Normal, conventional, old-fashioned lives now seem boring. What once served as relaxation no longer suffices in this new age. This is no longer the America of the 1950s. We see in Act I that Alvin tries to retreat into the television when Cleo gets feisty, but here they all admit that's no answer, either. Like the title character in *Pippin*, these couples seek some kind of abstract fulfillment, and they don't know yet that they aren't going to find what they're looking for in the place where they're looking. Eventually, they will learn the lessons of *The Wizard of Oz* (and hundreds of other hero-myth stories), that real contentment and fulfillment comes from *inside*.

In the finale, "I Love My Wife," Alvin finally figures out what he really wants, an emotional connection rather than a physical one. Just as "Lovers on Christmas Eve" is the only song in the show about romance, this is the only song in the show about serious, emotional connection. After a fast-paced evening of sex farce, suddenly in this last number everything slows down. We take a breath. Alvin has found the understanding he has been seeking and he is okay. There is peace. Balance.

The song continues and the story ends with a narrative solo from Harvey, tying up the loose ends, set to the same harmonies as the early verse, but in a different style and tone, both musically and lyrically. Cy Coleman has done some very subtle character work here in the music.

Both halves of the song are waltzes, but the naïve, easygoing Alvin gets a soaring melody over a lush traditional waltz, while the more cynical, wise-ass Harvey gets a nervous, bouncy melody over an offbeat jazz waltz.

There is a short requote of the "We're Still Friends" theme from the opening few bars of the first song, and then Alvin's verse returns as an instrumental under dialogue as we see the fallout from the evening's festivities. The dialogue is ambivalent here. Alvin and Cleo seem to be okay; it's harder to tell if Wally and Monica are. After all, there was a betrayal between Wally and Monica. Just as *Company* does, this show ends without resolving many things. Its very point is ambiguity. Life is complex, the authors are telling us. There are no easy answers and no neat resolutions.

And as the show ends gently, Alvin sings the title itself, "I love my wife, I love my wife, I love my wife." And we are reminded that this is a not a show about sex; it's a show about connection and safe harbor. Those critics who have complained that the ending is too tame don't really understand the show.

Sexually Free

Though this was the first time the veteran bookwriter was also writing lyrics, the virtuosity of Michael Stewart's lyrics is evident in every song in the show. In "By Threes," Stewart shows off his facility with complex interior rhymes:

If two, you say, is
Better than one,
Than logic guarantees
What two can
Do can
Better be done
By threes . . .

Just in this short section at the beginning of the song, he's got two almost hidden rhymes, matching "better than one" with "better be done," and also rhyming, in quick succession, "two can" with "do can." This announces to the audience that this is a show they have to really *listen* to. In terms of both content and form, the audience can't be passive or they'll miss a lot.

The Act I finale, "Sexually Free," offers a mini–master class in internal rhymes, subtext, and tone. Alvin, Cleo, and Wally have just decided that, along with Monica (who's notably absent here), they will have a sexual foursome. As mentioned earlier, the first thing you notice in this song is the number of *ifs*. It's an entirely conditional lyric, and because of that, it functions as a great cliffhanger as the audience goes out to intermission. This show as a whole divides neatly into two parts, *if* (Act I) and *then* (Act II), and this lyric explicitly tells us that:

If we could loose the ties that bind . . .

The first line of this song is a direct threat to the first line of the show, "Tied by links that can't be denied." In other words, if they could just ignore their longstanding relationships, sex would be far less complicated. We'll find out in Act II whether they will or not.

If we could liberate the mind,
If all the rules that hold us fast,
We could eliminate at last . . .

This was the whole reason for Wally to sing "By Threes" to Alvin, to get him to reject the "old-fashioned" rules of relationships, of love, of sex. It's a new world now, sexually speaking, and Wally has been trying to get Alvin to accept that.

If passions into which we're swept,
We could accept
Without misgivings . . .

This is the conclusion Cleo comes to, though tentatively, in her song, "Love Revolution." In other words, they all have to let go of the fear and guilt over the decision they've made and give themselves permission to break all the rules of morality they've always lived by, in order to find the fulfillment they all think they lack.

And moreover,
To Aphrodite give her due,
A pleasant hour—or maybe two—

Without forsaking what is due
Unto Jehovah . . .

With this line, Wally makes the dubious case that they can break the accepted rules of sexual morality without becoming generally immoral. They can have "multiple love experiences" without breaking their marriage vows or diminishing their love for their spouses—a dilemma Cleo and Monica sing about in "Someone Wonderful I Missed." Of course Wally also sneaks in a commercial for his own stamina with his line "a pleasant hour—*or maybe two*."

Then, after all these *ifs* from Act I, the chorus of the song offers up the potential prize ahead in Act II:

Then we'd be free, sexually free,
Free to let each urge
We suppress freely surge
And our inhibitions melt;

At least enough for all four to get in bed together . . .

Free, sexually free,
Free to cast our seed
On a stone, if the need
For a stone should be felt.

Probably a biblical reference to Onan, which has mistakenly been interpreted to be about masturbation, but it isn't really . . .

Free, sexually free,
Free to follow love,
Though it lead to above
Or below thy neighbor's belt.
See what it is to be
Satisfied and unfrustrated,
Free and at liberty
To be loved and stimulated.

How much more American could sexual freedom be?

Be unashamedly
Sexually liberated . . .

It's all about freedom. And what's more American than that? The idea here is that if these characters can just throw off everything they've ever been taught about love and sex, something wonderful awaits them. But is the prize worth it? That's what we'll find out in Act II. The second verse of "Sexually Free" continues in the same vein:

If we could drop the binding reins,

In other words, marriage . . .

If we could sever all our chains,

In other words, friendship . . .

If what the Puritans forbid,

"The Puritans," metaphorically meaning mainstream but old-fashioned Americans . . .

Just ev'ry now and then, we did,
If musty codes we learn to shove

In other words, the Old Testament, perhaps specifically Leviticus . . .

And look at love
Without that worn-out mystic aura,

In other words, religion and morality . . .

If we cut loose and have a ball
With orgies relatively small,

In other words, a foursome . . .

Because it's Trenton, after all,
And not Gomorrah.

In these last four lines, Alvin points us ahead toward Act II, when our four main characters will indeed attempt an "orgy relatively small." And here he also rejects Old Testament judgment.

The second chorus offers up even more incentives:

Then we'd be free, sexually free,
Free to lose our guilt,
Live it up to the hilt,
Be a Libertine or bust.
Free, sexually free,
Free to drop the pins

This is '70s gay slang for revealing one's feminine side, possibly evolving from the idea of taking out hairpins to let the hair down; in other words, acting openly gay.

There are just seven sins
And the best one is Lust.
Free, sexually free,
Free to go for broke,
Making love till you croak,
Or your parts begin to rust . . .
See what it is to be
Satisfied and unfrustrated,
Free and at liberty
To be loved and stimulated.
Be unashamedly
Sexually liberated.
. . .
Long as I'm here,
Let my time here
Be sexually free
Let me be sexually free!

And with this last line, these characters entreat, beg, pray that they can overcome all these *ifs* before the end of Act II, so they can get to the golden *then*.

By the Book

The dialogue scenes also appear to take *Company* as a model. Much of what's actually going on between these characters is underneath the dialogue, rarely explicitly stated. When these characters have a conversation, what they're talking about on the surface is often not what they're *really* talking about, just as it can be in real life. All the most important stuff in this story is subtextual.

Alvin is the central character of the story, the one who takes the most extensive journey and who learns the most. He's the one who follows the primal hero myth, the story form behind *Star Wars*, *The Wizard of Oz*, *Bat Boy*, *High Fidelity*, *Legally Blonde*, *Wicked*, *Cabaret*, *Tommy*, *Les Misérables*, *Evita*, *Jesus Christ Superstar*, and many others. The story begins with him and it can't end until his conflict is resolved. He starts in balance, is thrown out of balance by Wally and the scheme, and then at the end he finds his balance again. Alvin finds his Zen—and therefore, contentment—at the end of the show when he starts to sing "I Love My Wife," very much like a similar moment in *Sunday in the Park with George* when George and Dot sing "Move On." The trick for actors and directors is getting Alvin to that moment honestly and believably.

Throughout the whole story, the show's title seems like an ironic joke—these two husbands keep claiming they love their wives, although their actions sure don't support that—but in those last few moments, we realize the show's title is the very sincere central point of the show.

And it's really not about sex.

Here now the phenomenon is taking place: the beginning, the Genesis, of a cultural revolution. It is taking place out of utter necessity to survive . . . Personally, I have little hope for the survival of our civilization. But whatever hope we have lies with our artists. For they alone have the ability (if we do not continue to corrupt them) to withstand the onslaught of the mass media and the multitude of false gods. They alone have the ability to show us ourselves.

—Ralph Cook, quoted in Eight Plays from Off Off Broadway

On the surface, *Bat Boy: The Musical* seems to be a wacky, bighearted satire about American prejudice. But dig a little deeper, venture down into the dark caves and chambers of human emotion, and you'll find a bigger, more interesting idea that underpins everything else in the show: we all have an animal side, a primitive, primordial beast in us that lashes out when we're afraid, that drives our hungers for sex, for food, for power, for control—and our fear of the Other. The last line of the show implores us, "Don't deny your beast inside." And *that's* the heart of *Bat Boy*, the knowledge that we are, *all of us*, animalistic to one degree or another, and that we must embrace and integrate that side rather than fear it. The creators of *Bat Boy: The Musical*, Keythe Farley, Brian Flemming, and Laurence O'Keefe, have given us a hero who literally, physically embodies that dangerous mix. Edgar the Bat Boy represents every one of us, always trying to control our beast with only the thinnest layer of civilization as protection.

Every one of the characters gives in to his or her inner beast at some point in the story, but because Edgar is different on the surface, he is ridiculed, scorned, feared. We see in this beautiful, hilarious fable not only our own inner struggles, but also echoes of racism past and present (even the rationale for slavery), and as technology moves forward faster than our ethics can, who knows what next? We face our inner Neanderthal in the characters of *Bat Boy*, and it's a hell of a ride.

But *Bat Boy* is also about storytelling itself. In Act II of the show, a Pan-like figure called simply "King of the Forest" appears to sing the slyly subversive song "Children, Children." The opening lines, "Children, welcome home to where we all began," not only invite the young lovers Edgar and Shelley back to the roots of humanity and sex, urging them to embrace their more primal, animal natures, they also invite the audience back to the roots of theatre, back to mythic stories told around a fire, back to Grotowski's "poor theatre," where it's about the storytelling, not the budget, where originality is more important than money or technology, where the audience's imagination is the final vital ingredient.

In the late 1990s, the American musical began returning once again to the roots of George M. Cohan and the earliest musical comedies, though now with a postmodern layer of irony on top. With the musicals built on the Rodgers and Hammerstein model, the actors and audiences have all agreed for the last sixty-plus years to pretend what was happening on stage was real. Of course, that was always a big stretch since the orchestra kept firing up and the actors would break into song. But with the early musical comedies, and now again with what many are calling postmodern musicals, the artifice of musical theatre isn't just acknowledged (as the concept musicals of the '70s did), it's actively and aggressively referenced. These new shows remove the burden of "suspension of disbelief," acknowledging it as fundamentally silly, completely taking that issue off the table. These more recent shows (*Bat Boy*, *Urinetown*, *Avenue Q*, *Spelling Bee*, and others) essentially say to their audiences, "We know and you know that none of this is real. We're not pretending it is. We just want to tell you a great story." And without the burden of naturalism, which musical theatre never really conquered, endless new possibilities are opened up.

To be fair, *Bat Boy* is not about the conventions of Broadway musicals. Its authors have not written a musical about Broadway musicals. No, they wrote a show about a boy trying to find his place in the world, about the search for love, about past mistakes never really being past. But *Bat Boy* succeeds on more than one level, even on levels that may not have been contemplated by its authors. And while it tells its touching, wacky story, it also laughs hard at the conventions of traditional musical comedy—gently and affectionately, but it still laughs. The big Act I production number, "Show You a Thing or Two," recalls other time-telescoping sequences like the "Poor Professor Higgins" / "Rain in Spain" scene in *My Fair Lady* (the Bat Boy even exclaims "I think I've got it!") or the prologue in *West Side Story*. "Children, Children" was originally meant to wink at any play or movie that anthropomorphizes wild animals into cuddly human-like creatures, but today it's hard not to see it more specifically as a parody of the overly artsy pretensions of the stage version of *The Lion King* (a show that didn't yet exist when *Bat Boy* was created), which not only makes animals human but also projects onto them some kind of faux-primitive great art. *Bat Boy* laughs at big cast shows like *Les Misérables* and *Phantom of the Opera* by making so very obvious the practice of actors playing multiple parts, but in this case, switching gender and switching wigs in full view of the audience. *Bat Boy* laughs at big, unmotivated dance numbers by giving us a sudden, old-fashioned song-and-dance number ("Show You a Thing or Two") in the middle of a gothic thriller. It laughs at the oh-so-serious, tragic-poetic musicals like *Phantom of the Opera*, *Jekyll & Hyde*, and *Jane Eyre*, shows that try so hard to be dark and important, that fall flat most often because of uninspired lyrics that are only sometimes obscured by lush orchestrations and lavish sets.

Bat Boy composer Larry O'Keefe says:

> We did set out to foil people's expectations of what a musical does—making the love story perverse, the ending unhappy and the moral absurd—but we never intended to remind people of other songs or shows while watching ours. Unfortunately, our director for the off Broadway production misinterpreted our intentions and did occasionally play up some faint similarities to other shows: for instance, "Children, Children" contains a lot of singing celebrating forest animals, so he staged it like a parody of Julie Taymor using costumes and staging cribbed from *The Lion King*, but these were unnecessary surface references. We also unfortunately opened in NYC around the same time as *Urinetown*, which does in fact contain specific parodies of songs and shows, so we got tarred with the same brush.

Still, by rejecting some of the more ridiculous conventions of contemporary commercial theatre (musical or non-musical), by insisting on a theatre of imagination instead of high-tech machines, by using imaginative techniques from the world of improv and experimental theatre, *Bat Boy* does indeed comment on other musicals, intentionally or not. By its very existence and its success, *Bat Boy* argues that too many musicals have gone too far, have gotten too high-tech, have lost the simplicity and joy of storytelling. *Bat Boy* has a small cast, a small budget, no helicopters or chandeliers, no special effects, and yet it doesn't suffer for all that—it ends up being *more* fun, *more* transporting, *more* magical, *more* emotional, because it goes back to the roots of storytelling and relies on its audience to participate in the magic. Edgar the Bat Boy tries to teach the people of his town about tolerance and acceptance, while *Bat Boy* the musical tries to teach us, the audience, about what *really* matters in the theatre—people, emotion, relationships.

Birth of the Bat

It all started with the satiric supermarket tabloid, *Weekly World News*. This brilliantly funny newspaper boasted outrageous headlines over the years like "Dead Rock Stars Return on Ghost Plane!" and "Faces of Howard Stern, Pamela Anderson and Satan Appear in Volcano Smoke!" and the classic, "Bill Catches Hillary With Space Alien!," a story that claimed one of the best subheads in the history of newsprint: "I thought she was gay, says stunned ex-Prez." It did a story called "Surprising Bible Prophecies Your Preacher Doesn't Want You to Read," about a "turncoat Vatican librarian" who has revealed parts edited out of the Bible, including an unknown corollary to the Tenth Commandment: "Thou shalt not covet thy neighbor's wife unless you in turn are willing to share thine own wife with him."

In 2001, the *Washington Post* did a tribute article to the tabloid, saying, "Funnier than *Saturday Night Live*, deeper than Leno or Letterman, smarter than *Mad*, more outrageous than *The Onion*, *Weekly World News* just might be America's best purveyor of social satire. The fact that it's disguised as a sleazy tabloid just makes it that much more delicious."

In 1992, the *Weekly World News* began following every twist and turn in the bizarre life of a poor half bat/half boy who was found in a rural West Virginia cave, dispatching a crack team of twenty-four reporters and photographers assigned exclusively to the Bat Boy story. The paper described him this way: "Discovered in a cave in Hope Falls, West Virginia, this half-bat has escaped from captivity and is currently at large. He can be identified by large, pointy ears and oversized eyes that make him profoundly sensitive to sound and light. The creature has reportedly attacked at least three people with his razor-sharp fangs and should be considered extremely dangerous." The paper chronicled how he initially attacked a ten-year-old girl; how he was captured by the government and then got sick; how he received 17,402,901 get-well cards in the hospital from *Weekly World News* readers, how sympathetic nurses fed him flies; how he escaped from the hospital by crawling from a sixth-story window; how his abrupt withdrawal from hospital drugs caused him to go crazy and attempt to mate with a scarecrow; how he was chased by a bloodthirsty bounty hunter; how he was run over by an exterminator's truck; how he showed up mysteriously at Al Gore's campaign headquarters in 2000, wanting to officially endorse Gore; how he tried to sneak into the White House to visit Jenna Bush; and most notably, how he joined the US military in Afghanistan because his special bat vision made it easy for him to find the Taliban in all those caves.

In November 1996, two writers were standing in the lobby of the Actors' Gang Theatre in Los Angeles. Keythe Farley, Gang member and director, and Brian Flemming, a screenwriter and film director, were working the concession stand for intermission of the musical *Euphoria*, when in wandered Laurence O'Keefe, the composer-lyricist and music director of *Euphoria*, taking a break. Farley and Flemming told O'Keefe they liked his music and lyrics and asked if O'Keefe would be interested in a project of theirs, based on a character from the pages of the *Weekly World News* named Bat Boy. They showed O'Keefe a cover of the *Weekly World News* featuring the Bat Boy's picture, a baby with huge fangs, bulging eyes, and pointy ears. They were determined to tell this poor creature's story—from the beginning. O'Keefe was shocked. "That's the ugliest thing I've ever seen in my life," he said. "I'll do it."

More recently, O'Keefe said about the show, "It's useful to note there are no swear words in *Bat Boy*. So aside from the lust and rage and interspecies mating and the stage littered with bodies at the end, it's absolutely suitable for kids over sixty and adults under ten. They say that *Rent* is the musical for people who hate musicals. I think *Bat Boy* is the musical for people who hate everybody."

On Halloween 1997, *Bat Boy* made its world premiere at the Actors' Gang Theatre, perhaps the only place where this show could be understood and properly nurtured. The Actors' Gang is Los Angeles's premier repertory theatre company, creating original works and reinterpreting classics, through the prism of the Style, a performance method derived from *commedia dell'arte*, from the work of the Theatre du Soleil in Paris, from vaudeville, from the political agitprop theatre of the 1930s, and from the off off Broadway movement of the 1960s, particularly the work of the Play-House of the Ridiculous. The Style is artificial and presentational, yet insists on deep truthfulness and high emotional stakes. All the authors agree today that the Style was instrumental in both the writing and the execution of *Bat Boy: The Musical*.

O'Keefe says, "The Actors' Gang is a hyperactive and politically committed theater company that teaches if you show an emotion, always make it a ten on a scale of one to ten. People pay money to see a show portray terror, rage, despair, and joy, so we might as well sell it in mega-doses. We were consciously trying to dig up the deepest and most volcanic emotions, the most inflammatory questions—what is it like to be a scapegoat? What is it like to be loved by one parent and hated by another? What is it like to have no idea who your parents are? What is it like to have an insatiable hunger for blood?"

Director and co-author Keythe Farley developed what Flemming likes to call the "take-it-so-seriously-it's-funny-but-it-also-hurts" style of *Bat Boy*. Both Deven May (as Edgar) and Kaitlin Hopkins (as Meredith) were in this first production and, together with Farley, they found the extremely sincere approach that this outrageous musical demands. Farley's mantra throughout the development process was "the height of expression, the depth of sincerity," a style of truthful acting that has marked all the work at the Actors' Gang—something the cast took to heart and something which guided them throughout the L.A. and New York productions. Brain Flemming says of his partner, "Keythe's major contribution to *Bat Boy* has gone largely unmentioned, but it was great and permanent." Unlike musicals in which the goal is to be as silly as possible (*The Producers*, *Spamalot*, *Dirty Rotten Scoundrels*), with *Bat Boy* the goal is to be as serious as possible within the context of an utterly silly universe.

About half the songs from the L.A. production remained largely unchanged in the off Broadway production, including "Christian Charity," "Show You A Thing Or Two," and "Children, Children." The music for the opening number, "Hold Me, Bat Boy," was nearly identical to the final version, although the lyrics were changed over time. Other songs from 1997 were more substantially altered, or replaced, in later versions. Julio Martinez wrote in *Variety*, "The clever scenario, though outrageous, always contains an aura of intriguing plausibility. And to his credit, [director Keythe] Farley creates a supercharged mix of heightened realism, surrealism and fantasy that is always engrossing. The work is magnificently served by the emotion-charged, thoroughly realistic performance of [Devon] May [as the Bat Boy], who catapults himself body and soul into the seared psyche of this child who possesses the mind of a genius but the uncontrollable, blood-craving appetite of a beast."

Throughout 1999 and 2000, the show went through staged readings at the Directors' Company in New York, now with director Scott Schwartz at the helm. The pace of the work was stepped up, aiming toward a 2001 New York opening, with rewrites continuing even after opening. And the collaboration among the writers was an unusually close one, free of ego. O'Keefe says, "I would take a character's speech and replace it with sung lyrics, or sometimes even take a line of dialogue and set it verbatim to music. Sometimes it worked in the opposite direction—we'd try a song in one place and realize it stole ideas or energy from a better song later, so the song would disappear and be replaced by new dialogue."

Bat Boy: The Musical opened at the Union Square Theatre in New York in March 2001, where it was a big hit but suffered the same fate as many other New York shows after the terrorist attacks on September 11, 2001, and it closed that December. It's tempting to guess how long the show would have run if not for the terrorist attacks and whether it would have moved uptown to Broadway like *Urinetown* did. But in a post-9/11 world, the hatred and discrimination leveled against the Bat Boy in the show took on a whole new dimension, as anyone in America with a Middle Eastern background was now a potential victim of abuse, harassment, and even imprisonment, based only on their appearance, their ethnicity, their clothing. The metaphor that was *Bat Boy* now held a power wholly unanticipated by its creators.

One of the many achievements of the show's creators was their fierce adherence to the Ten-Minute Rule of Musicals. This rule says that you can do anything you want in a musical (or play or movie, for that matter)—talk to the audience, sing the dialogue, use obscene language, move out into the audience, establish a bizarre premise (as in *Little Shop of Horrors*, *Reefer Madness*, or *Urinetown*), anything you want, as long as you do it in the first ten minutes, to tell the audience what the rules are for the evening, to make clear how this show will function. As Frank Hauser writes in *Notes on Directing*, "In all the best material, the outcome is inevitable and inherent in the opening moment and in every moment in between. From the audience's perspective, this can only be understood and appreciated *backwards*, after the play has run its course." *Bat Boy* starts with a very short scene in a cave that establishes the central conflict—the Bat Boy against an uncivilized "civilization," the classic Man versus Society. The show then moves into its opening number, "Hold Me, Bat Boy," during which the faux-serious tone of the show is established. Several short dialogue scenes inside the song establish the community (arguably the show's antagonist), performance style, the central plot premise, the style of music, major musical themes, and the show's offbeat sense of humor ("They beat him like a gong, and he was kicked repeatedly. And that was wrong, *so wrong*."). The main textual themes are introduced as well. And they do all this while keeping the audience laughing and their toes tapping. All in the first ten minutes.

The structure of the show is also interesting. The whole story is told in flashback. The opening number, "Hold Me, Bat Boy," a sort of prologue (and later, epilogue), tells the basics of the story in the past tense. The singers already know the outcome. They have already learned the lessons. They sing to us, "You are here not to laugh, but to learn"—which is funny in context because clearly the show's first priority is laughs. One of the more subtle comic moments comes before the reprise of "Hold Me, Bat Boy" at the end of the show. The man from the institute finally shows up—too late—and asks what has happened. The sheriff says, "It's a long story. I don't where to begin." Of course, he *does* know where to begin. They've just finished telling us this story. Just a little bit of funny, self-referential playfulness.

And then there's the name of the town—Hope Falls—more descriptive than anyone living there would like to admit. The town is plagued with tragedy. It's there that Edgar finds love and loses it. It's there that Mrs. Taylor loses all three of her children, Rick, Ron, and Ruthie. It's there that the Parkers' family is torn apart. And there are those dead cows. The story starts out loaded with hope, but that hope falls before the story is done.

The *New York Times* said of the off Broadway show, "It's remarkable what intelligent wit can accomplish . . . the show is a jaggedly imaginative mix of skewering humor and energetic glee." The *New York Post* said, "*Bat Boy* soars! An instant classic!" The *New York Daily News* called it "an outrageously silly and totally charming show . . . wickedly funny! A wacky, hilarious musical!" USA *Today* called it "immensely satisfying." *Backstage* said, "Rarely do we see a piece of theatre that is at once so smart, silly, self-aware, and easy to enjoy as *Bat Boy the Musical.*" It ran 260 performances.

Ah, the Children of the Night

Among his many models, *Bat Boy* is primarily built on two classic horror models—Count Dracula and the Frankenstein monster—both models updated to the twenty-first century. The Bat Boy feeds contemporary, small-town, fundamentalist Christian anxieties just as Bram Stoker's Count Dracula fed Victorian English anxieties—about sex, promiscuity, pre-marital sex (not just immoral but deadly), and the passing of bodily fluids. Like Dracula, Edgar is both pathetic and dangerous, both lonely and predatory, both sexual and dangerous. In Victorian England,

Count Dracula represented a kind of unfettered sexuality, a freedom of sexual expression, a freedom of women to be fully sexual and to enjoy their bodies without responsibility. In today's world, the Bat Boy represents non-conventional sexuality, both in his mysterious creation and in his desire to love and marry a human girl and to make a family. The people of Hope Falls find all this disgusting, unnatural, morally wrong, just as many Christians today believe that cloning, another new kind of life creation, is wrong. Edgar's desire for interspecies sex offers up a not-so-veiled parallel to some fundamentalist Christians' claims that condoning and legalizing gay marriage will lead to widespread and uncontrolled bestiality. *Dracula* and *Bat Boy* are about a "moral" society's reaction to "outsiders"—ironic quotation marks noted—in the form of foreigners moving into London in Stoker's time, and non-Christians (particularly Muslims these days) moving into a "Christian America" in our time.

Bat Boy also raises the specter of the most recent Christian boogeyman—Darwin's theory of human evolution. In recent years, fundamentalist Christians have begun arguing aggressively that Darwin's theories of evolution are not "real" science, that they can't possibly be true, that the only possible truth is the story of spontaneous creation by God. They argue that our schools should teach Christian creationism, the idea that the universe was created in seven days by an intelligent God. But Edgar is a shadow figure who doesn't fit into theories of evolution or creationism, the worst kind of threat to the black-and-white world these fundamentalists yearn for. How could they explain God's creation of a bat boy that lives off the blood and death of others? Would they say he has a soul? If it's okay to kill animals but not humans, which category does Edgar fit into? Would it have been ethical to have aborted Edgar?

The song "Children, Children" is sung by a version of Pan, the Greek God of male sexuality (and an early model for the Christian devil), and its lyric is entirely about interspecies sex, shamelessly referencing the Bible in the process, both foreshadowing the secret of Edgar's birth, and simultaneously encouraging the fully human Shelley and the only half-human Edgar to have sex, thereby presumably creating *another* hybrid creature, this time only one-quarter bat? It conjures up the once very vocal fears of interracial marriage in America. The lyric could not be more explicit:

> Now let the turtle and the dove,
> Let the lion and the lamb,
> Let the owl and wolf and ram embrace

Across the countryside.
Fur and feathers making love,
Paws and claws and jaws and beaks.
. . .
The Earth's asleep, time to wake it.
If you have clothing, forsake it.
We want you breathless and naked!
Choose your mate;
And then let's see what we create!

"Let's see what we create" indeed—a throwaway phrase that invokes the bizarre premise of the story itself, the wacky-genius musical we're watching, but also the abomination of a half bat/half boy. This lyric slyly starts with a Bible reference, referring to Isaiah 11:6–7, which says, "The wolf also shall dwell with the lamb, and the leopard shall lie down with the kid; and the calf and the young lion and the fatling together; and a little child shall lead them. And the cow and the bear shall feed; their young ones shall lie down together; and the lion shall eat straw like the ox." But this song sexualizes this idea of interspecies fraternization and creates a comic, "natural" counterpart to the bioengineering that has been advancing by leaps and bounds in the real world in recent decades, which also scares many Christians, and which sits at the heart of this tragedy.

The interspecies sex is also quite humorously foreshadowed, in G-rated form, by the children's book that Meredith uses to teach Edgar to read, earlier in Act I. The book reads:

Here is a cat. There is a goose.
This is a rat. And that is a moose.
The cat crept up behind the goose
But then away it flew.
The rat was jealous of the moose
Who loved a kangaroo
The cat and rat made up and found
A flat in Timbuktu.

Might this be the moment that Edgar is taught that loving Shelley is okay because apparently all animals crossbreed? It's probably his first encounter with a story about love and it's illustrated by cute little innocent crossbreeding animals. This image will be developed later when those animals of the forest come to orgiastic life and sing "Children, Children" to Edgar and Shelley.

Bat Boy Superstar

The famous Polish theatre director and theorist Jerzy Grotowski says that all theatre is rooted in some shared myth, and what could be more powerful than the classic myths and stories of the outsider—Dracula, Frankenstein's monster, Jesus Christ, Hamlet, the Elephant Man, Sweeney Todd, *Hair*'s Claude Bukowski, *Rocky Horror*'s Rocky, and others. Edgar is the ultimate outsider, equally connected to all these characters but also to more ordinary, real world people—African Americans, immigrants, Muslims, any gay kid tormented by his peers, any teenage geek who can't get a date, people with disabilities, and many more. (We have to wonder if Edgar would be covered under the Americans with Disabilities Act . . .)

Edgar shares many parallels with Christ. He is born in a kind of "virgin" birth. He is the victim of profound persecution, false charges, insults, abuse, and a kind of metaphorical crucifixion. He lives a life of tolerance and tries to spread that message. There are two moments that are clear Christ references. First, at the end of Act I, during the extended musical scene, "Comfort and Joy," Edgar prays to God. He sings:

> But please my thirst grows every day.
> I feel it burn in my glands.
> Please won't you change the way I am,
> Or prove I'm human underneath;
> Or if you just don't give a damn . . .

This parallels Christ in the Garden of Gethsemane, where he prays to God, asking him to stop the process that he knows will lead ultimately to his death. Also, at the beginning of Act II, at Reverend Hightower's revival meeting, Edgar gets up to speak and sings, "Let me walk among you," a very clear reference to Leviticus 26:12, in which God says, "I will walk among you, and will be your God, and you will be my people." This subtly sets Edgar up as a god-like figure.

Edgar's similarities to Frankenstein's monster are just as interesting. He is made by an "unnatural" process, as a result of scientific experiments run amok. His creator rejects him. He is not allowed to love, though he is desperate to find a mate. He is gentle as a kitten when treated with kindness, and deadly as any madman when provoked. And as an example of science run amok, *Bat Boy* resonates with other contemporary scientific ethics issues—human cloning, genetic engineering of food, stem cell research, and more. *Bat Boy* has the same message as many 1950s science fiction movies, that technology is evil and will only cause heartache and death. Of course, *Bat Boy* doesn't really believe it. Still, the show's prologue, "Hold Me, Bat Boy," pretends to the same solemnity and pretension of some of the great sci-fi B-movies of the 1950s.

Bat Boy also finds its roots in another groundbreaking rock musical, *The Rocky Horror Show*. Like *Rocky Horror*, *Bat Boy* is full of Christ references, Dracula references, Frankenstein references, and deals with the issue of America's sexual puritanism. Both shows also set up parallels to Shakespeare plays—*The Tempest* in *Rocky Horror*, and *Romeo and Juliet* in *Bat Boy*. And the end of the *Bat Boy*, with the bodies of the main characters strewn about the stage, even pays comic homage to the final scene of *Hamlet*.

Touch Me, Bat Boy

Bat Boy opened in New York the same year as another satiric musical, *Urinetown*. Both shows satirized conventional musicals. Both shows were hilarious. Both shows kept audiences laughing by taking Broadway musical conventions and either turning them upside-down or taking them to such an extreme they no longer could be taken seriously. But the difference between the two shows was palpable. *Urinetown* was intellectually brilliant but cold as ice. *Bat Boy* was brilliant but also had a heart so big and tender that some audience members were crying at the end. And this is because, even though both shows are satires, they couldn't be more different at their cores. *Urinetown* is about overthrowing a corporate monster, and the love story at the side of the central plot is nothing but a target for derision.

Bat Boy is about a defenseless boy who, through no fault of his own, has been cast aside, a boy who wants nothing more than to be loved, a boy with a big heart and lots of love to give. Even through all the satire, even through all the craziness, you can't help but care about Edgar. He takes an incredible journey, not only to learn to be literate, to learn to be a part of a community, but also to learn self-respect, to stand up for himself, to improve himself, to demand equality, to rebel against injustice, and ultimately to learn (sadly) that the world is inherently unfair. Edgar is every great civil rights movement in America and around the world, all wrapped up in one person. O'Keefe says, "Keythe and Brian set out to build a darkly comic world around deadly serious themes, primarily the notion of scapegoating—how societies will blame their fears and failures on the unusual, the weak, and the gifted. We decided to make Bat Boy all three."

And to extend the metaphor a bit, Edgar's growing rage throughout Act II could be compared to the growing rage in the black civil rights movement in the 1960s, which gave rise to groups like the Black Panthers. As injustice grows, so too grows the fury against it. Still, as the show comes to a close, Edgar's last line before the finale is "I am not a boy. I'm an animal . . ." And in this resignation, it's not hard to hear the voices of thousands of gay teens who have committed suicide because they believed the lies about them, the thousands of blacks who accepted horrific racial prejudice for hundreds of years, the voices of millions of oppressed people around the world and throughout history. Yes, *Bat Boy* is largely funny and there are even jokes in the tragic finale, but there are also emotions too big to be contained and it's not unusual for a performance to end with some tears in the audience—partly because we love Edgar and partly because we know in our hearts there is truth in this strange morality tale.

Edgar takes the same journey as a normal infant, though much more quickly (because apparently the drinking of blood makes him an overachiever). He learns everything by imitation, just like a child. First, he learns to communicate with Meredith in "A Home for You" by imitating her singing. This is an interesting moment because it steps outside the reality of the story for a moment and offers a subtle wink at the conventions of musical theatre. In most musicals, characters are not aware that they're singing; music and rhymed lyrics are merely the language of the art form, just as iambic pentameter is the language of Shakespeare's plays. So logically, neither Meredith nor Edgar is aware that Meredith is singing in "A Home for You"—within the reality of the show, she's just talking to Edgar. And yet somehow, Edgar knows she's singing because he sings back in imitation. And then the two of them harmonize (illustrating their emotional connection), which certainly implies an awareness of the music. Or maybe, Meredith *does* know she's singing; maybe she is singing Edgar a lullaby—a really sophisticated one—making this song diegetic (music that exists *within* the story rather than just as an expression of the story, like the club numbers in *Cabaret*).

Edgar learns everything else by imitation too. He learns to talk by imitating Meredith. He learns his British accent by listening to and imitating

BBC language tapes. He learns to love by watching Meredith. He learns to dance by imitating Shelley. He learns to have sex by watching the other forest animals in "Children, Children." And, most importantly, he learns to hate by watching the townspeople of Hope Falls. And once again, O'Keefe's music and lyrics do some important storytelling work as Edgar learns more and more; the best contemporary theatre writers (especially those taking up the mantle of composer-lyricist Stephen Sondheim) write lyrics that tell us a great deal more than what's on the surface. Specifically, the best contemporary musicals follow the rule that the more intelligence and presence of mind a character has, the more he or she rhymes, and the more emotional or uneducated a character may be, the less he or she rhymes. As Edgar presents his high school equivalency essay to the Parkers in "Show You a Thing or Two," note the acrobatic rhymes that reveal his newfound genius. Edgar sings:

> I will discuss
> Copernicus
> Who ruined all our fun,
> And showed we're just
> A ball of dust
> That limps around the sun.
> Which brings me then
> To Darwin, when
> He bent us out of shape,
> As he began
> To prove that man
> Is nephew to an ape.
> We were annoyed
> When Dr. Freud
> Declared it's not a soul;
> It is your blind
> Subconscious mind
> That's always in control.
> But I submit
> That any twit,
> If he has eyes to see,
> Can seize his fate,
> Self-educate,
> And turn out just like me!

Real craftsmanship is evident here, as it is in the brilliant rhyme scheme of the flash cards list in the same song. Not only does O'Keefe cram these moments with fun, interior rhymes, but he does it without contorting sentences, without unnatural vocabulary, and all while maintaining a coherent paragraph that moves forward both character and plot. In another bit of hidden self-reference, Edgar's essay addresses the four central issues that swirl around the subtext of *Bat Boy*: the nature of God and the natural world, the idea that humans evolved from animals, the concept of the human soul, and the idea that education transforms.

O'Keefe has some strong ideas about musical theatre writing:

> In any show I try never to slow the plot down too much—I think audiences get bored and antsy when a character sings, "What is this feeling I'm feeeeeling," when we've just seen him get kissed, or shot at. We already know exactly what he's feeling; we want to know what he's going to do next. We should never let the audience get ahead of the characters. A song can make the audience feel the impact of an event much more strongly than just dialogue alone, true. But I think in general audiences are not as patient as they once were. So during my songs I always try to have the characters ask for something new, or change their minds violently, or sometimes die. My cliché is, you have a honeymoon during the first verse and chorus. If you get to the end of that first sixty seconds of singing without a major new plot development, your song is over; you should move on and get to that plot development.

One of the show's biggest moments, when Meredith names Edgar, is deceptive. It seems like a throwaway, like another laugh. But it's the turning point of the entire story. Consciously or not, Meredith's choice for a name for the Bat Boy means everything. By choosing a human name no one would use for a pet or other animal, Meredith humanizes Edgar for the first time, both to Shelley and to the audience. And this is, arguably, the beginning of Shelley's attraction to Edgar. We stop seeing Edgar as an animal and start seeing him as a person. Before Meredith names him, he's a bat boy; after she names him, he's a sweet young man. Shelley complains that they never know the names of the stray animals Dr. Parker has to put down, and she's too young to understand why that is—if they name the animals, they personalize them, and killing them becomes much harder. The naming of Edgar sets all of them down a path that leads directly to the climax of the show. And despite Edgar's apparent humanness later in the show, the authors of *Bat Boy* keep Edgar's animal nature in the back of our minds through the entire show by peppering animal references everywhere—Dr. Parker's geese, the sick cows, the animals in the children's book, the animals mentioned in "A Joyful Noise," in the orgy in the forest, in the flashback, and elsewhere. Animals are everywhere in *Bat Boy*, making it impossible for Edgar—and for us—to forget his animal nature.

And significantly, Dr. Parker himself becomes animal, becomes a "monster" like Edgar, as he pursues more and more fervently his plans to destroy Edgar. His desire to remove Edgar from his family's life becomes a metaphor for his fear of his own animal side; but the harder he battles, the more his animal side emerges, and eventually he must be destroyed just as surely as Edgar must be. Likewise, Edgar unintentionally drags Shelley into a fate parallel to what we see Meredith suffer in the flashback, due to the actions of Dr. Parker. Edgar and Dr. Parker not only share the same fate, they also force the women they love into shared fates.

Of course, the great challenge of performing *Bat Boy* is to play these very real emotions, very real relationships, hopes, fears, and desires, and to focus them through the lens of a bigger-than-life style of performance, to play the characters' inner lives honestly while playing their outer lives outrageously. There are only a few shows that require that dichotomy (*The Cradle Will Rock*, *Little Shop of Horrors*, and the stage version of *Rocky Horror* come to mind), perhaps because it's just so difficult. Larry O'Keefe says of *Bat Boy*, "Even in its first embryonic form, the show had already found its tone: a balance between farce and high tragedy, in which any given moment might elicit snorts and guffaws from one viewer, yet tears from his neighbor in the next seat over."

Perhaps the silliest and also most interesting aspect of Edgar's personality is that he's been raised by bats, so that as a result, as the show opens, he doesn't behave like other humans, he behaves like a bat. As actual bats would be, Edgar is afraid of humans at first—bats are not aggressive creatures and rarely attack people—but he eventually attacks when threatened. Big credit should go not only to the show's creators but also to Deven May, who created the role, for making real and logical the ridiculous, sublime premise upon which the show rests.

Sex and the Single Bat

It's fun to watch Edgar learn about human sex. The first reference to Edgar and sex is when Shelley sings, "I'm afraid he'll reproduce" (which is on the cast album, but not in the printed score)—a strangely prescient comment. Shelley's juvenile delinquent boyfriend Rick then references the idea of alternative sexuality when he threatens to dress Edgar up in drag and makeup. (Rick and Shelley also taunt Edgar by telling him his father was a pig and his mother was a snake, a statement that takes on entirely new meaning by the end of the show.) Edgar then sees Shelley and Rick making out and he tries to imitate their sexual behavior alone in his cage, which of course enrages Rick—it's too human and it implies an understanding that makes Rick uncomfortable. Later, living in the same house with Shelley naturally leads to feelings between the two. When they each see the other dressed up for the first time, late in Act I, they begin flirting. Shelley sees the "ugly boy" who was brought to her house in a bag suddenly now as boyfriend material. The more Edgar is "civilized," the more Shelley wants him. Finally, their eventual descent into the world of star-crossed lovers in Act II brings them even closer together and they consummate their love. Just as Edgar grows up and becomes civilized very quickly, he goes through an accelerated kind of puberty as well.

And Shelley changes too, as she is touched by Edgar's sweetness and as she slowly finds she loves him. Her Act I song "Ugly Boy" is transformed into "Lovely Boy" in Act II. Shelley's music tells us (very subtly) that she is more like Meredith than she'd like to think, that she is just as empathetic as Meredith, just as kind; it's just that Shelley fights being like Meredith and tries to hide that side of herself, especially in front of Rick. But once she switches her romantic interest from Rick to Edgar, her music changes as well, from the aggressive rap song "Watcha Wanna Do" and the dissonant "Ugly Boy" in Act I, to the gorgeous sweeping ballads she sings in Act II. Also, the melody of her big love song, "Inside Your Heart," is foreshadowed as the accompaniment to the second verse of Meredith's lullaby to Edgar, "A Home for You," and another part of the "Inside Your Heart" melody shows up as a short figure between phrases in the same song. On top of that, a piece of melody from "A Home for You" shows up as accompaniment in the last verse of "Inside Your Heart." This links Meredith and Shelley musically, and by extension temperamentally. (Maybe Shelley is what Meredith *would* have been if not for the great tragedy in her past.) Perhaps the first indication of this is that, very early in the show, Shelley joins Rick's rap song, "Watcha Wanna Do," but changes sides during the song and eventually tries to stop the song when she sees Edgar might be in danger, finally yelling for Meredith to come to the rescue and stop the song for her.

Like many of Shakespeare's young lovers, Edgar and Shelley run away into the woods, where the rules of civilization no longer apply, where sexuality is open and unfettered, where love can find its way without the obstacles of polite society. And *Bat Boy* even follows a common Shakespearean structure, with Act I set in town and almost all of Act II set out in the woods. The major difference is that there is no return to civilization in *Bat Boy* the way there always is in Shakespeare. The other difference is that in this case, there's one obstacle Shakespeare's lovers never faced—Edgar and Shelley aren't of the same species. And that's why the animals of the forest must assemble to sing to the lovers and let them know that in nature there is no morality, that civilization has created layers of shame and control over sexuality that are, in fact, unnatural. In this story, it is the town's bloodlust and hatred that is unnatural, not Edgar and Shelley's love.

An example of how Edgar's dramatic arc changed over time: one of the last changes to the show before opening in New York was a rewrite of the surprisingly powerful "Apology to a Cow," Edgar's soliloquy of despair and rage. The number, interestingly, had never gotten much audience reaction in its previous incarnations, and the problem was at last identified. The audience didn't want to see Edgar in despair; they wanted to see him rise again to fight. The ending was changed, and instead of a mad scene and a collapse into an animal state of howls and rage and dissonant crashing chords, now Edgar resolves to take revenge on all humanity (like Sweeney Todd and Dr. Parker), singing his heroic/vengeful high notes as he accepts his animal nature and raises the severed cow head in triumph. After the show has made the audience fall in love with Edgar, he is now revealed to be as dangerous as Dr. Parker warned, a genuine monster. Edgar is now fully active, not passive; the moment is still tragic (though with comic echoes of the final scene of *Hamlet*), but much more dramatically satisfying.

Dr. Jekyll and Mr. Todd

Dr. Parker has two literary forefathers—Dr. Jekyll and Sweeney Todd. Part of the comedy of Dr. Parker's character comes from his abrupt shifts from mild-mannered veterinarian into crazed madman, and sometimes right back again. And his tragedy parallels Sweeney Todd's, both men beat up by the world, their lives ruined by forces outside their control, their lives now controlled—obsessed—by an event from years earlier that they are still trying to resolve that robbed them of a happy family life. Long ago, Dr. Parker and Meredith were truly in love, but their marriage began in tragedy and it never recovered. Still, all these years later, the wounds have not healed. As much as Dr. Parker still loves Meredith, she cannot love him in return; or perhaps, more accurately, she cannot face whatever love she may still feel for him. She avoids sex with him because it conjures up terrible images from the past that she just can't face. He can only win her affection by making a deal with her, by promising her something in return; and even then, it's not real affection, just the appearance of it. When Edgar shows up, he's only one more reminder of how alone and unloved Dr. Parker is. And Meredith's deep and tender love for Edgar only makes it worse for Dr. Parker. His tumultuous character arc is illustrated by two parallel coming-home scenes. In the first, he arrives home to find an empty, dark house. He calls out into the darkness, but no one answers. He is utterly alone. But the second time we see him come home, in the middle of "Show You a Thing or Two," he enters to a *Leave It to Beaver* cheerfulness that makes the earlier scene even more potent:

> Parker: Honey, I'm home!
> Shelley: Hi, Daddy! How was work?
> Parker: Great! How is Edgar coming along?

This stands in stark contrast to his first entrance, and the immediate reference to Edgar reminds us that this sitcom happiness will continue only as long as Parker keeps Edgar alive and happy. The happiness is artificial and Parker knows it.

We laugh at the extremity of Dr. Parker's madness, at the increasing level of "evil" in him, but it's not hard to see what has driven him to this place. Every time he asks for love, Meredith turns to Edgar instead. Over and over, Dr. Parker is rejected, humiliated, and in some way he must blame himself for all this as well—and we can assume this is how it's been their entire marriage. Is it enough to explain his violence, his madness? Maybe, maybe not. We can't forget, despite the English accent, that Edgar *is* part animal and that he attacked both Ruthie Taylor and Dr. Parker. But Parker's love for Meredith does give us some insight into Dr. Parker's situation. Even as he plots murderous acts late in Act I, their commission depends on how he thinks Meredith will react, whether or not it will affect Parker's chances at winning her back. He is single-minded, just like Sweeney Todd—he must put things right again. He must have loved her very deeply, and now knowing that he may never be loved in return again, it is torture for him to live in the same house with her, especially now seeing her display such affection to Edgar. As with much of *Bat Boy*, Dr. Parker is funny, but there is a very sad, very dark, very *dangerous* underside to his character that can't be dismissed.

Parker is a fascinating villain, one you can't totally hate, one you can't totally judge, and yet one who threatens the safety of our hero and those he loves. He shares more with Edgar than is immediately apparent—he too just wants to be loved and live a normal life, but the prospects are just as bleak for him as they are for Edgar. As they both sink into despair and then rage, Dr. Parker and Edgar both get their *Sweeney Todd* epiphany moments, Parker with "Parker's Epiphany" and also "More Blood," and Edgar with "Apology to a Cow." Just as Sweeney declares in "A Little Priest" that the world is divided up into who gets eaten and who gets to eat, so too Edgar declares in "Apology to a Cow" that he must "eat or be eaten." And interestingly, both Edgar and Dr. Parker sing about the impact of the smiles of their beloved on them. In "Dance with Me, Darling," Parker sings to Meredith:

> But there was a time, you know,
> When you would smile at me.
> Once long ago there was love in your eyes.

Similarly, in "I Imagine You're Upset," Edgar sings of Shelley:

> Once in a while, she would meet my stare.
> Then I'd forget the cage.
> Surely her smile wasn't meant for me . . .

Sadly, though Dr. Parker and Edgar both want the same things, each of them can only have those things if the other one doesn't get them, or, more to the point, if the other one is eliminated. But even at his most feral, it's clear that only one thing ever motivates Parker—his love for Meredith. Perhaps the most heartbreaking moment in the entire show is at the end when Parker sings, "Your eyes, Meredith, he has your eyes . . ." It's at that moment that we forget the ranting, the drunken rage, the savage side of Parker; at that moment, all we see is his deep, dark, unrequited, unconditional love for Meredith and the uncontrollable tragedy that has forever stained that love. And there, *Bat Boy* rises confidently to the level of Greek tragedy.

Christian Charity

The actors playing the townspeople, as they repeatedly change characters in full view of the audience, and with only the slightest change in appearance, become a physical metaphor for the transformations that Edgar, Dr. Parker, Shelley, and Meredith undergo. As one actor constantly changes from Rick to Lorraine to Mr. Dillon, as another actor switches between Bud, Daisy, and the King of the Forest (sometimes with only one dialogue line separating characters), these quick costume/character changes underline the theme of inner transformation that informs the entire story. Edgar transforms from animal to human, from lonely individual to family member, and from outsider to insider. Dr. Parker moves from neglected husband to megalomaniac to latter-day King Lear. Shelley changes from selfish teenager to empathetic girlfriend to tragic lover. Meredith changes from passive housewife to proud mother to terrified mother to strong-willed rescuer. And, as with the end of *West Side Story*, we hope at the end of *Bat Boy* that the townspeople will soon change their ways as well. Although, in one of the great comic strokes in the show, as the townspeople list the lessons they've learned in the final song, it's clear that some of them haven't really learned the right lessons . . .

In talking about the population of Hope Falls, co-author Keythe Farley recommends a book called *Depth Psychology and a New Ethic* by Erich Neumann. Farley says, "Neumann argues that the repression of the shadow in society causes a deep need for that energy to find a target, someone, other than us, to be the shadow that we can't own, someone who we can destroy in the hopes of creating a feeling of stability for ourselves. This dynamic is at work from our first playground scuffle to the mightiest wars of our age. Neumann goes on to identify the three types of people that society tends to scapegoat: those whom we perceive as being different (immigrants, people of color, most notably today, Muslims), those who appear weaker ('welfare mothers,' 'wimps,' the homeless) and those who we see as 'better than us' (holy people, do-gooders, rich people, smart people, 'the elite'). Edgar is all three—a sweet, sensitive freak of nature with a fierce intellect and a nasty bite."

Like the town in Stephen Sondheim's *Anyone Can Whistle*, Hope Falls, the setting for *Bat Boy*, is a town in crisis. Its primary industry, coal mining, is gone, and the people of Hope Falls have turned to ranching, at which they do not excel. Their cattle are dying because they don't know how to raise cattle ("A mountain's no place to raise cows," the finale reminds us), but rather than accept their own inadequacies, they look for a scapegoat. Edgar shows up in town and they get their scapegoat.

Bat Boy satirizes religious extremism and also religion as a misused sociopolitical force, but it doesn't really poke fun at Christianity itself or at people of genuine faith. The people of Hope Falls frequently proclaim their "Christian charity," but it's clear from their behavior that they aren't nearly as Christian as they claim to be. It seems everyone in town loves exclaiming, "Sweet wounded Jesus!" when they're surprised, and yet one would assume that a serious Christian would not take the Lord's name in vain. They initially blame the death of their cows on God, rather than recognizing how bad they are at cattle ranching. They talk about doing horrible things to Edgar, and later they threaten Dr. Parker, all the while pretending that their actions reflect their "Christian charity." The song "Comfort and Joy" shows how misguided the people of Hope Falls are. Second Corinthians 1:23–24 says, "Our strength and ability are owing to faith; and our comfort and joy must flow from faith." But these people are asking God to give them comfort and joy outright. They've got it backward; they don't get that it must come from faith, which they don't have. They believe their comfort and joy will result from the destruction of an innocent life—Edgar's. They sing:

Comfort and joy,
Comfort and joy!
Kill the bat boy,
Kill the bat boy!

On the other hand Meredith has it right. She knows that comfort and joy comes from faith. She sings:

He will show them he's not
What they're terrified of.
He will show them a love
They can never destroy.
If we prove that they're wrong,
They'll come 'round before long,
And we'll all sing a song
Full of comfort and joy.

It's significant that Meredith understands the teachings of the Bible and that she alone in Hope Falls *practices* actual Christian charity by insisting on caring for Edgar, by teaching him, by making him a part of the family. In the first dialogue scene in the show, Meredith even quotes Romans 6:23 at Shelley: "For the wages of sin is death . . . ," though she conveniently leaves out the more positive rest of the sentence. In *this* story, the wages of sin *are* death, and maybe Meredith's past and present circumstances lead her in that direction unconsciously. In this world of faux Christians, only Edgar sincerely seeks God, first praying to him in "Comfort and Joy," then hoping for divine healing at the revival meeting, then in his testimony before the congregation. Edgar believes that God can help him. But the people of Hope Falls practice a poisoned, hypocritical brand of Christianity, one that has arguably corrupted American culture today, and because this is the only kind of Christianity Edgar experiences, it prevents Edgar from finding God as he had hoped.

It's also significant that the one explicitly religious figure in the show, the Reverend Hightower, is not a source of satire. He is completely sincere. He accepts Edgar without reservation. Even though the people of Hope Falls have asked him to come to town for all the wrong reasons, he's still there hoping to do some good. And like Meredith, he accepts Edgar unconditionally. The Reverend Hightower, the one *genuine* Christian in the story, invites Edgar up on stage to be healed and urges the congregation to accept him. They do, if only for a moment.

He Shoots, He Scores

The *Bat Boy* score is one of the most sophisticated, most carefully and artfully built theatre scores of the 1990s, matching in its artistry some of the great scores of the American theatre—*Sweeney Todd*, *Ragtime*, *West Side Story*, *Carousel*, *Show Boat*. Its music succeeds on three levels at once. First, this beautiful, emotional, soaring music delivers an emotional punch only a few musicals can equal. Second, it's skillfully enough built that it uses music to reinforce drama, to make dramatic connections, to foreshadow events, to define characters and relationships, to give us more information than the dialogue and lyrics alone supply. Like the legendary theatre composer Stephen Sondheim, O'Keefe doesn't use a reprise in *Bat Boy* unless it has a very different meaning and dramatic function from the first time we heard it. Third, *Bat Boy* is unashamedly funny. There are musical jokes everywhere and the frequent and sudden explosions of melodramatic horror-movie chords at just the right moments throughout the show supply both dramatic intensity and inevitable laughs at their aggressive obviousness.

One of *Bat Boy*'s greatest strengths is the depth of characterization its music achieves. One example of this can be found in the song "A Home for You." Meredith is singing to Edgar, showing him his first-ever taste of human tenderness. The song is almost a lullaby, yet also a powerful ballad. It sets up musical themes that will be used throughout the evening. But one moment in the song defines the relationship between Meredith and Edgar better than any line of dialogue ever could. As Meredith sings to him, she is interrupted by Edgar singing for the first time, picking up her melody, trying to communicate with her. At this point, he still hasn't learned to talk; he's only been in the house a short time. But he wants desperately to communicate and so he picks up the language Meredith is using, the language of the pop ballad. As he will through much of Act I, he communicates by imitation.

That by itself would be a powerfully dramatic moment—the first time Edgar sings, the first time he communicates, even if only in an abstract way. But composer Larry O'Keefe develops this moment further. Meredith tries to communicate further. She sings another line and waits for his musical response, which comes quickly. Then the two of them sing together—no words, just *ooo*'s—but we see that they have made a connection. It's only a basic connection—they're not singing any harmony yet—but it's a connection. (Actually they do sing harmony on the cast album, but not in the printed score, which is a better dramatic choice.) This subtle, sweet, funny moment not only begins to develop what may be the most important relationship in the show, it also foreshadows the surprise at the end of the show. Then O'Keefe goes even further. Meredith returns to her words in the next verse and Edgar sings a complex baroque countermelody. They are developing their relationship, both emotionally and musically. Their connection is more complex than it first appeared (again, foreshadowing). The music tells us that these two people are very different—they don't sing the same melody—but they fit together. They belong together. They are in harmony with each other.

And once again O'Keefe scores laughs in two separate directions. First, it's funny that this boy who can't even talk yet understands classical harmony and counterpoint and can improvise a countermelody; it could only happen in a musical comedy. Second, it's funny because his countermelody is so sophisticated, so artful, and though we don't know it yet, it foreshadows the genius and quick mind that we will discover Edgar possesses later in Act I. And as the song ends, Meredith hits her final note and holds it while Edgar sings a lovely final countermelody that ends in perfect, simple harmony. In fact, it's important to notice that Edgar sings and harmonizes with both Meredith and Shelley, but never with Dr. Parker. He does not have the same connection to Dr. Parker that he has with the two women (even more foreshadowing).

O'Keefe says of his songs, "I noticed something I did unintentionally throughout the score: just about every song contains a right-angle turn, a plot development that interrupts or completely wrecks the emotion that was just building. The animal celebration turns pornographic. The optimistic mother-daughter gonna-get-out-of-here song turns ugly. Bat Boy's aria pleading for acceptance asks for too much and horrifies the townspeople. And in most of the songs, someone makes a big mistake or miscalculation too. Maybe one of my major themes is that life doesn't stop just because someone opens his mouth to sing . . ."

Making a Connection

One interesting element of the *Bat Boy* score is the fact that several songs in the show don't actually end. This kind of musical coitus interruptus focuses dramatic incidents, intensifies the twists and turns the plot takes throughout the story, and, most importantly, it also dramatically increases the level of tension, frequently robbing the audience of their chance to applaud, to respond, to release their tension. Stephen Sondheim's *Passion* does the same thing, but in *Bat Boy* the effect is both dramatic and often very funny. The opening number, "Hold Me, Bat Boy," ends normally, but it's a prologue, not part of the main story, and this normal ending sets up audience expectations that will get intentionally frustrated later on. At the end of "Christian Charity," instead of a conventional "button" (the final chord or note that signals the end of a song), the music segues directly into the horror-movie chords. The next song, "Ugly Boy," never finishes but just moves into underscoring music. Edgar's reprise of "A Home for You" isn't allowed to finish because Edgar is not allowed to finish his argument; Dr. Parker cuts him off and refuses Edgar's request. Rick's Act II song, "All Hell Breaks Loose," is interrupted by Edgar's attack, so it never finishes. "Three Bedroom House" is interrupted by Shelley dropping a bombshell on Meredith. And then there are other songs that the soloist doesn't get to finish because the ensemble jumps in to finish it for him with lots of scary chords.

Even though there are many wonderful elements in this score, the most interesting and probably least obvious element is its dramatic structure. One of the primary ways composer Larry O'Keefe uses music in *Bat Boy* is through musical themes (longer musical passages used and developed throughout the score, connected to an important idea or character) and musical leitmotifs (shorter phrases that do the same), music that clearly defines action and relationships. Most of these work subliminally on an audience. Most audiences won't consciously recognize or assign meaning to these themes and motifs, but they will work on the audience's ears and subconscious nonetheless. It's a device born in the world of opera but adopted by the best musical theatre composers as well, including Stephen Sondheim (really the first to make it his modus operandi, to do it consistently, intelligently, and fully), Adam Guettel, Stephen Flaherty, and others.

The first major leitmotif in *Bat Boy* is a short phrase (just four notes) repeated four times as the introduction to the opening number, "Hold Me, Bat Boy," and it accompanies and often presages danger throughout the show. It shows up inside the accompaniment throughout the rap song "Watcha Wanna Do," which precedes an attack by Rick against Edgar. It shows up again in the accompaniment at the end of the song "Another Dead Cow," after the townspeople have decided Edgar is responsible for their cows dying, a decision that will lead to great danger for Edgar later in the show. It shows up in "Dance With Me, Darling" as Dr. Parker slits the throats of the geese and feeds Edgar blood for the first time. It shows up in the accompaniment in the middle of "Mrs. Taylor's Lullaby," in which she demands Edgar be destroyed. It shows up under dialogue before the reprise of "A Home for You," as the Parkers tell Edgar he can't go to the revival meeting. It shows up again in "Comfort and Joy" before the sheriff sings about the revival meeting. It appears, sung by the chorus, at the end of "Comfort and Joy," after Dr. Parker arranges to frame Edgar for murder. It appears again in an Act II musical sequence called "All Hell Breaks Loose," right after Edgar attacks Rick. We hear it as scene change music (labeled "Babe in the Woods" in the score) as Shelley goes off into the woods by herself to find Edgar, and again right before Mrs. Taylor sets the slaughterhouse on fire. It appears in the accompaniment to Edgar's "Apology to a Cow," as Edgar embraces his dark side. (Also, in the middle of that song, the accompaniment refers back to Rick's rap song, telling us that Edgar is turning mean like Rick.)

The second major motif is also found in the opening number, accompanying the lyric "hold me, Bat Boy; touch me, Bat Boy." This melody shows up again at the end of Act I, near the end of "Comfort and Joy," only now the lyric has changed to "stop the Bat Boy." It's also the last thing we hear in Act I. It shows up again in Act II in a piece called "Stop the Bat Boy," with the lyric "find the Bat Boy, stop the Bat Boy." Later, in Act II, the same melody comes back, this time with the words "find the Bat Boy! Kill the Bat Boy!" The melody stays the same but the words grow progressively darker and more deadly as the story moves forward. A close variation on this melody shows up at the end of "Apology to a Cow" as Edgar's life starts to crumble.

Another motif is a phrase from "A Home for You" that accompanies the lyric "then we will find a home for you" at the end of the first verse. This shows up, though in a very distorted, dissonant version (that's somewhat reminiscent of *Sweeney Todd*) in the accompaniment of the song "Dance With Me, Darling," right after the lyric "I know how you feel," the first time Dr. Parker has expressed his sadness at the terrible state of his marriage. This is a love motif, but Parker's love for Meredith has been horribly distorted by past events. This motif shows up again in the accompaniment for "Inside Your Heart" as Shelley discovers her love for Edgar.

Shelley and Edgar's big Act II love song, "Inside Your Heart," is based melodically on "A Home for You," connecting the two women who show love to Edgar. Also, most significantly, Shelley's early song "Ugly Boy" is transformed in Act II into "Lovely Boy" as she declares her love for Edgar. Edgar's testimony at the revival meeting ("Let Me Walk Among You") is also related melodically to "A Home for You," though less exactly than in other instances (however, the accompaniments are very closely related). Another phrase from "A Home for You" shows up in the accompaniment in the middle of "Three Bedroom House" as Meredith and Shelley dream of a new house for them and Edgar.

The opening melody for Edgar's Act II "Apology to a Cow" is foreshadowed several times during the show, but always sung without words, on open vowels, by the "scary chorus." O'Keefe establishes this melody so firmly as "bad news" that when it finally shows up in "Apology" with words, it packs quite an emotional wallop. There's also a very sad musical motif in this song. Edgar's melody to the lyric "deep in a cave under miles of stone," later turns into rage in the finale, under the lyric "is that what you call it, that empty pit." The great sadness here is that the melody first shows up in "A Home for You," early in Act I, as Meredith sings to Edgar, "Poor little person with eyes so sad." By the end of the story, that first touch of kindness shown to Edgar has now festered and soured as he loses his family, and that sweet lullaby turns to a blistering rage. Very sad.

Because the song "Revelations" late in Act II happens entirely in flashback, it uses melodies from throughout the show, effectively flashing back musically as well to reveal the secret truths behind many of the scenes we've already witnessed. ("Revelations" also starts with a funny-creepy nod to "Tubular Bells," the theme from *The Exorcist*, to set the mood.) Here we find out what has *really* been going on, and by returning to these melodies we see everything that's already happened in a new light as we hear music we've already heard now used in a new context. This musical scene begins with a requoting of Edgar's "Apology to a Cow," the moment that necessitates this flashback. As Meredith and Dr. Parker begin to tell their story, we start with "Dance with Me, Darling," a song that not only returns to their first scene together in Act I, but also back to their earlier, more romantic days when their future seemed bright. Next we hear a very funny, very creepy quotation of "Three Bedroom House" set to a frantic waltz tempo as Meredith tells her story of the destruction of her dreams of blissful domesticity. Soon, the piece moves into a scene of Meredith giving birth, musically quoting the melody of "A Home for You" but this time with the accompaniment figure from Mrs. Taylor's lullaby to Ruthie. As horror comes to Meredith's world, we hear again the horror movie music from the Act I finale, and finally move into an even sadder quotation of "Dance with Me, Darling," as Dr. Parker finishes the tragic tale.

As the final scene of the show continues, Edgar sings again his melody from "Apology to a Cow," his anger and hurt growing even deeper and more painful now. Soon, Edgar moves into a requoting of his redemption and forgiveness theme from "Let Me Walk Among You," a theme Dr. Parker will pick up moments later as he asks Meredith's forgiveness for all he's done wrong, this time with Meredith singing a heart-wrenching countermelody. Even though Edgar and Dr. Parker have still never actually sung together, at long last they share a melody. They do have some connection, the music tells us; but though this melody was hopeful and openhearted when we first heard it, now it's tragic and full of doom.

Is all this interweaving of themes and motifs just musical overkill? Is it just a way for O'Keefe to avoid composing new music for these moments?

Not at all. First of all, most people won't even hear this stuff the first time they hear the score; it's very subtly done. Second of all, it achieves dramatic purposes. These themes and motifs don't just appear at random (as they do in shows like *Phantom of the Opera* or *Jekyll & Hyde*). The reason the "Home for You" melody seems to show up everywhere in the score is that the desire for a normal, loving home is the engine that drives the entire story, both from Edgar's side and from Dr. Parker's side. That idea is everywhere and so is its accompanying motif. Just as Shakespeare dealt with recurring images in his words with each of his plays, so too do the best modern musical theatre composers deal with recurring images in their music. It's the same practice, just in a different theatrical language.

And not only does all this provide structural signposts for the audience, it also provides a strong dramatic structure for the actors. And again, even though it may not be consciously recognized by the audience, it does the job of making the score sound like a unified whole, like it all belongs together, like it's all in the same language, the same musical world, and it allows the audience to stay inside that world (and its emotions) more easily. And certainly, the danger motif accompanies bad things so often in the show that it turns the audience into Pavlov's dogs; they hear those four notes, in whatever context, and they get the feeling that something bad is coming. They may not know why they feel that way, but they do. And perhaps the mark of a truly talented composer is that he or she can do all this, make it work, make it function effectively, and still make it effectively invisible to the audience's ears.

Sondheim did it in *Sweeney Todd*, *Passion*, and *Merrily We Roll Along*; Bernstein did it in *West Side Story*; Flaherty did it in *Ragtime*; and O'Keefe does it with *Bat Boy*.

Hedwig and the Angry Inch

She makes her entrance like a star dying to be born—goose-stepping through the audience with the arrogant aplomb of Marlene Dietrich and Jim Morrison; decked out like a trailer-park tart's idea of a glam-rock fox, in stonewashed denim, an Aryan-yellow, blow-dried mane and red-glitter lipstick; accompanied by the refried Queen strains of "America the Beautiful" and a marvelously surly introduction by her crusty Serbian valet boy toy, Yitzhak: "Ladies and gentlemen, whether you like it or not—Hedwig!"

That's how *Rolling Stone* described the first moments of the monumentally innovative, "neo-glam, post-punk, rock musical" *Hedwig and the Angry Inch.* Real rock and roll—glam, heavy metal, a little punk—had come to the American musical theatre without being diluted. And if there was any question about its intentions, the show stated its musical manifesto in its first moments, as the lead guitar wailed a heavily distorted "America the Beautiful." This was real rock and it was uniquely American.

Glam rock was a mostly British genre that brought theatricality and show biz back to rock and roll. Its music and lyrics were less artsy, less sophisticated, more playful and more accessible. Though authenticity had been the measure of quality, at least in American rock, glam admitted its falseness; it spit on authenticity and borrowed from everything, including bubblegum pop, hard rock, guitar rock, folk rock, heavy metal, and progressive rock. Glam rock admitted the artifice and artistic cannibalism that its predecessors tried to hide. It embraced the elevation of form over content. Glam celebrated the mask, the playing of a role, and in admitting its artificiality, it was really the most honest of all genres. Some compared the glam rockers to Oscar Wilde and Quentin Crisp. And of course, glam also erased the line (some would call it an *arbitrary* line) between genders. Just as *Rocky Horror* used glam and its descendent, punk, as its models, *Hedwig* uses the language of glam because it was the only genre and the only time in rock and roll history in which gender lines were erased; there was no male and female in glam. It was the only language really made for Hedwig's story.

Punk rock emerged from glam in the mid-1970s as the yang to glam's yin, as a conscious rejection of the excesses and homogenization of commercial rock and roll, as well as those of glam (which is why the punk-inspired "Exquisite Corpse" in *Hedwig* literally explodes out of the more glam-inspired introspection of "Hedwig's Lament"). The history of rock and roll has always been the story of the struggle for supremacy between the beat (and "bad" content) versus the melody (and "good" content). As the art form has evolved, its pendulum has swung reliably back and forth, as the beat first gained the upper hand in the 1950s, but then that rowdy energy of early rock and roll was commercialized and made palatable. As each new rebellion in music gains an audience, that rebellion is appropriated and commercialized by the music companies, as the rebel music of one generation becomes the sanitized pop music of the next. The same thing happened with punk, and most recently with hip-hop. Once again today, the beat has taken prominence, almost eliminating melody in much of hip-hop music.

By the early and mid-1970s, mainstream rock had become so commercial, so *manufactured*, so middle class, so tied to money, and it had been largely taken away from the real artists by multinational corporations. *Hedwig ant the Angry Inch*, one of the most innovative, most shocking, most brilliant new musicals in years, was created for similar reasons. It rejected the spectacle of *Miss Saigon*, the overearnestness of *Jekyll & Hyde*, the pretentious self-awareness of *The Lion King*, the mind-numbing emptiness of *Phantom of the Opera*, and the boy-gets-girl myth of old-fashioned musical comedy. *Hedwig* even references the famous phrase "filthy lucre," which was how London's *Daily Express* described a 1976 appearance on British TV by the punk rockers the Sex Pistols—who later adopted the phrase themselves as a badge of honor. *Hedwig*, in other words, was the punk of musical theatre.

Hedwig and the Angry Inch was born at the same time that *Rent* was being developed. John Cameron Mitchell and Stephen Trask's rock musical began its life in January 1994 at a new drag rock club in Manhattan called Squeeze Box. Mitchell and Trask had met not long before and had talked about working on a piece together. Trask was a gay songwriter and front man for the alternative rock band Cheater. Mitchell was a gay actor, a veteran of shows like *The Secret Garden* and *Big River*, as well as many non-musicals. Mitchell told Trask he wanted to create a theatre piece that used a real rock band playing real rock music. Trask was interested. And because Trask knew the rock and roll idiom intimately, he created a theatre score of unusual sophistication. As an example, several of the key songs in the score are based on chords that are missing the third degree of the scale, the note which defines a chord as major or minor. Without that third in these chords, they are impossible to hear as major (happy) or minor (sad), and the resulting musical ambiguity parallels the gender ambiguity at the heart of the story. Few composers on Broadway today are skilled enough to use a device this skillfully and this subtly. It's not a device that registers consciously in the audience's ears, but it does affect how they hear and react to the show. It's a musical device used by emo-rock artists, and Kyle Jarrow's *Love Kills* was one of the few emo-rock musicals that used this same device to a similarly potent dramatic effect.

At first, talk between Mitchell and Trask centered on an autobiographical character Mitchell had been working on, Tommy Speck, the son of a military general (as was Mitchell). But Trask was more fascinated by Mitchell's transsexual character, appropriately named Hedwig (*head* plus *wig*), inspired by an East German immigrant woman named Helga who used to babysit for Mitchell while turning tricks in a Junction City, Kansas, trailer park. Later on, *Rolling Stone* would call *Hedwig* "a way off Broadway hybrid of Sandra Bernhard, Nina Hagen, and Courtney Love." They missed Marlene Dietrich. Eventually Tommy and Hedwig would come together. As the two writers began work, Mitchell bought Trask a copy of Plato's *Symposium*; showed him the central story, which explained the origins of gay, lesbian, and heterosexual love; and asked him to write a song based on that story. Trask came back with the moving, fiercely multicultural, fairy tale–like song-story "The Origin of Love." This became the spine of their show.

Part Ziggy Stardust, part Frank N. Furter, and part Marlene Dietrich, Hedwig made her first appearance in January 1994 at Squeeze Box, where Trask was the music director and his band, Cheater, was the house band. The club was unique because drag performers did not lip synch there; they actually sang. And Hedwig was unique because she was quickly becoming a fully formed, fully emotional, fully human character with backstory, not just a drag creation with a funny name. Mitchell would bring Hedwig back every six months or so, to develop the material and to try out new songs. Mitchell and Trask had created their own Broadway musical workshop, in the tradition of Michael Bennett. The show was conceived as a concert at which Hedwig tells her life story, so no traditional set was necessary, just a stage for the band and Hedwig. Its minimalism was, perhaps unconsciously, an echo of the very first productions of *Rocky Horror*.

Soon, Peter Askin came on board as director. He said in an interview, "It was a mess, but it was a wonderful mess"—the same thing people said about *Rent.* With producers on board, they planned to mount the first full production, on the tiny budget of $29,000.

Looking back, Askin said, "Hedwig is really divided into three things. It's standup comedy with some hoary, cheap jokes. It's Stephen's wonderful music. And then it's also this unexpectedly poignant love story. And it was a question of first recognizing that, and then shaping it so that the comedy came in certain sections, and whatever happened between the comedy and the music, it never took us away from Hedwig's journey." By now, Hedwig's story had a clear through-line. She began life as Hansel, a boy in East Berlin before the Berlin Wall came down. An American soldier meets Hansel and they fall in love, but for the soldier to bring him back to America, Hansel has to go through a physical exam and be proved a woman. So the soldier takes him to a back alley surgeon for a sex change operation, which gets horribly botched, leaving Hansel with just a stub of a penis—an *angry inch.*

Back in America, the soldier abandons Hansel—now Hedwig—and she is left in a trailer park in Kansas. There she meets Tommy Speck, the general's son, they fall in love, and Hedwig transforms him into the rock star Tommy Gnosis. But Tommy also abandons Hedwig, and she is left playing small tacky venues, as Tommy plays major stadiums. Now, with her band, the Angry Inch, and her eastern bloc husband, Yitzhak (played by a woman), Hedwig tells us her confessional story in the context of a concert. *Hedwig* was unusual in so many ways, not the least of which is that the entire show, every note of music, is diegetic. It is a fully naturalistic musical because Hedwig always has a fully naturalistic reason for singing—she's performing a concert for us. It was also unusual because it used genuine hard rock, a little punk, some guitar rock, and some piano power ballads. Trask said, "Most rock musicals are just silly because they're made by people who don't know anything about rock music." That was not the case here.

This was the first musical to treat a transgendered character seriously, but true to Mitchell's Broadway background, the show's structure mirrored other Broadway musicals, offering its audience a first half full of comedy and a second half full of darkness, just like *Camelot*, *Into the Woods*, *The Fantasticks*, and others.

Hedwig and the Angry Inch first opened off off Broadway at the Westbeth Theatre Center in February 1997. But the team wanted a special space for their show, not just a typical theatre. Mitchell heard about an old hotel down by the Hudson River that might have a theatre. He visited the Hotel Riverview in Manhattan's meatpacking district (where the Titanic's surviving crew had once been taken), and found it had an old, rarely used ballroom. It was there that the new *Hedwig* family decided to set up housekeeping. The show opened at the newly christened Jane Street Theatre on Valentine's Day 1998, but it didn't catch on right away. "People weren't coming. It was really slow," Mitchell said. "It was too rock and roll for some of the uptown theatre people. It was too rock and roll for maybe the gay audience. And it was too 'theatre' for the rock audience." But soon, the show picked up steam.

It ran 857 performances and won the Obie Award and the Outer Critics Circle Award for Outstanding New Off Broadway musical. The *New York Times* said, "*Hedwig and the Angry Inch* brings theatre alive with the pounding sounds of rock and the funny sad voicing of a painful past. It is also an adult, thought-provoking musical about the quest for individuality." *Time* magazine called the music "the most exciting hard rock score written for the theatre since, oh, ever," and called the show itself "a poignant mediation on loneliness, gender confusion, and the Platonic notion that sex is the effort to reconnect two halves of one ideal being." *The Village Voice* called it "the absolutely fabulous glam rock musical." Later, in 2004, critic Damien Jacques wrote in The *Milwaukee Journal Sentinel*, "To reach its potential, the show needs an audience that will growl back at the stage. It is the brilliant genius of *Hedwig* that in such an atmosphere, the musical becomes a beautifully delicate and multi-layered piece."

Mitchell was succeeded in the lead by Michael Cerveris (of *Tommy* and *Titanic*, who also took it to London), Kevin Cahoon, Donovan Leitch, Ally Sheedy, Asa Somers, and Matt McGrath. A rabid fan base rose up around the show, dubbed "Hed Heads." David Bowie and Madonna came to see it. New Line Cinema bought the screen rights and released it in July 2001, in the midst of the movie musical rebirth. The film won the Audience Award and the Directing Award at Sundance.

Whether You Like It or Not . . . Hedwig!

Hedwig Schmidt is one of the most interesting, complex characters ever to assault the musical stage. From the moment she speaks her first words, the audience hears the German accent and Hedwig is automatically, perhaps unconsciously, branded as "other" by the audience, just as the world has branded her an outsider, always on the outside looking in, searching for the American Dream yet not fully American in too many ways. Some later regional productions of the show dropped the accent, but with it they dropped the most prevalent symbol of her outsider status, and the show became less poignant, less complex, and ultimately less triumphant.

Hedwig is not a drag queen. She is not a man, though she was born a gay boy named Hansel. Hedwig is a woman, even if the plumbing is not there. But unlike most transsexuals, Hedwig was never "a woman trapped in a man's body." She got her sex change operation in order to escape Communist East Berlin. In fact, she only gets the operation because she feels the "absolute power" (her words) she holds over the American soldier, Luther, and his desires. But absolute power corrupts, as her mother tells her early on, maybe even more so when it comes to love and lust, and this feeling of power over Luther will ruin her life in many ways.

The proof of her gender confusion is in a throwaway line before the song "Wicked Little Town." As the song begins, Hedwig says, "This is the first song I've ever written. And it's written for a guy to sing." Hedwig has written this extremely autobiographical song and, quite interestingly, it's from a man's point of view. Hedwig feels she owes the audience an explanation for singing it herself. In her mind, it's not written for her to sing, even though it's about her life.

Hedwig's journey—and the thing that gives the show its unexpected unity and dramatic punch—is the search for her "other half." She subscribes to the Platonic idea that humans were once double creatures that came in three sexes—one was what we'd perceive as two males, one was two females, and one was both male and female. The gods were jealous of our happiness, so they cut us in two, and forever after, humans have searched for their other halves. Hedwig believes this search is for another person to complete her, first in the person of Luther, then Tommy Speck, and finally Yitzhak. Tommy, in his desperate attempt to understand Christianity, points out a similar story in Genesis, when Eve is literally pulled out of Adam's body, fashioned out of his rib, a story that parallels the older story.

But the Genesis story plays an even bigger part in the show. It begins with Tommy's reinterpretation of the story of Adam and Eve. He tells Hedwig that God should not have forbidden Adam and Eve to eat from the tree of knowledge (for most Christians, a metaphor for sexual intercourse, or "original sin"). As Tommy sees it, "Eve just wanted to know shit. She took a bite of the apple and found out what was good and what was evil. And she gave it to Adam so he would know. Because they were in love. And that was good, they *now* knew!" He then asks Hedwig to give *him* "the apple." This is Tommy's way of telling Hedwig he loves her, even though he may not be ready to say the words. But what kind of knowledge is Tommy asking for? Literal knowledge or sexual knowledge? And later when Hedwig bestows Tommy's new name upon him—the Greek word for knowledge—is it because Tommy has gained literal knowledge or have they made love?

In a way, Hedwig is making two journeys, one a search for her spiritual "other half," but also a search for the physical maleness she lost back in East Berlin in her botched sex change operation. What she eventually discovers is that she must find both halves *within* herself. She is that Platonic creature who is both male and female.

Of course the Berlin Wall, violently cutting the once world-famous arts center of Berlin into two parts, mirrors the story of "The Origin of Love," and also Hedwig's own life. In the song "Sugar Daddy," Hedwig even makes a reference to Erich Honecker, the leader of East Berlin, and Helmut Kohl, the leader of West Berlin, as a metaphor for the gods who split humans in half. Of course, Hedwig doesn't know at that point in the story that Honecker and Kohl will be the leaders who will reunify Berlin in 1989, that in fact they are also a metaphor for healing. But in 1988, before reunification, Hedwig has to escape. And her escape from this town cut in two can only happen if she cuts herself in two as well. The opening number, "Tear Me Down," positions the Wall as a metaphor for Hedwig herself. Her first words in the show are, "Don't you know me? I'm the new Berlin Wall. Try and tear me down!" In the song, Yitzhak says, "The world was divided by a cold war and the Berlin Wall was the most hated symbol of that divide." The show is extending the metaphor—now, the Wall doesn't just represent Hedwig; it represents *all* of us. We are *all* divided, the show says, both within ourselves and across the world. Yitzhak says, "Hedwig is like that wall, standing before you in the divide between East and West, Slavery and Freedom." And interestingly, Hedwig and Yitzhak also represent Berlin—a German and a Jew, the two halves of another infamous split in Berlin's history. Ironically, Berlin is reunified shortly after her escape, making her sacrifice unnecessary, and also making her own splitting in two that much more tragic. She even refers to her wig (representing her femaleness) as her own personal hell.

The emotional center of the show, the song "Wicked Little Town," is the first song Hedwig ever wrote, she tells us, and it is also the most autobiographical. It describes Hedwig's life in Junction City, Kansas, but it does so in very philosophical terms. In keeping with the central metaphors of the show, it is also about pairs of opposites. The first image shows both sun and black skies co-existing in the same place. But do these images of dark and light co-exist in Tommy? Or since Hedwig "wrote it for a guy to sing," are we meant to believe the *you* of the song is Hedwig herself? Later in the song the lyric speaks of wind so cold it burns. This split personality is so much a part of her, it even comes out in her metaphors.

Another pair of opposites can be found in the songs "Tear Me Down" and "Hedwig's Lament," which is actually a much-altered reprise of "Tear Me Down." The first version of the song is defiant, the second defeatist. The first is powerful, the second powerless. They form the perfect bookends to Hedwig's story. The only songs lying outside these bookends are "Exquisite Corpse" (a nervous breakdown); the reprise of "Wicked Little Town" (which actually happens at Tommy's concert, not here at Hedwig's); and "Midnight Radio," Hedwig's final healing and her offer of healing to us. None of these three songs works *inside* the show's autobiographical framework; they operate outside of it. While the rest of the show exists in the past, telling a story that has already happened, the last three songs happen in the present. We actually witness Hedwig's breakdown, we hear Tommy's rendition of "Wicked Little Town" as it happens, and we see before us Hedwig's healing.

The Gods Would Be Terrified

But we can also see Hedwig as a god figure herself, paralleling the gods discussed in "The Origin of Love." She even sees the parallel herself. But those classical gods were destroyers and Hedwig is a creator. She can't find her other half, and so, like a god, like Dr. Frankenstein (and the back alley surgeon?), she must create him. And like a god, she creates Tommy in her own image. She tells us in the show that their eyes are the same color. In the original off Broadway production, John Cameron Mitchell played Hedwig and recorded the sounds of Tommy's concert, so Hedwig and Tommy had literally the same voice. She puts her words and her music into his mouth and she puts her philosophy into his persona.

Hedwig takes the blank slate that is Tommy Speck and, like Pygmalion and Henry Higgins, she remakes him into the international rock star

Tommy Gnosis. She transforms him (or thinks she does) by changing his name—and therefore his self-image—from the inconsequential nothingness of a "speck" to the cosmic significance of "gnosis," a word meaning mystical knowledge or intuition. She creates his look, his persona, even his songs, and like her literary forebears, she falls in love with her own creation, a creature in her own image, and this is the most dangerous kind of narcissism. In fact, both Tommy and (at the end of the show) Hedwig wear a silver cross on their foreheads, the universal symbol of death and rebirth, or to take it even further, persecution, crucifixion, and divine resurrection. The film's last image also strongly suggests a rebirth. Biblical parallels are also referenced in "Wicked Little Town" with a line about "Mrs. Lot." Hedwig is being persecuted in Junction City, Kansas, just as the angels were persecuted in Sodom, further reinforcing the suggestion that Hedwig is somehow divine.

And there is an implied connection between Hedwig and Tommy through Tommy's name and the early Christian Gnostic sects. The Gnostics believed that a secret knowledge (gnosis) of God was what would bring salvation, that the Old Testament God was evil and the New Testament God would save us, and they believed in most of the teachings of Jesus. There are many Gnostic Gospels that were widely read and studied before the current Bible was codified, excluding much of what was once considered legitimate religious texts. Those excluded gospels include the Gospels of Mary, Peter, Thomas, James, Judas, and even a Gospel of Jesus. Some were excluded by church leaders because they contradicted the teachings of those in power at the time. Some were excluded because their authorship couldn't be authenticated. Some were lost; others were among the Dead Sea Scrolls discovered centuries later. To connect *Hedwig*'s characters with the Gnostics is to imply that Hedwig and Tommy need only to *understand* themselves and their world in order to be saved. In fact, Mitchell and Trask include an excerpt from the Gnostic Gospel of Thomas in their published *Hedwig* script. They quote the following:

> Jesus said to them, "When you make the two one, and the inside like the outside and the outside like the inside, and the above like the below, and the male and the female into one and the same, so that the male be not male nor the female female; and when you make eyes in place of an eye, a hand in place of a hand, a foot in place of a foot, and an image in place of an image; then you will enter the kingdom."

How appropriate that this cosmic union happens in a place called *Junction* City. Hedwig tells us that Tommy wore two contact lenses, one blue and one pink, again referencing the maleness and femaleness in all of us, the two-sided nature Hedwig is searching for. Tommy is literally Hedwig's words made flesh. Everything about Tommy comes from Hedwig. He is a character more than a real person (as many of the famous glam rockers were). Tommy himself contributes nothing but raw materials. Of course, in the context of the show, this creates so many levels of reality: an actor playing Hansel who has become Hedwig, who is in turn portraying Tommy Speck, who has become Tommy Gnosis.

Hedwig's transformation of Tommy brings us back to Plato's *Symposium*, in which the philosophers discuss the idea that in true love, one lover will make the ultimate sacrifice to make the other lover happy, even if the other lover is unworthy of that sacrifice. Here, Hedwig sacrifices her own career and instead expends all her energy on making Tommy a star. What Hedwig doesn't see until much later is that if everything Tommy is came from Hedwig, then she already has that other half she seeks inside her. The Gospel of Thomas also says:

> Jesus said, "If you bring forth that which is within you, what you bring forth will save you. If you do not bring forth what is within you, what you do not bring forth will destroy you."

The whole show is about the relation of the part to the whole and of one part to its compliment: man and woman, male and female, gay and straight, spiritual and physical, East and West Berlin, sacred and profane, creator and creation, god and mortal.

Exquisite Corpse

Throughout her adult life, Hedwig has found healing, even salvation, in the act of turning her many tragedies into art (not unlike Eugene O'Neill and other theatre artists). Her songs are the tale of her life. But she doesn't see at first that the creation of songs from her pain mirrors the creation of Tommy from her need.

She also doesn't see until late in the show that her relationship with Tommy is very close to her relationship with Yitzhak. Like many people, she's repeating her mistakes without knowing it. Hedwig married Yitzhak to get him out of Croatia, just as Luther married Hansel to get him out of East Berlin. Tommy started out singing backup for Hedwig, then became the star himself and left her behind. In "The Long Grift" and in other moments throughout the show, we see that Yitzhak is actually a strong performer himself. And he also has begun as Hedwig's lover and backup singer. Might Yitzhak break out like Tommy did, or is Hedwig determined to prevent that? Yitzhak *becomes* Tommy in "The Long Grift," now singing the lead with Hedwig as backup—just as it once happened with Tommy—and we find ourselves both inside that past narrative (reliving Hedwig's demotion to backup in the shadow of Tommy's ascension) and also outside that narrative in the here and now. Those who ignore history are doomed to repeat it, they're telling us.

Hedwig does finally realize that all the heartache may happen to her again, if she doesn't change course. But when she tries to reconcile with Yitzhak and suggest a more equal partnership, Yitzhak spits in her face. He knows why she's worried, and he also knows he doesn't need her anymore. He certainly doesn't need her abuse. In the film version, Yitzhak sees an audition notice for *Rent* and, like Tulsa in *Gypsy*, decides to go off on his own.

Just as Frankenstein's monster did, Tommy turns on Hedwig, in a way "killing" her career. But finally Hedwig understands that she doesn't really need Tommy, that in fact she *is* Tommy, as much as he ever was. When Tommy at last offers an apology in the form of a reprise of "Wicked Little Town," Hedwig is finally able to let go of her anger and her hurt.

Now, for the first time in years, Hedwig can see clearly. She finally understands that she can be whole without another person. She makes peace with her past tragedies, with her gender deformity, with her place in the world, creating art and sharing it with an audience. Interestingly, when Tommy sings this musical apology, he introduces it as a song Hedwig wrote—the first time he's ever publicly acknowledged her help—but that fact gives the song so many layers of meaning. If Hedwig wrote it, we have to read it in several contexts. Certainly, it applies to the Hedwig/Tommy relationship the way a pop song may seem to be written just for us at any given moment in life. But it could also be Hansel singing to his mother. Or it could be Hansel singing to Hedwig.

The wicked little town that Hedwig must escape is *inside*, not outside. It's not about running away; it's about changing the way she sees the world. And of course, in Hedwig's life the stranger, the person who causes pain, has always been Hedwig herself. Tommy was created by Hedwig in her own image; Tommy *is* Hedwig in many ways. Luther treated Hansel just as Hedwig treated Yitzhak, so again, Luther *was* Hedwig in certain ways. And when Hansel left East Berlin, he took on his mother's identity and name; here again, Hedwig *is* her mother in certain ways. But the reprise of "Wicked Little Town" could also be the older Hedwig singing to her younger self, telling her that Luther was not the "other half," that he was not worth the profound sacrifice.

Notably, the first time we hear "Wicked Little Town," it doesn't really end. The music does stop, but it never comes to a satisfying close as most songs do. It is, in a sense, unfinished, perhaps because the journey it describes is still unfinished. In most musical theatre scores, we hear the full version of a song first, then later a shorter version as a reprise. But in *Hedwig and the Angry Inch*, the first version we hear is the incomplete version (because Hedwig, its author, is still incomplete), and only when we hear the reprise of "Wicked Little Town" do we finally get a full version, with a longer bridge in the middle, and a clearly delineated, extended ending. Are we to understand that one of Hedwig's most deeply felt songs can only be finished—can only be *whole*—when Hedwig herself is finally whole?

Lift Up Your Hands!

The ending of *Hedwig and the Angry Inch* is a source of great debate. Mitchell refuses to analyze it or define it, hoping that audiences will take from it what they need. It is, in many ways, a fairy tale as scary, as violent, as cautionary, and as hopeful as the original Grimm Brothers' stories. And like the great children's fairy tales, audiences take from Hedwig's story and its ending what they need at that moment in their lives. Just as there are multiple lessons and interpretations of the great fairy tales (read Bruno Bettelheim's excellent *The Uses of Enchantment* for more on that topic), so too there are many different lessons and interpretations left wide open at the end of *Hedwig*. Each of us sees in it what we need to see; each of us finds in the show the healing we seek.

The end of the show leaves so many questions open. Did the action of the show actually move from Hedwig's concert to Tommy's concert, or is that in Hedwig's mind? Has Hedwig actually *become* Tommy? Or is the actor playing Hedwig now playing Tommy? Or has Hedwig found the Tommy inside herself? Has something magical taken place at the end, or are we watching two brilliant theatre artists (Mitchell and Trask) constructing an overarching metaphor? The fact that Hedwig finally rejects the magical and metaphysical in the "Wicked Little Town" reprise might suggest that something magical has not taken place at the end.

If the scene actually changes to Tommy's concert, that raises another question. Since we are the audience at Hedwig's concert for most of the show, in effect playing a role ourselves, have *we* switched roles and are we now the audience at Tommy's concert? Since the entire show takes place in this theatre as we're watching it, why would the authors suddenly insert the show's only scene change just minutes before the show ends? The rest of the show is brilliantly constructed enough to suggest the authors wouldn't do that. But can we draw that conclusion with certainty? No. *Hedwig* breaks other rules; maybe it breaks this one too.

Or is this transformation entirely an *internal* one for Hedwig? Since Tommy came from Hedwig, since literally everything that made Tommy a star was Hedwig's invention, what does it mean when the stage direction in the script says, "She has become Tommy in concert"? Are we to take that literally or metaphorically? Perhaps she has rediscovered her male side—the side she "gave" to Tommy—and is finally whole again, healed, reborn, connected once more with her other half. That the script refers to her after this as "Hedwig/Tommy" suggests that Hedwig's two halves have at last made peace with each other in the same body, that she is now a whole person with her male and female sides finally in balance. Hedwig and Tommy now co-exist inside Hedwig. At last, she has reclaimed her male half—her Hansel—and she/he is going to be okay.

Hedwig's Foremothers

Finally, the reprise of "Wicked Little Town" segues without dialogue into the finale, "Midnight Radio," Hedwig's declaration of independence, a paean to singing your own song, a visceral Patti Smith–style anthem. Now healed, now whole, perhaps Hedwig may even end her performing career, since she no longer needs the healing it promises. And like Prospero freeing his servant Ariel at the end of *The Tempest*, here Hedwig releases Yitzhak from his indentured servitude, giving him the same freedom she is claiming for herself. But in the moment when Hedwig sings, "Lift up your hands," and everyone in the audience throws their hands in the air, many with tears streaming down their faces, some with eyes closed, it's clear that this is healing as religious experience for everyone in the theatre, recalling the effect the great tent revival preachers of the 1930s had on their audiences.

Or maybe Hedwig will continue her career, but with a new message for audiences. She's not just whole now; she's also been healed artistically, becoming one with her idols, and now that *she's* healed, she can heal *us*. From the first moments of the show, when we meet Hedwig in a denim patchwork costume reminiscent of *Foxy Brown*, we know that this is a show about female strength and independence. In this final song, Hedwig toasts to the great divas of rock—strong, independent women who made their own way, most of them *after* their men were gone. She invokes the names of Patti Smith, Tina Turner, Yoko Ono, Aretha Franklin, Nona Hendryx, and the iconic, once ubiquitous Nico. And finally, Hedwig toasts to herself; now *she* belongs among the pantheon of great divas. She too can now heal through her rock and roll.

Interestingly, most of these divas led lives similar in some details to Hedwig's. Patti Smith began as a painter, became a playwright while dating Sam Shepard, then began performing accompanied poetry readings and, finally, early, proto-punk rock songs. It wasn't until she left behind the influences of the men in her life that she became a force to be reckoned with, as one of the leaders of the New Wave movement. Tina Turner came to fame as part of a duo with her abusive husband, Ike. In 1975 she divorced him, but her career was in trouble. Finally, in 1984, she staged a rock-and-roll comeback like few had ever seen, and she became a bigger star than she had ever been with Ike. Like Hedwig, Turner never shied away from her ugly past and was willing to talk about the dark places she had been and her journey back to the light.

Yoko Ono was for a very long time seen as nothing more than John Lennon's wife, but she was a serious artist in her own right, and it wasn't until after his murder in 1980 that Ono, now relatively free of the shadow of Lennon's genius, was finally taken seriously. Aretha Franklin came from a broken home. Her career, under the management of her husband Ted White, began to hit the skids in 1966 and Columbia records decided not to renew her contract. White left her, and in her despair she considered leaving the music business. But now on her own, without White managing her, she got picked up by Atlantic Records and was given almost complete artistic control of her work. She recorded several songs, including the now legendary "Respect," and she soared to the top. Though Nona Hendryx had success for years singing backup for and working with men like David Byrne, Alice Cooper, and Bootsy Collins, she found her greatest success in her own solo career, writing and performing some very innovative rock and roll. The singly named Nico was a model, film actress, and singer with the Velvet Underground before going on to her own solo career. It is rumored that she had affairs with Bob Dylan, Brian Jones, Iggy Pop, Lou Reed, Jim Morrison, Jackson Browne, and several other rock icons, but she found lasting success and legendary status as a solo artist. Significantly, in the 1995 film *Nico Icon*, she said, "I don't have any limits, I don't need to be outside to feel like I'm outside . . . My only regret—I was born a woman instead of a man."

Hedwig also mentions LaVern Baker, the great 1950s R&B singer, in the song "Wig in a Box." But this brief reference holds more meaning that one might expect. Baker's career mirrors Hedwig's in interesting ways, including a surprising parallel to Tommy's theft of Hedwig's songs, and the discrimination that both Baker and Hedwig faced. According to the Rock and Roll Hall of Fame:

> A versatile vocalist, LaVern Baker proved capable of melding blues, jazz and R&B styles in a way that made possible the emergence of a new idiom: rock and roll. During her time at Atlantic Records (1953–62), Baker cut half a dozen singles that rose to high positions on both the pop and R&B charts, including "Tweedle Dee" and "Jim Dandy." Coming at a time when jazz singing was swiftly evolving into an earthier, more down-home and emotionally fervent style known as rhythm & blues, Baker proved to be one of the key vocalists who furthered that transition. As an R&B pioneer, Baker suffered from the segregationist impulses of the larger culture by having her songs "covered" by a white singer, Georgia Gibbs, whose sanitized versions greatly outsold Baker's own. Because mainstream white pop stations were reluctant to play "race records," artists like Baker and Little Richard lost considerable airplay, sales and income from the cover syndrome.

But these rock divas aren't Hedwig's only foremothers. Though glam rock seems to be the most pronounced influence on *Hedwig and the Angry Inch* and its central character, another less obvious but still very important influence is the great Marlene Dietrich. Like Hedwig, Dietrich was famous for her heavy eye shadow, her exaggerated eyelashes, her deeper than usual voice, and her overt yet still somehow subtle sexuality. Like Hedwig, Dietrich left Germany for America, in Dietrich's case, just before the rise of the Nazis. (Hitler actually invited her to return to make movies for the Third Reich. She refused.) Like Hedwig, Dietrich's sexuality was very ambiguous. She was often seen in men's formal wear, both on-screen and in her private life. In her first film, the now legendary *The Blue Angel* (1930), Dietrich not only performed her signature tune, "Falling in Love Again," in full men's evening wear, she also flirted shamelessly during the song with the women in her audience. Later in her career, Dietrich became even more famous for her one-woman concerts—and for her furs. She often sang songs written for men about women ("I've Grown Accustomed to Her Face," for example), and was always relatively open about her very intense lesbian love affairs while in Hollywood. Interestingly for *Hedwig* fans, Dietrich appeared in one film with glam rocker David Bowie, 1979's *Just a Gigolo*. The great film director Billy Wilder described her as "a strange combination of the femme fatale, the German hausfrau [housewife] and Florence Nightingale." Mightn't the same mix apply to Hedwig?

The other major influence on Hedwig and *Hedwig* is Bowie and his character Ziggy Stardust. His 1972 album, *Ziggy Stardust and the Spiders from Mars*—and the subsequent concert tour and film—revolutionized rock and roll. First of all, the album told a fully formed story about the doomed messiah, Ziggy Stardust. It's true, The Who had done it first with *Tommy*, but Bowie took it further. *Ziggy Stardust* was also the beginning of the marriage of science fiction and rock that would last through the '70s and into the '80s. And *Hedwig*'s song "The Origin of Love" has its parallels in the *Ziggy Stardust* song "Soul Love." Another song on the album, "Lady Stardust," extols the virtues of cross-dressing. The other big innovation was the confident and skillful transformation of rock and roll into a theatrical experience. CultureVulture.com says of Bowie and *Stardust*, "What's surprising, viewing this film after reading innumerable magazine articles looking back at the then-shocking theatricality of the *Ziggy* performances, is how straightforward a rock show this actually is. Aside from Bowie's wardrobe, there's very little of the spectacle that bands like Kiss and Alice Cooper would bring to American arenas only a few years later. It's not the kind of overblown, Vegas-esque extravaganza so many acts, from U2 to Britney Spears, take on the road these days. It's just a really good rock concert. In 1973, that was enough."

But it was also *dramatic*, giving audiences not just an evening of songs, of many separate experiences, but instead one full, unified, dramatically coherent experience. There was a unity to the *Ziggy Stardust* album and concerts that was still pretty new. British commentator James Littlewood wrote:

> Of all David Bowie's many distinctive personae, none have done more to lodge this most ingenious of British artists in the world's consciousness than his 1972 amalgam of the alien visitor and Christ-like rock star: Ziggy Stardust. Cheap glamour, spacemen and ambiguous sexuality surface throughout the loosely conceptualised collection that is *The Rise and Fall of Ziggy Stardust and the Spiders from Mars*. If its premise sounds faintly ludicrous, then inspired and dramatic songs such as "Starman" and "Five Years" dispel all doubts about Bowie's genius, and the theatrically tragic "Rock 'n' Roll Suicide" brings the album and its fictional protagonist to a close. As a cultural and musical signpost, *Ziggy Stardust* points simultaneously backwards to early rock & roll and forward to the simpler, tougher inclinations of late-1970s punk and New Wave rock. As one of the defining rock albums of the 20th century, its influence is immeasurable.

Like Dietrich's, Ziggy Stardust's sexuality was ambiguous, his performances electrifying, his influence impossible to fully comprehend. Much of rock and roll had become rather safe and commercial by 1972. Bowie changed that. Rock again became dangerous, sexual, ambiguous, rebellious, angry, and, most importantly, confusing and annoying to adults. Most subversively, it argued that sexuality *can* be fluid and ambiguous, that sexuality doesn't have to fit comfortably into preordained categories. That scared the hell out of many parents. Bowie and his experiments not only helped give birth to the glam-rock movement, but also to the slightly later but parallel punk movement.

The other big musical influence on *Hedwig* is the godfather of glam rock, Iggy Pop, who, along with his band the Stooges, redefined rock and roll from 1969 to 1973 and created the musical and thematic vocabulary of glam rock and, later, punk rock. *Rolling Stone* says, "Iggy Pop once billed himself as the 'world's forgotten boy,' but that is no longer the case. From fronting the proto-punk Stooges—the most despised band of the peace and love Sixties—Pop has gradually attained a position of veneration, and permanence, in the rock pantheon." The website IggyPop.org says:

> During the psychedelic haze of the late '60s, the grimy, noisy and relentlessly bleak rock & roll of the Stooges was conspicuously out of time. Like the Velvet Underground, the Stooges revealed the under-

side of sex, drugs and rock & roll, showing all of the grime beneath the myth. The Stooges, however, weren't nearly as cerebral as the Velvets. Taking their cue from the over-amplified pounding of British blues, the primal raunch of American garage rock, and the psychedelic rock (as well as the audience-baiting) of the Doors, the Stooges were raw, immediate and vulgar. Iggy Pop became notorious for performing smeared in blood or peanut butter, diving into the audience . . . In essence, the Stooges were the first rock & roll band completely stripped of the swinging beat that epitomized R&B and early rock and roll. During the late '60s and early '70s, the group was an underground sensation, yet the band was too weird, too dangerous to break into the mainstream. Following three albums, the Stooges disbanded, but the group's legacy grew over the next two decades, as legions of underground bands used their sludgy grind as a foundation for a variety of indie-rock styles, and as Iggy Pop became a pop cultural icon.

As with Dietrich and Bowie, so much of this could apply to Hedwig. But *Hedwig* also finds its roots in the surrealist movement of the 1920s, from which the phrase *exquisite corpse* comes, the name of the show's climactic number. It began as a parlor game, in which each player would write a phrase on a sheet of paper, then pass it to the next person to continue the phrase. The game expanded to images as well as words, and the surrealists adopted the game as a way of creating art. The name *exquisite corpse* or, in its original French, *cadavre exquis*, came from an early playing of the game that resulted in the now famous phrase "*le cadavre exquis boira le vin nouveau*"—"The exquisite corpse will drink the young [or newly made] wine." Nicolas Calas called the result of this kind of work "unconscious reality in the personality of the group" resulting from a process of "mental contagion." Hedwig certainly sees herself as that kind of creation, a perhaps awkward stitching together of the influences of her life—her mother's telling of the origin of love, Luther's initial love than abandonment, Hedwig's botched surgery, the various wigs (and resulting personalities) over the years, the harsh rejection by Tommy Speck, her final healing—all these pieces held together by Hedwig's courage and survivor's instinct, to form a mangled but proud human being—a sex-reversed Frankenstein's monster who, like Mary Shelley's original, does not want to harm anyone but just wants companionship. The label also refers to Hedwig's belief that she was separated from her "other half" and must be stitched back together again in order to be truly happy. It's not only a disturbing image but also a perfect one for the show.

Hed-Aches

Once *Hedwig and the Angry Inch* left its creators' loving arms, once rights were released to theatres across the country and around the world, Trask and Mitchell lost control of their baby. Productions of *Hedwig* began appearing everywhere, some very true to the creators' intent, others less so. Various websites went up with photos of dozens of Hedwigs and Yitzhaks from around the world. Unfortunately, too many actors who were in love with the show mounted their own vanity productions without the understanding or know-how to make this complex theatre piece work.

Despite the strength of the material, many of these productions suffered from major drawbacks. Many of these actors thought *Hedwig* was just a concert rather than a piece of theatre, just a chance to crack some jokes and do some glorified karaoke. While it's true that the show *appears* to be a concert, and that, in fact, audiences need not be consciously aware of more, the show is actually a carefully built piece of theatre with a relatively conventionally structured linear plot, including backstory, character development, rising action, a clear dramatic climax, falling action—all the elements of any good play or musical. That it looks like a concert on its surface is no excuse for directors and actors to give its dramatic elements short shrift or to ignore its complicated, naked, honest emotion. Some of these productions also view Yitzhak as nothing more than a backup singer, when he is clearly far more. As discussed earlier in this chapter, Yitzhak and Hedwig's relationship is not only dramatically but also thematically central to the story. To ignore Yitzhak's dramatic content and context is to lose a big part of Hedwig's journey.

Some productions took the few references in the show to punk rock and made that central to the show, refashioning Hedwig as a punk rocker instead of a glam rocker, making her more angry, flipping off the audience, cursing at the audience, and more. But this ignores two of the most important elements of the show. First, Hedwig must be genuinely warmhearted or the audience doesn't get emotionally involved and the show's payoff at the end loses all its impact. We need to *want* her to find her great love. Second, Hedwig chooses glam rock as her musical language specifically because glam was the only rock and roll movement in which gender was erased. Gender came fully back to center stage with the punkers in the '80s, so the gender-confused Hedwig would have never chosen a form of rock in which aggression and masculinity play so central a part. Again, placing Hedwig in a punk context robs the show of almost all its emotional heft and much of its thematic punch.

This show is deceptive. It seems so spontaneous, so casual, almost careless; but it's really a very carefully built show that doles out tiny details of character and plot, one by one, sometimes unnoticed, and those details slowly become a magnificent mosaic in which a clear picture of Hedwig and her life journey emerges in the second half of the show. A careful, thoughtful look at the show and its influences offers proof positive that *Hedwig and the Angry Inch* is one of the richest, most intelligent, most literate, most beautifully wrought pieces of theatre in years, full of such complexity, such immense philosophical questions, such profound emotions. This is where the American musical theatre is headed, and it is a cause for celebration.

At the climax of *Hedwig and the Angry Inch*, the musical about the healing power of pop music, Hedwig sings "Midnight Radio," a reassuring power anthem about community and connection for those who love rock and roll. And the three central characters of *High Fidelity*, Rob, Dick, and Barry, are the guys Hedwig is singing to. To them, music is life. Unlike most musicals, *High Fidelity* is not a love story; it's not about whether Rob and his girlfriend Laura will get back together. This is a story about one man and his struggle to grow up, to learn to put others first. Rob is on a classic hero's quest to find his own best self, and rock and roll is there to help him.

High Fidelity is a story about experiencing music autobiographically, about using music to connect to others, about how music makes your personal pain somehow transcendent, but also about how music cannot supplant real life. What better form in which to tell that story than a rock musical? In this case, the form of storytelling is as important as the story itself—it is told in music, exclusively from Rob's point of view, and the narrator and hero are the same person, even though the hero has virtually no self-knowledge through much of the story. In the book *Jung and Shakespeare*, Barbara Rogers-Gardner describes Hamlet in a way that illuminates Rob as well: "All through the play, Hamlet has to look to others for identity, for knowledge of himself, and fails to find it. When he compares himself to others, he can suffer only pain and humiliation. Ultimately, philosophic abstractions do not solve his problem; only what Jung calls maturation can do that, and Hamlet runs out of time before maturation can occur."

But Rob doesn't.

Given all that, what better way to construct this score than in the musical vocabulary and language of Rob's life? Rob doesn't have a voice of his own yet, but his favorite artists can speak for him. The show's creators, Tom Kitt (music), Amanda Green (lyrics), and David Lindsay-Abaire (book) avoided the mistake that too many movies-to-musicals make: instead of rewriting the screenplay for the stage, they found a new form for this story that is organic to its narrative. Instead of just putting a movie up on stage and sticking some songs into it (as too many have done, for example, *The Full Monty*, *Dirty Rotten Scoundrels*,

Big, *Urban Cowboy*, and others), this team created something original that has a life—and rules—of its own. This show traffics in genuine rock and roll, with a score that delivers dramatically but that is also peppered with musical references to some of the great rock and pop artists of our time, the muscular American rock sound of Bruce Springsteen, the raw rage of Guns N' Roses, the intellectual playfulness of Talking Heads, the fierce defiance of Aretha Franklin, the smoky groove of Percy Sledge, the naked emotion of Ben Folds, the driving cynicism of Billy Joel. But the use of music isn't always straightforward; sometimes it's ironic, even snide. Since we're witnessing this story through the filter of Rob's mind, the musical models for the various songs in the show even tell us how Rob feels about the people singing, through the voices and sounds his subconscious mind assigns to them. This score isn't just pastiche for its own sake, a crazy quilt of past musical sounds; this is a show that uses music as carefully and cleverly as it uses dialogue to tell its story—comically, sarcastically, and also movingly.

Though some will object to the label, the music of *High Fidelity* is the music of the so-called slackers, America's latest Lost Generation, those on the cusp between the Baby Boomers and Generation X, men (usually) for whom popular music forges a deep emotional connection in ways that most people would never understand, men who choose not to play by the majority rules, rejecting money, family, and career as life goals, in favor of an obsessive dedication to the music of their lives. In Nick Hornby's novel on which the *High Fidelity* movie and musical were based, Rob says:

> It's not like collecting records is like collecting stamps, or beermats, or antique thimbles. There's a whole world in here, a nicer, dirtier, more violent, more peaceful, more colorful, sleazier, more dangerous, move loving world than the world I live in; there is history, and geography, and poetry, and countless other things I should have studied at school, including music.

But what is the cost of this obsession, of this "relentless triviality," as the novel puts it? In Act I, Rob says, "People worry about kids playing with guns or watching violent videos, but nobody worries about kids listening to thousands—literally *thousands*—of songs about heartbreak, rejection, and loss. Did I listen to pop music because I was miserable or was I miserable because I listened to pop music?" Perhaps both are true—and not just for Rob, but for many Americans who came of age in the 1960s and 1970s. Before the 1960s, pop music was an accompaniment to life; but from that point forward, pop music was an integral, elemental *part* of life.

High Fidelity is a show that loves pop music fervently, but one that also recognizes its addictive dangers and its false promises. Is it enough to know that someone else is in pain, too, if they don't offer a roadmap out of that pain? As Pete Townshend says, "Music changes the way you live in the world. It changes the way you see it. But it doesn't change the world itself."

Page to Stage

Hornby's brilliant 1995 novel wowed the critics. The *New York Times Book Review* said, "Mr. Hornby captures the loneliness and childishness of adult life with such precision and wit that you'll find yourself nodding and smiling. *High Fidelity* fills you with the same sensation you get from hearing a debut record album that has more charm and verve and depth than anything you can recall." London's *Guardian* said, "Reading *High Fidelity* is like listening to a great single. You know it's wonderful from the minute it goes on, and as soon as it's over, you want to hear it again because it makes you feel young, and grown-up, and puts a stupid grin on your face all at the same time. If this book was a record, we would be calling it an instant classic. Because that's what it is." Salon.com wrote, "*High Fidelity*, the popular first novel by British author Nick Hornby, is like reading from an old diary—at once hilarious and pathetic, the stories of romantic engagements and disengagements are often an embarrassing reminder of who you once were." A film version was released in 2000 starring John Cusack and Jack Black.

Rock composer Tom Kitt (who would go on to write the Pulitzer Prize–winning rock musical *Next to Normal*) and lyricist Amanda Green (daughter of legendary Broadway and film lyricist and bookwriter Adolph Green) began working on a stage adaptation of the novel, and found a willing partner in up-and-coming New York playwright David Lindsay-Abaire (*Fuddy Meers*, *Rabbit Hole*). *High Fidelity* the musical became the new *Company* for a new generation and a new American culture, the story of a single man trying to make a human connection in an increasingly frenzied and digitized world. The musical ran for a month in Boston, then moved to Broadway, closing after only eighteen previews and fourteen regular performances, in a wildly overproduced physical production and with sadly conventional musical comedy direction, chock full of frantic, almost farce-like speed; broad, shallow caricatures instead of real individuals; a gigantic trick set (the kind often designed to camouflage the flaws in a weak show); and a surprising lack of love for the music at the heart of the story. The achingly, beautifully underwritten script, full of heavy words often left unsaid, was bulldozed under, and raced through as if it were *Dames at Sea*. And though every number in the show is its own rock concert in Rob's head, the Broadway production staged the songs as if they were in *Beauty and the Beast*. Conventional, standard, not worthy of the fireworks of Aretha Franklin or Pat Benatar. The show's script and score both love and respect the music, but the Broadway production *mocked* the music.

The director Walter Bobbie was quoted in an essay by Zachary Pincus-Roth for the (never printed) Broadway souvenir program, saying, "I almost hate to say this but I'm going to: It feels to me like *Seinfeld: The Musical*. *Seinfeld* was a glorious celebration of just ordinary lives being lived." He couldn't have been more wrong. *High Fidelity* isn't about ordinariness and it's not glorious; it's about acute pain and loneliness, and the connective and destructive power of art. The one thing it's *not* is a musical comedy.

Is it possible that Bobbie didn't understand the show any more than the critics did? Did he fail at the most fundamental rule of musical theatre, that all the collaborators always have to be doing the same show? Looking back, it's now clear that Bobbie was directing a completely different musical than Kitt, Green, and Lindsay-Abaire were writing. Bobbie's artistic influences were shows like *Guys and Dolls* and *Footloose*. The writers' artistic influences were *Rent* and *Hedwig and the Angry Inch*, along with Bruce Springsteen, Aretha Franklin, and The Who. Who thought this marriage would work? The producers' efforts at mainstreaming the show, at making it palatable to the tourists, were exactly what sunk it.

It seemed clear to many observers that had the show opened as a more intimate, modest production off Broadway and if it had been accepted for what it was, a dark but funny rock concept musical, it probably would have enjoyed a more respectable run. But soon after closing, thanks in part to its cast album, theatres across America and abroad were clamoring for production rights.

David Kaufman wrote in the December 2006 *Vanity Fair*, before the show opened:

> The last thing theater mavens need is another pop-rock musical based on a cult film. But with a book by the wily David Lindsay-Abaire, *High Fidelity* is apt to have the gnawing fascination of both the original Nick Hornby novel and the 2000 film starring John Cusack, concerning a record-store owner and troubled soul. Lindsay-Abaire defied categorization and stunned theatergoers last season with the searing *Rabbit Hole*, about a family coping with the death of a child. When the playwright first heard that a musical version of *High Fidelity* was in the works, he thought it sounded misguided. "I had read the book and seen the movie and I had loved them both immensely," he said during the show's Boston tryout, prior to its December opening on Broadway. "Frankly, I was quite dubious about the idea of someone turning it into a musical." He was converted, however, when he heard several of the songs written by Tom Kitt and Amanda Green. "They were really ironic and soulful and very, very funny," he added.

Variety said of the show in New York, "*High Fidelity* is a musical that celebrates the power of pop culture with wit, verve and a killer beat . . . It's really about growing up while still honoring one's self-defining music." Michael Kuchwara of the Associated Press said, "Its charms are considerable and don't be surprised if you fall under its spell." But most of the critics didn't understand the show, its cultural references, or its musical sources. They mistook the shallowness of its direction and design for shallowness in its writing. The show's most honest, most truthful elements were those most under attack from the mainstream critical establishment.

Several reviews of the Broadway production complained that the role of Laura was underwritten, that we don't spend enough time with her, that she mostly only appears inside songs. What none of them understood is that this isn't a story about Rob and Laura; it's a story about Rob. The original production tried too hard—in this regard but also in others—to make it a musical comedy and to make it a love story. It's not. And neither was the novel or the film. Additionally, the audience is getting this story through the filter of Rob's mind. If Laura can be two-dimensional at times, perhaps it's less the show's latent sexism and more that Rob only understands her on a two-dimensional level (at least at the beginning). And arguably, we never actually meet Laura, just Rob's obviously biased *perception* of who Laura is. But with Rob's emotional growth comes more complex storytelling. And since Rob is the sole conduit for information to us, we go through the same gradual awakening and understanding that Rob does.

When a musical operates the way *High Fidelity* does, when its opening number makes musical references to U2, REM, Lenny Kravitz, Talking Heads, The Who, Otis Redding, and Fountains of Wayne, how could anyone expect the aging critics of the old media to understand it? *High Fidelity* doesn't use music the way Rodgers and Hammerstein used it. In old-fashioned musicals, music was just a vehicle; here, it is the point. Here, the conventions and mechanics of theatre music are deconstructed. In a certain way, *High Fidelity* works very much like *Hedwig and the Angry Inch*, with stand-alone rock songs. In *Hedwig*, these presentational songs are justified because we're at a rock concert. In *High Fidelity*, they're justified because we're at the rock concert in Rob's head. Pop music isn't just Rob's *voice*; it's his *soul*, for better or worse.

The Heart of Rock and Roll

But a pop/rock score isn't all that makes *High Fidelity* special. After all, the early years of the new millennium brought the rock musical back to commercial prominence, even on staid, old-fashioned Broadway. After a brief period of mediocre revivals of *Man of La Mancha*, *The Music Man*, *The Pajama Game*, *Bells Are Ringing*, *Brigadoon*, and other (now creaky) classics, Broadway opened its arms again to rock musicals. It wasn't *Rent* or *Hedwig* that changed New York commercial theatre, but more likely the "new" *Rents*: *Jersey Boys*, *Hairspray*, *Spring Awakening*, *In the Heights*, and others.

What made *High Fidelity* special was the one thing its Broadway team seemed to miss entirely—its *soul*. This was a genuinely alternative show, one that avoided "show tunes," linear storytelling, and the fourth wall, one peppered liberally with the word *fuck*, and one that offered up only the most tentative of happy endings. This was a show that followed Stephen Sondheim's prime directive that content dictates form, a lesson the show's Broadway director and design team apparently had not learned. These characters are people who live outside the confines of mainstream American life, outside the mainstream economic system, outside the mainstream culture. And so the creators of *High Fidelity* wrote a show that lives outside the conventions of mainstream musical theatre, a show that uses music as more than accompaniment, a show that plays around with structure in the way many recent American indie films have, a show that grapples head-on with real human pain. Everyone in this story is damaged. And though Rob is our hero, he's also a real jackass sometimes. Many musicals today can claim that they reject the Rodgers and Hammerstein model, but only a few can claim that they use music and lyrics in genuinely new ways.

Tom Kitt and Amanda Green haven't just imitated Aretha Franklin in the song "She Goes"; instead they've actually written an Aretha Franklin song, a song Franklin might actually sing. It's not a Broadway version of Franklin's style or a parody; it *is* that style. Likewise, they don't just imitate Al Green and Percy Sledge with the finale, "Turn the World Off"; they've actually written a new R&B anthem worthy of Green or Sledge. In a review of the first regional production at New Line Theatre in St. Louis, Paul Friswold wrote in the *Riverfront Times*, "The music's homage to real-world rock songs achieves perfect pitch when Bruce Springsteen arrives to provide Rob guidance in the greatest Springsteen song Springsteen never wrote."

Instead of just writing a score that references lots of pop/rock songs and artists for comic effect—or worse yet, as a commercial gimmick upon which the whole show has to stand or fall—we actually hear the world through Rob's ears. We get inside Rob's brain and think about how this pop music snob hears the world around him. The musical choices are *dramatic* choices, not entertainment choices. Just as Rob does in his conscious life, in his subconscious life (i.e., the show) he uses pop music to try and figure out the people and events around him. Music is how he makes sense of his world, although he eventually learns that his music doesn't hold all the answers. For that, he has to dig down into his own heart.

As most good musicals (and films and plays) do, *High Fidelity* follows Sondheim's Ten-Minute Rule: that writers can do anything they want—directly address the audience, establish a half boy/half bat or a post-op transsexual as the hero, fracture time, use four-letter words, introduce a man-eating plant or a town where you have to pay to pee, ignore the fourth wall, play scenes out in the audience, use rock music, really *anything*—as long as they establish the rules for the evening in the first ten minutes. And *High Fidelity* is a textbook example. The show's opening number accomplishes so much: it introduces the main characters and the central conflict, but it also introduces the way music will be used for the evening.

Where the Music Takes Us

The show's opening song, "The Last Real Record Store on Earth," establishes the central conflict of the show, that Rob and his cohorts see themselves as more "real," more honest, more legitimate than the world around them, and that this warped self-image has led to exclusionary, sheltered, walled-off lives. The hyperbole of the song's title says it all. It's not just a record store, it's the only record store left *on the planet* that is authentic, whose staff understands the value of great music. But here also is the overarching metaphor for the entire story, in these guys' obsessive deification of vinyl, a symbol of the past. Rob is still living in his childhood, when vinyl was everything. While 8-tracks came and went, vinyl rules over all. But Rob must break with the past and join the rest of humanity in the present. Only in the end when Rob sells his 45s late in the show—breaking with at least *part* of his vinyl collection, the *core* of his collection—can he find emotional maturity and real human connection.

But this opening number doesn't just tell the audience how the show will use music; it also tells us a great deal about *what* music these guys like, which of course is one of the most important things to know in this world. Rob hears himself and his friends in the voices of a surprisingly varied array ofartists. "Last Real Record Store" is built on so many real-world models: "Where the Streets Have No Name" and "In God's Country" (U2), "Drive" (REM), "Are You Gonna Go My Way" (Lenny Kravitz), "Won't Get Fooled Again" (The Who), "Try a Little Tenderness" (Otis Redding), and "Bright Future in Sales" (Fountains of Wayne). There's even a short quote of "Life During Wartime" by Talking Heads, a song about the oppression of social and cultural expectations on young people. What other song could ever incorporate such diverse sounds and yet still function as satisfying theatre, doing all the heavy lifting of establishing style, plot, and character? The *High Fidelity* writers are no tourists in this world. They live here with Rob, Dick, and Barry. But they also really know how to tell a story in the theatre.

In "Desert Island Top 5 Breakups," Rob sees himself as a real rock and roller in the classic sense—masculine, strong—as he channels The Who and Elvis Costello. But Rob's best friend Liz is a ballbuster, so Rob hears her song "She Goes" as an aggressive Aretha Franklin anthem, in the tradition of "Think." He's in control of the situation when he's channeling The Who, but he isn't when Liz is channeling Aretha. Rob's rival, the faux-Eastern therapist Ian, sounds like the Eastern experiments of

George Harrison and the Beatles, a group Rob mocks in the novel. (Barry thinks the Beatles belong on the list of Top Five Bands or Musicians Who Will Have to Be Shot Come the Musical Revolution.) The models for Ian's song are Beatles' songs like "Within You Without You" and "Across The Universe," but also maybe a little Styx (what would Barry say about that?), and a passing reference to Michael Jackson.

When Rob feels defeated by Laura, her voice in his fantasies is the sexy, hard-rocking sound of Pat Benatar or Heart. And in "Number 5 with a Bullet," the Dream Laura is teasing Rob—in his own lingo—declaring that though she was lower on his chart before ("Desert Island Top 5 Breakups"), she has now risen up into his Top 5. For those who don't follow the Billboard pop charts, a bullet (a black dot, really) next to a song on the chart means the song is higher this week than last week. Perhaps this is language the real Laura would never use, and might not even know, but in Rob's nightmare the Dream Laura knows all.

The club singer Marie La Salle, on the other hand, is far less intimidating, and enters Rob's consciousness with a more mellow, more soulful Indigo Girls sound. Finally, as the first act draws to a close, and the boys see the possibility of some sort of individual successes, they became joyful and playful, evoking the pure pop sounds of Bow Wow Wow and Coldplay.

In Act II, Rob's song "I Slept With Someone Who Slept with Lyle Lovett" becomes a Lyle Lovett song (obviously). Laura's companion song, "I Slept With Someone Who Handled Kurt Cobain's Intervention," even quotes Nirvana's "Smells Like Teen Spirit" at the end. Rob gets musical advice from both Neil Young and Bruce Springsteen, both in fantasy and both singing songs you'd swear they had actually recorded. The fantasy Young's "Exit Sign" could easily sit beside the real Young's forlorn ballad "Heart of Gold," and you'd almost think the fantasy Springsteen's "Goodbye and Good Luck" might have been on an album alongside "Thunder Road," "Born to Run," and "The River"—except that it ever so gently mocks the Boss's blue collar persona. Rob's cry of despair, "Cryin' in the Rain," evokes the sad/angry songs of Billy Joel and Rufus Wainwright. When Rob fantasizes about assaulting Ian, where the movie shows us three fantasy beatings, the stage show gives us three acts of musical violence, suggesting Guns N' Roses, then the Beastie Boys, then Snoop Dog and Dr. Dre. These aren't Rob's usual musical personas, but this is violence to Rob, *musical* violence. When Rob finally achieves the rumblings of nascent self-awareness, his heartfelt apology to Laura for his emotional shortcomings comes in the form of a ballad in the style of Ben Folds. As the show draws to a close, Barry emerges as the pop star he always dreamed he'd be, first channeling some Jim Morrison (to shore up his pop music street cred), then the powerful, emotional, sexually charged R&B anthem "Turn the World off (And Turn You On)," taking inspiration from Marvin Gaye, Al Green, and Percy Sledge. This is, after all, what pop does best—expresses deeply felt, soul-cracking emotion.

But the lyric of this song says more than it pretends. Barry, Dick, and Rob have all learned that other people matter, that a life of self-absorption is a life lived alone. They guys have always turned the world off, but only now do they understand the joy in turning someone else on. Dick has found Anna, Barry has found his audience, and Rob is ready to grow up and put Laura before himself. It's not a fully happy ending, but it's a start.

Altogether, the score for *High Fidelity* is extremely well-wrought and easily passes the primary test of the strength of a theatre score: If the songs are removed, does the story still make sense? If the story makes sense without the songs, that means the songs aren't doing their share of storytelling and don't need to be there. With *High Fidelity*, as with most of the best musicals, a great deal of story and character is developed inside and through the songs. The opening number, "The Last Real Record Store on Earth," is equal in many ways to the great opening numbers in shows like *Into the Woods*, *Ragtime*, *Company*, *Bat Boy*, and *A Chorus Line*, establishing the main characters, the central situation, the tone of the show, the musical language of the show, and any rules that may be broken during the evening. It interweaves music and dialogue, it gives us important information about personalities, lands some solid punch lines, establishes its street cred in the rock and pop world, and establishes the energy and intensity for the rest of the show. The number also tells us straight out that Rob is the main character, not Rob and a girlfriend.

But music is also used as mood, as commentary, as joke. There is great care and intelligence behind the intentionally empty lyric to "Exit Sign," the cultural cluelessness of the fictional Springsteen's "Good-bye and Good Luck," and the grand flamboyance of the meek Dick's grand musical moments. But there's also Marie LaSalle's two songs: "Ready to Settle" foretells her own future one-nighter with Rob (or is it more of a commercial?), and her song "Terrible Things" starts as black comedy and becomes deadly serious as Rob tells us how everything got screwed up in the first place. The music for that song becomes a musical theme throughout the show, always adding color to a moment when Rob starts to understand himself better. It's a kind of self-knowledge theme that underlines the central story of whether Rob will finally start to grow up. Likewise it's the music that lends violence to Rob's fantasy attacks on Ian, allowing a live stage show to be less realistic with the violence, since the violence of the music already increases the intensity—and the humor—of the moment. In the movie, Dick throws an air conditioner at Ian; in the stage show, they throw Axl Rose at him.

High Fidelity

Like the titles of *Rent*, *Follies*, *Company*, and many other shows, the title of *High Fidelity* virtually swims in meaning. The phrase came into the American consciousness in the 1950s as a term that meant pure, authentic sound reproduction, after decades of AM radio and 78-rpm records.

But the technology of high-fidelity sound reproduction is, at its heart, a cheat—the idea is to imitate the sound of a concert hall, to fake the reality of a live performance, to fool the human ear. Obviously there is great value in that for music lovers, but it isn't real; it just *imitates* reality. And perhaps in that fact lies yet another metaphor for the life Rob is living when our story begins.

Still, the title goes much deeper than just technological considerations. To Rob and his cohorts, *fidelity* means more than faithfulness to sound quality; it means faithfulness to music as art, as spiritual experience, as religion, as life itself. They cling to the technology of LPs as many audiophiles still do today, believing that the sound is warmer and realer than the digital sound of CDs. Are they right, or is their position more emotional than factual?

Their fidelity to their LPs takes on even greater meaning, a kind of fake heroic outsider stance that fits nicely with the mindset of the true pop-music snob. We can argue with them over the LP versus CD issue, but now there's an even newer form of the debate, as more and more young people turn to MP3 digital audio files to be played on the ubiquitous iPod (the sound quality of which is actually inferior to that of CDs but still arguably better than LPs). In that context, what does Rob's fidelity to LPs mean? Does the LP stand in for his relationship to Laura—comfortable, familiar, though not really as good as it should be?

High Fidelity is about thirty-something misfits who have stopped growing after adolescence, who value descriptions and interpretations of life over life itself. These are men who honestly believe you can't be a serious person if you own fewer than five hundred records. But this story uncovers the worth in these guys as they find it in themselves and then finally find some success in life, love, and music. Here, as in real life, pop music is a double-edged sword, a haven for those who feel misunderstood or ignored, a place where someone else understands what we feel, both at our highest and at our lowest; but also an emotional trap as powerful as your parents' basement, a place to hide from the real world of real emotions too complicated for a pop lyric.

In the show, Rob can only win Laura after he sells his 45s (symbolically standing in for his vinyl collection as a whole) in order to pay her back the money he owes her. He must move from a world of self-gratification, exclusionary trivia, and obsessive list-making into a world of self-sacrifice and acceptance of the unknown and unsafe. And this happens at a funeral, marking the death of the Child Rob, so that he can be reborn as the Man Rob.

Part-Time Stoner

Rob is a quirky leading man for a musical, not nearly as happy as most musical comedy leads (Nathan Detroit, J. Pierrepont Finch, Harold Hill), but also not as tragically Shakespearean as most musical drama leads (Billy Bigelow, Sweeney Todd, Gaylord Ravenal). But they weren't nearly as dark or as complicated as Rob. He's closer kin to Chuck Baxter in *Promises, Promises*, the antihero who narrates his own story and on occasion even lies to us. And he shares a lot with Bobby in *Company*, a leading man taking a mostly interior journey, making a choice at the end of the show, but an ambiguous one. Watching both Rob and Bobby we are compelled to ask: Will his choice be the right one? Will he be happy? Will he stick with his decision? Will he finally commit to another person? All we see in these two shows are decisions at the final curtain, no firm resolution, no guarantee of a happy ending. After all, there are no happy endings in life; there's always a morning after.

But Rob is an unusual character for another reason. Though he is the narrator, he actually loses control of the story sometimes (somewhat like the Leading Player at the end of *Pippin*). Not only are we watching Rob in this show trying to grow up and find a real relationship, trying to navigate his way back to Laura; but we're also seeing Rob trying to navigate his own inner terrain. He is in charge here as narrator, but the characters he conjures up often do and say things Rob doesn't like. We see the first real cracks in his omniscient armor in the song "Number 5 with a Bullet," when his ex-girlfriend Jackie steps out of the number and refuses to go on. Rob tries to push her back into the line of his Top 5 Breakups, but she gives up her spot to Laura, despite Rob frantically screaming, "Not on the list, not on the list, not on the list!" He's neither omniscient nor omnipotent.

As the show progresses, more and more of the numbers get out of hand. The show sends the audience out to intermission with a palpable sense of hope; maybe Rob's going to be okay. But Act II takes it all back as we watch Rob fall victim to one humiliation after another. *High Fidelity* shares this structure—a happy Act I, and a dark Act II—with other shows like *Hair*, *Rent*, and many others.

As Act II of *High Fidelity* gets underway, Neil Young shows up to sing some nonsense about a tollbooth and chipping his "ol' tooth." Then Springsteen shows up and sings about plant closings and Veterans Day. The pop music is becoming less and less helpful and the story is becoming less and less controllable. But all this is in Rob's head, so *really* it's Rob's own mind that is becoming less helpful and less controllable, as he tries more and more to grapple with the complexity of the real world.

As Rob is subjected to repeated humiliations, as he slides and skids his way to rock bottom, his music becomes less able to save him. But this is the process Rob has to go through. He has to hit bottom before he can be "reborn" in line with the great hero myths. Many of the great world religions, myths, legends, and stories are built on the model of the hero myth, not incidentally including the Christ story, *Star Wars*, *The Wizard of Oz*, *Hair*, and other stories. Rob is Luke Skywalker. His beloved pop artists are his collective wise wizard, his Obi-Wan Kenobi. His music is his magic amulet, his light saber. Barry and Dick are his companions, his C-3PO and R2-D2. Perhaps Ian is the evil wizard he must do battle with, or maybe it's Rob himself who is his own evil wizard (as in many hero myths). And like every good hero myth, when Rob accomplishes his task (restoring balance to his own Force), he returns to his "village" (his fellow music fans) to share his new wisdom with them—in the form of *High Fidelity* itself.

But maybe the surface message of the story—that the key to a real relationship is to value the other person more than yourself—is only part of this story. Maybe the other part is that sometimes two people love each other and they still don't belong together. Maybe it's a lesson Rob hasn't yet learned before we leave him. It's important to remember that the novel actually takes the story one step further than the show and lets us see Rob and Laura back together for a while. Even though they may care about each other, do they really belong together? Late in the novel, Rob and Laura have a conversation that tells us pretty much all we need to understand about their relationship:

> "You used to care more about things like Solomon Burke than you do now," I tell her. "When I first met you, and I made you that tape, you were really enthused. You said—and I quote—it was so good that it made you ashamed of your record collection."
>
> "Shameless, wasn't I?"
>
> "What does that mean?"
>
> "Well, I fancied you. You were a DJ, and I thought you were groovy, and I didn't have a boyfriend, and I wanted one."
>
> "So you weren't interested in the music at all?"
>
> "Well, yes, a bit. And more so then than I am now. That's life, though, isn't it?"
>
> "But you see . . . That's all there is of me. There isn't anything else. If you've lost interest in that, you've lost interest in everything. What's the point of us?"
>
> "You really believe that?"
>
> "Yes. Look at me. Look at the flat. What else has it got, apart from records and CDs and tapes?"

But what's really going on here? If the relationship was begun on false pretenses, and if their future happiness depends on Rob changing himself completely, then how strong is this relationship? At the end of the novel, Rob says, "I'm always going to feel miserable about Laura going. That's what I've learned. So I should be happy that she's staying, right? That's how it should work, right? And that's how it does work. Kind of. When I don't think about it too hard."

It's the classic double-edged sword, and it's what makes *High Fidelity* not just a great novel but also a great work of musical theatre. After all, what separates musicals from plays is the abstract language of music itself, so powerful and so abstract that only it can express deep human emotions fully. Words alone can never express the love, longing, loss, or joy that music can, because those emotions are bigger and more complicated than mere words; it takes the primal language of music. And that's why, the cries of the music snobs notwithstanding, *High Fidelity* was always meant to be a musical. Not a Jerry Herman, happy-feet musical comedy, but an honest, adult, complicated piece of musical theatre. And that's exactly what it is.

The Mix Tape

Some pop music aficionados will tell you that the world is divided into two parts: those who understand the beauty and artistry of a great mix tape, and those who don't. Early in the *High Fidelity* script, Rob lays out some of the basic rules of making a mix tape:

> This, in case you don't know, is called a cassette. And yes, they still exist. I've used them pretty much my whole life to make mix-tapes. Very old school, I know. This one happens to be for Laura. I'm sorta in the dog-house with her, so . . . But you don't really need to know about that. What you do need to know is that the making of a great mix tape, like breaking up, is hard to do. You gotta kick off with a killer song, to grab attention. Then you gotta take it up a notch. But you don't wanna blow your wad, so then you gotta cool it off a notch with something soulful. Also, you can't have two tracks by the same artist side by side, unless you've done the whole thing in pairs and . . . Anyway, there are a lot of rules. I still haven't mastered them all yet, but . . . I'll figure it out eventually.

But what does a mix tape really mean? To some guys, a mix tape (or today, a mix CD) is the most personal, most heartfelt gift imaginable. On the surface, the mix tape is a gift, meant for the recipient's enjoyment, but really it's also for the giver of the gift. The guy wants the girl to know and understand him, but he doesn't have enough self-knowledge, at least consciously, to just explain himself in words. So he makes a mix tape, an expression of himself, a kind of autobiography, an explanation of his joys and fears and yes, his most awkward, most embarrassing emotions, those that could not be expressed in any other form. It's the most fully many men are ever able to reveal their innermost feelings, and in many ways it's a very potent window into its maker. But also, because this music is a part of his very soul, he is giving a girl a piece of himself. Like a class ring, but better. At least that's how the guys see it. At the end of the *High Fidelity* novel, Rob realizes he'd like to make Laura a mix tape with songs *she* would like instead of only songs *he* likes. He had been trying to change her with his mix tapes, *educate her*, but the purpose of a mix tape should be to share and to reveal oneself. Rob finally understands that.

A mix tape is a lot like meeting the friends, that pivotal moment in many relationships. The guy introduces his new girlfriend to the music he likes to listen to, and he hopes that she likes it as much as he does—or that she is at least open to hearing more of it. If she really doesn't like his music, that may reveal incompatibilities that wouldn't otherwise be discernible.

But a mix tape is also an artistic expression, connecting the maker of the tape to his favorite artists, making him almost a collaborator with them. In the same way that hip-hop artists sample other people's art to make new art—and the way the makers of musicals and films sometimes take the art of novelists and make new art from it—so too does Rob make new art from the work of other artists by giving the existing art new context and new meaning.

In a way, *High Fidelity* the musical is a mix tape itself, with Rob's record collection as its source material. We spend the evening listening to the voices of his rock and pop gods, to their music and lyrics (in fictionalized form, obviously). For two hours, we hear the world through Rob's ears. We hear a pissed-off woman as Aretha Franklin. We hear a hot girlfriend as Pat Benatar. The score is Rob's autobiographical mix tape, to share with us his love of music, and to reveal himself to us. Some audiences will love it; others won't completely understand it. Which is one of the reasons it didn't have a successful commercial run on Broadway. This show has a target audience that isn't the same audience that goes to Broadway shows. The people who embrace *High Fidelity* (and *Bat Boy*, *Assassins*, and *Urinetown*) are often the people who thought they didn't like musicals.

But like real mix tapes, *High Fidelity* the musical reveals Rob in ways he doesn't expect. In opening song, Rob sings, "I went where the music took me, and oh God, it took me here." The music didn't just take him to this physical place, running a used record store; it also took him to this emotional place, miserable and lonely, unable to connect to anyone except through music (and then only with fellow music lovers), full of too many romantic expectations, and most notably, a world built entirely on vinyl and cassettes, both outdated forms. He says in that same number that he's "sitting on a business that has zero growth potential." But at this point, his life itself also has zero growth potential. Just as his concrete life is centered on outdated forms of recording technology, so too is his inner life centered on outdated emotions and ideas about relationships that come from his high-school days. He tells us late in the show that he's been listening to his gut since he was fourteen, and also that he hasn't been able to forget a girl since he was fourteen. That seems to be the age where he's stuck emotionally—an incredibly turbulent, confusing age.

It's significant that Rob sees his store as the *last* real record store. Everyone else has moved on—in life and in sound-reproduction technology—but him. Early in the story, he has pride in that; later, he sees what's wrong with it. Only at the end, when he sells his 45s to pay back Laura, when he finally lets go of his vinyl (symbolically at least), can he heal his relationship with Laura and start to grow up.

It's a Problem

Once upon a time, Broadway welcomed complex, nuanced musical theatre, including shows like *Company*, *Follies*, *Cabaret*, *Nine*, *Sunday in the Park with George*, *Big River*, *Grand Hotel*, *Assassins*, *Jelly's Last Jam*, and *Hedwig and the Angry Inch.* But in the early years of the new millennium, nuance was not always welcome on Broadway, certainly not by the critics and tourist audiences. *High Fidelity* is a prime example. And the song "It's No Problem" is a perfect case study.

"It's No Problem" is a song that operates almost entirely on a subtextual level, like many of the songs in *Company*, *Follies*, and other intelligent musicals. And yet some critics used this song as an example of how *High Fidelity* is "about nothing." In reality, the exact opposite is true. This song is about so much, if you just listen to the lyric.

As the song begins, Rob has asked Dick to tell Barry that Laura broke up with him. Rob has just attacked Barry and he wants Dick to explain the extenuating circumstances to Barry, as a kind of apology. In Dick's mind, this is a real honor, an important assignment, to be Rob's "ambassador" to Barry, to be a solution to a problem. Dick doesn't have a lot of human interaction outside the record store, so this new and complicated situation is not only dramatic but exciting for him as well. He takes this seriously:

It's no problem,
No problem, Rob, you're on.
I'll tell him when I see him next:
"Rob says to tell you Laura's gone."
My schedule's pretty open,
So I've got some time today.
Plus I've got some other stuff to tell him anyway.
So I'll tell him when I tell him all the other stuff,

Or I could even call.
So it's no problem,
No problem at all.

As the song continues, Dick considers the optimal time and place for telling Barry, though as he thinks through the logistics of his assignment out loud, he worries that he may have offended Rob, who he knows is still hurting from the breakup. He even takes time to reassure Rob that he and Barry on are on Rob's side.

Part of the "joke" of the song is that Dick's life is so empty (by mainstream standards) that this offhand request from Rob seems monumental. But it also reminds us that Dick simply *feels* too much (as evidenced earlier by his "Hiroshima of the Soul"), and that he is profoundly empathetic, which is what will later save his relationship with Anna. This song tells us a lot about Dick, about his relationships with Rob and Barry, about the qualities Anna will find attractive in him, and about how closely intertwined Rob's, Dick's, and Barry's lives are.

And later in Act II, the reprise of "It's No Problem" goes even further in defining Dick, showing us how he has grown and changed, as any fully drawn character does. The reprise is Dick's declaration of independence from the "authority" of Barry. Long before either Rob or Barry learns the lessons they have to learn, Dick has learned his: "And I'm thinking it's not what you like that counts, but who you are . . ." Anna may like John Tesh—an unthinkable crime in this world—but she's also smart, pretty, nice, the right height, she has a great laugh, and she really likes Dick. Surely all those things outweigh John Tesh. Dick has finally realized that when pop music defines the world, the world can be pretty narrow. He now knows that actual human connection is more important and more satisfying than just listening to songs *about* human connection. He rejects the safe, insular world of Championship Vinyl for the less predictable, harder-to-navigate, real world, and in the process he becomes a whole person. Rob won't learn this lesson for two more scenes yet. There's even an argument to be made that Rob only learns his lesson by watching Dick's transformation. If Dick can suffer through John Tesh for Anna, maybe Rob can suffer through Art Garfunkel for Laura.

Without this song and its reprise, Dick's character would be far less well drawn; but, as with the rest of the show, too many of the critics refused to see what's going on under the surface, to recognize the complexity and honesty and truthfulness of the writing. Was this because the world of *High Fidelity* is just too foreign to the senior citizens who review most New York theatre? Or was it because Broadway has been so dumbed down in recent years that the critics are no longer accustomed to giving musicals the same thoughtfulness and respect that they routinely give to plays that lack music?

Ben Brantley wrote in his *New York Times* review, "The seeming credo of this production at the Imperial Theater can be found early in its lyrics: 'Nothin's great, and nothin's new, but nothin' has its worth.' This declaration is sung by the show's hero, the romantically bereft Rob, as he describes his uneventful life as the owner of a vinyl record store in Brooklyn . . . And that's a problem."

No, the problem is that Brantley can't see that that lyric reveals the central conflict of the show. It's not that Rob's life is uneventful; it's that his life is too self-involved and lacking in the joy that comes from a giving, two-way, adult relationship. The "nothin' " of the lyric refers on the surface to Rob's outer life, but also subtextually to his inner life. He is emotionally empty, running on the fumes of a once great (though immature) relationship. The "nothin' " that his and Laura's relationship has become has the comforts of familiarity and little effort, but it can't sustain either of them. Rob doesn't have enough self-knowledge at the beginning of the story to assess his own problem, so we have to read between the lines—as audiences do routinely with plays by Tennessee Williams, Arthur Miller, Edward Albee, and Lanford Wilson.

That the opening number ends with all the guys singing, "I wouldn't change a thing," tells us exactly what this show is about: the stagnation of a generation. Could there be a more powerful or clearer metaphor for stagnation than a used record store in the mid-1990s? Rob's story is the story of millions of people on the cusp between the Baby Boomers and Generation X, caught between cultural forces, the expectations of the previous generation, and world-shaking changes in technology. This is not a show about nothing, as some critics charged, and it's not the *Seinfeld* of musical theatre. It's a deeply felt, deeply authentic show about America (the UK in the novel) at the turn of the millennium.

Messing With Your Mind

One of the most interesting aspects of *High Fidelity* on stage is that the entire story takes place inside Rob's head. He is telling us his story, functioning as hero, narrator, even God figure now and then as he actually manipulates the people and circumstances he presents to us. Though the original Broadway production somehow missed this central device, the script and score make it quite explicit.

So how do we know that we're actually spending the evening inside Rob's head, as opposed to Rob simply being a narrator? The answer is that Rob does things throughout the show that narrators aren't able to do, and, unlike most narrators, Rob frequently takes us off on tangents as his mind races through the emotions and associations that the story conjures up in his mind. And though most narrators are there to fill in the gaps in the narrative, to establish time and place, to add important information, in contrast to that, Rob shares his deepest, most closely held feelings, his fears and insecurities, and much more. Rob goes way beyond the normal job description for a narrator.

In the opening number, Rob not only tells us where we are and who the other characters are, he also tells us how he *feels* about it all. He compares his stereo to *our* stereos. We learn in this opening that we will not be told a story this evening; we will have a conversation. We become Rob's friends, his confessors. We are immediately involved. As in Shakespeare (and many of the great musicals), these characters frequently tell us directly what they're thinking. It's interesting how often the word *you* and its variants are used in the opening number. The audience is neither invisible nor passive in this show; they are a part of the proceedings. Another thing the Broadway production didn't understand.

In the second scene, in which Laura walks out on Rob, he continues to talk directly to the audience. With tremendous humor and skill, Lindsay-Abaire places Rob into two competing conversations, one with us and one with Laura. He even interrupts his conversation with us at one point because he realizes he needs to talk to Laura before she leaves. Throughout the scene, Rob bounces back and forth between these two conversations, something no ordinary narrator ever does. On occasion he even comments to us on what he's just said (or is about to say) to Laura. He's both in the scene and outside of it at the same time.

In the middle of that scene, as the song "Desert Island Top 5 Breakups" reaches its climax, Laura re-enters, interrupting the song. We watch in silence as she crosses the room, disappears into another part of the apartment to retrieve the toiletry bag she left behind, and then returns to a pleading Rob. The ex-girlfriends, now Greek chorus and backup singers, have to wait for Rob and Laura to play out their scene before the song can finish. On Broadway, the director sent the exes off stage so that the story could return to the real world, but that defeats the purpose and the joke of Laura's interruption of the song. Rob has been fantasizing about telling Laura off, and that fantasy is interrupted by Laura's return. But even then, we're still not in the real world—Rob's in the middle of a song, after all—we're still in Rob's head. Significantly, the script does not call for the exes to leave the stage at this point.

The next scene returns us to the record store, but we're still not in the real world. Several times, Rob turns to us to comment on the action, and the story simply stops and waits for him. This doesn't make sense unless we're still in the unreality of Rob's mind. He even steps out of the scene to deliver one of his philosophical treatises, this time on the psychic dangers of listening to too much pop music. Liz's big song in this scene, "She Goes," is the first time we're introduced to the device that informs most of the show, that each of the people in Rob's life sounds to him like one of his pop gods. Liz and Rob are actually having a conversation, but in his mind, he's talking and she's belting out an R&B number. Liz the ball-buster lectures Rob on his romantic incompetence, but in his mind he hears her scolding him as one of those Aretha Franklin, girl-power anthems (not surprisingly influenced by Aretha's "Respect"). Not only is "She Goes" a showstopper, but it also tells us a lot about Rob: to him, an angry, defiant woman sounds like Aretha Franklin, and he sees his ex-girlfriends as mere accompaniment to his life story, easy to manipulate. But that will soon change.

When we meet Ian, Rob's rival, we are even patched in to Rob's memories of Ian's sex noises when he used to live above Rob and Laura's apartment. Rob doesn't just tell us about Ian's noise, we actually hear it just as Rob does. And for the first time, now only halfway through Act I, Rob's fantasy numbers start to become uncontrollable. In "Number Five with a Bullet," Rob finds himself unable to manipulate the proceedings anymore. Laura and the exes are taunting him. Ian enters and begins an Eastern-flavored orgy with Laura and the exes, driving Rob crazy. The horror escalates until Rob turns off the song (interrupting it just as Laura interrupted "Desert Island"), by screaming, "Stop! Show me no more!" in great Dickensian terror. Rob is certainly no ordinary narrator here; he has literally lost control of the storytelling. The exes, who had been on Rob's side in "Desert Island," are now on Laura's side.

In the club scene with Marie LaSalle, Rob again ducks in and out of the scene, talking to us, taking us into flashback, even admitting that he's altering what Liz said to Laura. ("Liz may not have used those *exact* words, but it's what I like to *imagine* she said.") For the first time, we realize that Rob may not always be telling us the truth. Rob even replays one moment in the scene, after he has explained it to us. But before he explains it, he asks something of the audience, that we think about some terrible thing we did to our partner, so that we will forgive Rob the transgression he's about to reveal to us. What narrator would do that? When the scene ends, Rob delivers a long monologue telling us in detail what led to the fight the night before our story started. Here, late in Act I, Rob finally reveals the answer we've been wondering about since the show opened: What happened "last night" that led to Laura leaving Rob? Now we know. Maybe the whole show is just Rob sitting in his apartment replaying the events of the last few months, trying to make sense of it, trying to figure out where he went wrong and how he can fix things. Maybe, as with Bobby in *Company*, Rob reviews the mess that is his life in the briefest of moments before he decides to take action.

The last scene of Act I contains most of the devices the show's creators have been using throughout the act. But even though the song "Nine Percent Chance" is largely about Rob getting Laura back, he ends the song (and the act) by telling us that he goes out and sleeps with Marie LaSalle. Rob still hasn't grown up. He's still a jerk. He's still emotionally stunted. In most musicals, the audience goes out to intermission, hoping that the two lovers will get past their misunderstanding and eventually find true love. But this isn't that kind of story. In this show, the audience goes out to intermission wondering if these three idiots will ever grow up—and knowing that we've all got some Rob, Dick, and Barry in us deep down. At the least the men in the audience do.

TMPMITW and Friends

As Act II proceeds, Rob tries to bring balance and sanity to his life, and though Neil Young and Bruce Springsteen show up, they're no help at all. Rob is finally in the real world now, and his music no longer saves him. He understands now the complexity of actual human interaction and that knowledge makes it impossible to live in his music anymore.

Though the song the Springsteen doppelganger sings is pure Boss, Rob doesn't live in a steel town, there is no plant nearby, and it's not Veterans Day, so the working-class metaphors offer him nothing. Rob has begun to realize that his depressing pop songs don't really help as much as he thought they did. Rob is on his own from now on. But he has learned one lesson here—it's time to move on down the road, to stop standing still, to take action. Trouble is, Rob still doesn't know what action to take.

To Rob's embarrassment, both Dick and Barry are chasing their dreams now and they leave Rob to his lonely stagnation. By the end of the scene, TMPMITW (the character known only as The Most Pathetic Man in the World) is offering Rob his sympathy and declaring that he and Rob are kindred spirits. This disturbs Rob to his core, but perhaps he sees the truth in it. In some ways, Rob, Dick, and Barry dislike TMPMITW because they see themselves in him—lonely, socially awkward, musically obsessed, and unable to fit comfortably into the real world. Left alone in his record store, Rob finally sees the truth and he knows what to do—not to win Laura back, but to grow the hell up. Rob finally sees that this journey was not about Laura; it was about him. Like many heroes in many hero myths before him, Rob finally confronts his own demons and faces them down.

In the climactic song, "Laura, Laura," a dead-on Ben Folds invocation, Rob tells Laura how he feels in the simplest, most unadorned, most honest, most unguarded, most self-aware moment he's ever had. He doesn't ask her to come back; he merely asks her forgiveness. And *that* was the lesson he had to learn, not just to get his girlfriend back, but to try to become a better person. In the final scene, we see that Rob has turned his life around and he just might be okay in the end. There are no promises of a happy ending here, merely a new beginning under better circumstances. In the last few scenes of the show there is far less direct narration because Rob is getting closer and closer to the truth, and he needs less and less to complain and justify to us. We have been his therapist for two hours and now he's ready to end his therapy session.

The finale tells us a lot about how Rob's worldview has changed. At last, Rob is not the center of attention. Barry has taken center stage musically because Rob is now ready to change his focus from his own happiness to Laura's. Rob's lines near the end say it all: "I've started to make a tape in my head for Laura. Full of stuff *she'd* like. Full of stuff that'd make her happy. For the first time, I can sorta see how that's done." Music can still be central to his life, but if he wants to share a life with Laura, he has to share her music too—both literally and figuratively.

This is an adult musical, and though Broadway couldn't see its value and its beauty, the show lives on in regional theatres across the country, anywhere there are men who haven't yet grown up.

Some old-school musical theatre scholars and commentators are convinced that the golden age of musical theatre lasted from 1943 (*Oklahoma!*) to 1964 (*Fiddler on the Roof*), and that musical theatre has been careening downhill ever since. They talk about the "rise and fall" of musical theatre, as if the art form somehow mirrored the decadent last days of the Roman Empire. They bemoan that theatre songs no longer sound like Richard Rodgers or Jerry Herman songs. They dismiss most of the concept musicals and other experiments of the 1960s and '70s, and they despise rock musicals.

What they don't fully understand is that their golden age is really just the Rodgers and Hammerstein era. Because that model was considered the ideal for so long, it has been mistaken by some as the *only* model; and so the heyday of that one model is assumed to be the golden age of the art form as a whole. This period started with Rodgers and Hammerstein's first show, *Oklahoma!*, which did indeed change many of the rules, and its influence reached far, spawning dozens of imitators who followed in their footsteps and even surpassed them, as the veteran team's own work got less and less interesting over time. The period ended with the last great practitioners of the Rodgers and Hammerstein model, Jerry Bock and Sheldon Harnick, whose last hit was *Fiddler on the Roof*. The end of the era didn't remove this model from the stage entirely; some examples are still with us today, like *Wicked* and *Beauty and the Beast*. But that old model no longer leads the art form.

The year 1964 was a pivot point for the art form. That year, Broadway saw the openings of an old-school musical comedy (*Hello, Dolly!*), an almost pure example of the Rodgers and Hammerstein school (*Fiddler on the Roof*), along with several R&H revivals, two radical concept musicals (*Marat/Sade* and *Oh, What a Lovely War*), and the first of the Sondheim experiments (*Anyone Can Whistle*), which tinkered with structure, flirted with self-reference, comically deconstructed the musical-comedy love story, and explored the kind of political content that would change the musical theatre from a passive mirror of our culture into a more conscious observer and commentator. From that point forward, most serious musicals, and even many musical comedies, would offer up social and political commentary on our culture.

The musical moved past the Rodgers and Hammerstein era to the concept musicals of Hal Prince, Stephen Sondheim, and the team of Fred Ebb and John Kander; and also toward the rock musical, which quickly became its own subgenre. Those today who mourn the so-called "golden age" really just miss Rodgers and Hammerstein's midcentury morality and that ubiquitous Broadway foxtrot that underpinned too many Rodgers and Hammerstein scores. But arguably, the real golden age of musical theatre began in the mid-1990s and we're still in the midst of it today, with brilliant, adventurous rock musicals like *Spring Awakening*, *American Idiot*, *Bloody Bloody Andrew Jackson*, *Passing Strange*, *Love Kills*, *Next to Normal*, and others.

And unlike many of the early rock musicals (with the exception of *Hair*), today's shows no longer have to make musical concessions to the "Broadway sound." Now rock musicals sing in the authentic voice of real rock and roll, not watered down, not adapted, just pure rock. And as the rock musical finally comes of age, more and more of the most interesting shows are coming from young, new writers, writing about coming of age themselves, and bringing along with them a new, re-energized audience for the American musical theatre.

The Capeman

As this second golden age got underway with brilliant, rule-busting shows like *Rent*, *Songs for a New World* (both of which are explored in the book *Rebels with Applause*), *Hedwig and the Angry Inch*, *Bring in 'da Noise, Bring in 'da Funk*, and *Bat Boy*, the 1997–1998 season saw an unlikely rock musical come from a very unlikely source, and it was not at all welcomed by the Broadway community, though it can be seen in retrospect as quite a ballsy experiment and a fascinating link between *Assassins* and *Love Kills*, both of which are ultimately better shows.

Legendary songwriter Paul Simon stormed onto Broadway with *The Capeman* in 1998, a deep, dark, true-crime Latin rock musical, with music by Simon and book and lyrics by Simon and Nobel Prize–winning West Indian poet Derek Walcott. The show told the true story of Salvador Agron, a damaged, sixteen-year-old, cape-wearing Latino kid, victimized by abusive nuns, an absent father, and an abusive stepfather; who brutally stabbed two white youths in 1959 in New York City. Agron was tried, convicted, and sentenced to death, until Governor Rockefeller commuted his sentence to life in prison. Released after twenty years, he found God, became a model citizen, and died seven years later. Significantly, and perhaps both to its credit and its detriment, this tough, difficult musical never passed judgment on Agron or his horrific crimes, much like its artistic forefather, Sondheim and John Weidman's *Assassins*.

While it had its considerable flaws—just like *Rent* did—*The Capeman* was more often than not thrilling, transcendent theatre, with a sensory-confounding production design; dark, troubled, emotional music and lyrics invoking the sounds of 1950s doo-wop and Latin rock; and the perfect cast: Ruben Blades as narrator and the adult Agron, Latino pop star Marc Anthony as the young Agron, and Ednita Nazario as Agron's mother. Simon had been working on songs for the show since 1989 and he began working with Walcott in 1993. Walcott said in an interview with *In Theater* magazine, "I thought it would be extremely challenging for Broadway. I always associate Broadway with an upbeat kind of formula. Even when something is supposed to be daring, it's normally safe in its daring." In 1997 Simon began work on a new album, his first in seven years, on which he sang many of the *Capeman* songs, with occasional help from Blades, Anthony, and Nazario.

Simon approached several Broadway veterans for their advice in mounting the show. They all told him to stop working on the recording, get a director, and do a workshop. But rather than heed their advice, he took offense at the implication that they didn't think he knew what he was doing. Perhaps in reaction to that, he strayed far from Broadway to hire avant-garde modern dance choreographer Mark Morris to choreograph the show. To direct, Simon first hired Argentine-born Susana Tubert, then fired her and hired Eric Simonson, who had directed *The Song of Jacob Zulu*. A workshop was done in late 1996, but soon the team decided to fire Simonson too. Then Morris and Walcott directed as a team for a while. Then they decided to let Morris do both jobs. After the workshop, twenty-two of the forty-five actors in the cast were fired. Meanwhile, the end of 1997 was spent giving interviews, trying to ignore the naysayers, and put up what was fast becoming an eleven-million-dollar Broadway musical.

A month before the opening, Morris was replaced by veteran musical-comedy director Jerry Zaks and choreographer Joey McKneely. Under Zaks, several songs were cut or changed, and the running time was cut from almost three hours to a little over two and a half. But this stubbornly unique piece could not be mainstreamed, and it certainly wasn't a musical comedy. They learned too late that Zaks was the wrong director for the material, just as he had been for *Assassins* a few years earlier.

During an unprecedented fifty-nine previews the work continued, and *The Capeman* finally opened in January 1998, running only sixty-eight performances before shuttering. The critics unfairly savaged the show. In the *New York Times,* Ben Brantley wrote, "It's like watching a mortally wounded animal. You're only sorry that it has to suffer and that there's nothing you can do about it." And yet, of the score he said, "Intricately weaving Latin American rhythms and inflections with the doo-wop harmonies in vogue in the 1950s, these songs have a contemplative, sensuous elegance all their own and remain a pleasure to listen to." Greg Evans suggested how to save the show in *Variety*: "Scrap the irredeemable book, make peace with the static nature of the show, and dispense with any foolhardy attempt to flesh out one-note characters or raise the barely-a-footnote real-life tale to the stature of social significance."

The critics didn't understand that this was a different kind of show, not really a Broadway musical, sometimes a staged oratorio, other times a concert, still other times a full-fledged rock musical, spinning out this primal tale of predestination, remorse, forgiveness, salvation. It was ritual, even exorcism, as much as theatre. But it was controversial outside theatre circles as well. Some people in New York still remembered the Capeman murders and families of the victims protested the show—without having seen it, of course. Friends of Agron argued with how he was portrayed. But as Simon later said in a television interview, "Artists are supposed to raise questions. We're *supposed* to."

Simon, Walcott, Morris, and the others were trying to break through to a new kind of storytelling—more fragmented, more dreamlike, less linear—a kind of impressionistic musical theatre. They were trying to use music in a new way, more culturally authentic, more purely ethnic, and often more diegetic (arising organically from the action). They were trying to expand the limits of scenic art, to make it more abstract, more sculptural, less interested in literally representing time and place. They were trying to work in another cultural language, no longer content to see a minority culture portrayed strictly in terms of the dominant culture (as it was with older shows like *Flower Drum Song* and *Dreamgirls*), to let these New York Puerto Ricans speak in their own voice and music. Still, several Latino political groups protested what they called a perpetuation of stereotypes by the mostly white creators. The show's creators were trying to see just what else was possible within this ever-evolving art form, trying to break through to a new theatrical language. But the commercial theatre community seemed inexplicably threatened by it all.

Simon said in a January 1998 *Vogue* interview, "I really couldn't care less what the theater community, or whatever it is that they call themselves, thinks about this work. Because, quite frankly, I didn't write it for Broadway. I wrote it for me."

Did every experiment in the show work? No. Did most of them? Yes. As unconventional as it was, this was serious, adult, emotionally compelling storytelling and the Broadway community just could not embrace the breaking of so many rules of commercial musical theatre, even if the end product was as insightful and original and powerful as *The Capeman*'s audience found it. During its brief run, audiences routinely leapt to their feet at the end of the show, cheering, deeply moved by what they had seen and heard. Still, *The Capeman* ran for a couple months and gave up. An announced national tour was converted to a concert tour, and then canceled altogether. A cast album was recorded but not released until years later and then only on iTunes. It's tempting to wonder how *The Capeman* would have fared if it had started life at a more daring regional theatre and enjoyed a little success before braving the waters of Broadway. Maybe it just wasn't a "Broadway musical," but really neither was *Bring in 'da Noise, Bring in 'da Funk* or *Contact* or *Movin' Out*, all of which were embraced by critics. It would be left to younger voices than Simon to move the art form forward, and there were plenty standing in the wings.

Bare

One such show had about as much luck in New York as *The Capeman*, but it survived anyway. Before the Internet there was generally only one way for a show to get produced in theatres around the country: it had to run on or off Broadway and get a cast album recorded. Major regional theatres usually won't produce a show unless it has a decent New York pedigree. But that leaves a lot of cool, interesting shows unproduced.

Today, everyone can read on the Internet about some new, offbeat musical produced in a sixty-seat basement theatre somewhere in Colorado or Ohio. No longer is that New York imprimatur necessary for a show to have a long life. Many large regional theatres are still timid about untried shows, but there are so many smaller, more adventurous theatre companies in the US now, less constrained by multimillion-dollar budgets, subscriber bases, and the placating of major donors. And as long as these smaller, alternative companies can find the shows, they revel in producing this less conventional, less commercial work. Perhaps more than any other show, *bare* has been a beneficiary of this technological revolution.

The pop opera *bare* (usually spelled in lower case), written by Jon Hartmere Jr. and Damon Intrabartolo, first opened in Los Angeles at the Hudson Theatre in October 2000, where it won the L.A. Weekly Award for Best Musical, the Ovation Award for Best Musical, and the L.A. Drama Critics Award for Best Score. Originally called *bare: a pop opera*, it was supposed to run in L.A. for thirty-two performances at an eighty-seven-seat theatre on Santa Monica Boulevard. Four months later, it had become a multi-award–winning sensation created by two twenty-six-year-old writers and a twenty-three-year-old director. The show then opened off Broadway at the American Theatre of Actors in 2004, but ran only a few weeks before closing. The off Broadway reviews were very mixed, but the *New York Times* wrote, "*bare* has youthful promise written all over it." The Associated Press called the show an "ambitious and original creation." TalkinBroadway.com said, "The show is breathlessly energetic, and an obvious labor of love crafted with care down to its smallest details." Now with a shortened title, *bare* has had an active life since then, with productions in Sacramento, Houston, and Seattle in 2008; Amherst, Denver, and Toronto in 2009; Sydney, Australia, in 2010; and Minneapolis and St. Louis in 2011.

Bare has been described as a mix of *Rent* and *Dead Poets Society*, exploring sexuality, self-expression, guilt, jealously, teen pregnancy, female body image, and religion, all overflowing with the kind of urgency and intensity that comes with being seventeen. The show follows six seniors at a Catholic boarding school, all struggling with various issues. At the center are Jason and Peter, who are forced to deal with their mutual romantic attraction while trying to live up to the standards of their parents and the Catholic Church. The show's first director, Kristin Hanggan, said in an interview, "Its real allure for audiences is the commonality of experience—alienation, fear of rejection, confusion of sexual identity and the poignancy of marginalization." Hartmere said in an interview, "There are still kids killing themselves. There's a long way to go. One kid calling you a faggot where you're nine is enough. You pray that you survive high school, and then you begin your adolescence in college, maybe. I don't think that's the best we can do, so hopefully, something like *bare* will bring us a step closer."

Though the show's authors have tried more recently to distance themselves from their own label of "pop opera," that's what they wrote. The score is reminiscent of *Rent*, but where *Rent* mined the sounds of 1980s pop, *bare* speaks more in the language of twenty-first century alternative pop and emo-rock—very minimalist, very melodic, relatively simple harmonically. Like much of emo, many of the chords in *bare* are missing the third, the note that makes a chord major or minor; these open fifths are ambiguous, neither entirely happy (major) or sad (minor). There is complexity and gray area here in the music as well as the lyrics, and there is no Broadway in this sound. Despite its aborted run off Broadway, *bare* quickly became a cult favorite across the country, especially among younger musical theatre fans, through bootleg audio and video recordings and YouTube.

Bare helped move forward a trend toward musical authenticity in contemporary pop and rock musicals. Where shows like *Miss Saigon*, *The Full Monty*, and *Hairspray* forged a commercially safer Broadway-pop hybrid sound, *bare* is pure alt-pop. And that may account for its fervent cult following and its simultaneous dismissal by much of the musical theatre establishment. Like emo, most of these lyrics are about pain, isolation, loss. Though there are laughs (including two very funny dream sequences), those laughs come at a cost, and early in Act I, we know this story will not end well.

And like emo, *bare* takes its teenage characters seriously. The show never laughs at their pain, never suggests that their problems are trivial or ridiculous (as shows like *Bye Bye Birdie* used to do), and it never doubts the depth of their love. The musical within a musical, the school's production of *Romeo and Juliet*, may be a cliché, but it is exactly the right reference here. How many of us first encountered *Romeo and Juliet*'s teen angst in high school? Unlike most of us, at least these kids see relevance to their own lives in the passion and tragedy of the Shakespeare play. It's just as hard to be a kid now as it was then, the *bare* writers are telling us. In fact, it's *always* hard. Adults can look back cynically and see only puppy love here, but these struggles are real to these characters and to the millions of young fans the show has across the United States.

A workshop of a revised version of *bare* was held in New York in November 2010, with an eye toward a possible new production on Broadway. Producer Randy Taradash said at the time, "We approached the team about taking a fresh look at their musical, whose universal themes of acceptance, tolerance, and unconditional love, whether from a lover, parent, peer, or from personal faith, have been at the forefront of so many of the discussions our nation has faced in recent times. As we've read with great sadness the headlines of the past few weeks concerning the struggles and despair facing today's LGTBQ youth, we have been struck by how ahead of its time *bare* was in 2000, and how, sadly, the world has caught up with *bare*. With a newly revised work in hand, the entire *bare* team is united in shaping a thrilling and emotional theatrical experience that allows anyone who feels their issues are singular to know that they are not alone." And isn't that the whole point of human storytelling? With or without a Broadway run, *bare* will no doubt have a long life.

Taboo

No one ever expected to see a stage musical—particularly a good one—from pop singer Boy George (née George O'Dowd). But he surprised everyone by giving them one anyway. His autobiographical but fictionalized pop musical, *Taboo*, showed us the free-spirited, sexually omnivorous London club scene in the mid-1980s, the self-dubbed New Romantics, and their spiritual and creative godfather, Leigh Bowery. But far from being another catalog musical, *Taboo* was a serious story about living life as performance art, about what fame can do to an underground artist, and about the dark side of a life built on style over substance. Boy George took on the role of his artistic mentor Leigh Bowery, giving the storytelling a weird, postmodern, metatheatrical layer of irony and self-awareness. This was a fable, not history. This was Boy George's own *8½*, a surrealistic, clear-eyed, but self-indulgent summing up of his life, following in the footsteps of Fellini's famous film, but also Woody Allen's *Stardust Memories* and Bob Fosse's *All That Jazz*.

Though a few of Boy George's pop songs appear in the show, the score is largely original and extremely well crafted. Still working entirely in his own unique pop-music vocabulary, with a touch of Brecht and Weill here and there, he wrote everything from comedy numbers to anthems to gut-wrenching, emotionally naked ballads like "Stranger in This World."

The show opened in London in January 2002, with a score by Boy George, a book by Mark Davies, and direction by Christopher Renshaw. Lyn Gardner of the *Guardian* saw many problems with the show but wrote, "This could so easily have been a vanity project, but while there is plenty of narcissism and self loathing on view as the characters flutter too close to the bright lights, get their wings burned and crash so spectacularly to the ground that most wouldn't get on the guest list to their own funerals, the evening is sufficiently light and witty and so deliciously bitchy and ironic that you cannot help warming to it." It ran fifteen months.

Comedian and Broadway gadfly Rosie O'Donnell saw the show in London, fell in love with it, and decided to produce it on Broadway to the tune of $10 million. Unhappy with Renshaw, O'Donnell brought in choreographer Jeff Calhoun as a show doctor, but it didn't help. Too much tinkering destroyed what once made *Taboo* special.

The show opened on Broadway in 2003 with a revised, bitchier book by Charles Busch, now focused less on the working-class life of London and more on the rise of Boy George as a pop star. It ran only a hundred performances, despite its first-rate cast featuring Euan Morton (as George), Raul Esparza, and Boy George. Many insiders blamed the show's insurmountable problems and dramas all on O'Donnell, who controlled the show with an iron fist, got into very public fights, cancelled performances, and threatened to fire staff, all while publicly fighting a lawsuit over her magazine, *Rosie*. The rewrites and Rosie's insanity did not help the show, sapping much of its original honesty and rawness, presumably in an effort to make it a big splashy Broadway show. But that's not what Boy George had written. *Taboo* was nominated for four Tonys, but won none of them. It was nominated for four Drama Desk Awards but only Raul Esparza took one home. The show lost its entire investment.

Richard Zoglin wrote a mixed review in *Time*, but noted that "the real triumph of *Taboo*, however, is O'Dowd's music and lyrics, among the best I've heard on Broadway in the past few seasons . . . Ten years from now, I can see a cult developing around the music for *Taboo* the way it has around the score of *Chess*. Count me a charter member." But Ben Brantley in the *New York Times* called the show "a disastrously overcrowded tableau of a show about hedonists who hide their hearts, [that] can keep your head spinning for any number of reasons . . . there's no denying that the show is a crazy, mixed-up mess in tone, structure and rhythm. Its first act inspires a kind of open-mouthed fascination, as such messes often do. By the second act, the numbness descends that comes from overdosing on plot lines."

But the critics didn't understand what *Taboo* was. It doesn't operate along traditional musical theatre lines. This is a rock musical about extreme people who hide behind extreme facades, and cause each other extreme pain. The show isn't melodramatic, as several critics complained; these characters' *lives* are melodramatic. Old-school musical theatre lovers couldn't grapple with this subculture, whose behavior and social norms were so foreign to them, where everyone *performed* real life. As they did with *The Capeman*, the Broadway establishment refused to consider that a piece of musical theatre could be fashioned using completely different rules and different aesthetics, that it could have a voice and agenda uniquely its own. *Avenue Q* was doing much the same thing at the same time, but in a far more mainstream, commercial voice. *Avenue Q* kept a safe, ironic distance from its characters' pain, while *Taboo* assaulted its audience with the raw emotion of its cultural outcasts. *Taboo* was a better piece of art, but arguably *Avenue Q* was a better Broadway musical. Broadway is, after all, a commercial enterprise. As Bowery says in the show, "I am art; you are parody."

Unfortunately, regional productions of *Taboo* are not possible because O'Donnell still holds the rights and swears she will bring the show back to Broadway again. But no one wants to get involved with her after the train wreck she created. The real shame is that the show is fascinating and outrageous and honest and original, and it should have had a longer life. O'Donnell's tinkering was destructive and the show probably never belonged on Broadway to begin with. An off Broadway production with a producer who understood how to leave artists alone might have given *Taboo* more of a chance to find its audience. We'll probably never know.

Jersey Boys

In October 2004, another fascinating experiment in musical theatre opened at the La Jolla Playhouse in California, the unexpectedly thrilling *Jersey Boys*, with a book by Marshall Brickman and Rick Elice, music by Bob Gaudio, lyrics by Bob Crewe, direction by Des McAnuff, and pitch-perfect choreography by Sergio Trujillo. This was the story of the 1960s pop group the Four Seasons, using their own music to tell their story. Like *Mamma Mia!*, *Rock of Ages*, *Million Dollar Quartet*, *Come Fly Away*, and many other recent musicals, *Jersey Boys* is a "catalog musical" or "jukebox musical," using pre-existing popular songs and building a plot around them. The problem with most catalog musicals is that they're built backward, trying to fit a coherent story and characters to existing lyrics. The creators of this subgenre forget that the art form is musical theatre, not theatrical music. *Theatre* is the noun, the subject; *musical* is just a modifier. By definition, the storytelling is primary. But with a catalog musical, the songs are primary, and that almost always results in weaker, often contorted, or shallow storytelling.

But *Jersey Boys* was the first genuinely mature catalog musical, one that didn't fall into those traps, and it seemed to many that this subgenre, which has been around since the 1970s, might finally be finding its voice as serious, legitimate musical theatre, laying the groundwork for other outstanding examples of the genre, like *American Idiot*, based on the Green Day album. With *Jersey Boys*, the book did not contort itself to accommodate the songs; instead the book and music entwined around each other so organically it seemed as if these songs had been written just for this show.

And more than any other catalog musical Broadway had yet seen, the script boasted insightful, complex, sophisticated, deeply emotional writing about the artist's eternal struggle of art versus life, about women, alcohol, success, crime, and loyalty. This was a tough story about real people's lives. And the music in the show almost never stopped, incorporating part or all of more than thirty songs, used in so many different, interesting ways. The songs were sometimes just musical fragments, sometimes background music, sometimes moments of fantasy or memory, sometimes ironic Brechtian commentary. We saw diegetic "performances" of songs in clubs or concerts, and we also saw songs being written, rehearsed, and recorded. This was a story about these four guys, but it was also a story about making art. This time, the *music* was telling the story of the music. Very few other musicals that had come before were this truly and entirely about the life force and emotion and power of art and its effect on people, its ability to reflect, to mourn, to celebrate, to illuminate. (*Avenue X* comes to mind. *The Sound of Music* doesn't.)

Jersey Boys was an authentic commercial home run and it opened on Broadway in November 2005 to cheering audiences and great reviews. The critics all raved about John Lloyd Young in the role of Frankie Valli, and he became an overnight Broadway star thanks to this show. And significantly, many of the critics were shocked by the excellence of the script. That certainly didn't happen with the mindless *Mamma Mia!* or the duds *Good Vibrations*, *All Shook Up*, or *Lennon*. Clive Barnes's review in the *New York Post* was headlined, TOO GOOD TO BE TRUE, and he wrote, "It's a Broadway commonplace that the most important thing about a musical is the book—but no one goes out singing the book, so it's a commonplace often forgotten. Then comes a show like *Jersey Boys*, with a book that's as tight and absorbing as an Arthur Miller play . . . It's a show still dynamically alive in music while, as a drama, it catches the very texture, almost the actual smell, of its time." Linda Winer of *Newsday* wrote, "Unlike the dim-bulb shows that use made-up stories as excuses to plug in hits by Elvis or the Beach Boys, this one is a straightforward biography of the group that defined a slick, street sound. Unlike the recent John Lennon bio, *Jersey Boys* doesn't get artsy with the material or overly selective about history. Nor is this a sanitized, glitz-revue in the tainted tradition of the long-running *Smokey Joe's Cafe.*"

Jersey Boys was nominated for eight Tony awards and won four, including Best Musical, Best Book, and Best Direction. It was nominated for seven Drama Desk awards and won two. As of this writing, it has run more than two thousand performances on Broadway and shows no signs of stopping.

Next to Normal

Next to Normal was surely the most adult, most mature rock musical to hit Broadway in decades, an unrelentingly intense, brutally honest story about a bipolar woman undergoing electroshock therapy, about the impact of her illness on her family, and about the shortcomings of the medical profession's understanding of mental illness. But this score wasn't Broadway pop; this was hard-driving rock and roll, authentic enough to match the authenticity of its emotion. It was the second rock musical to win a Pulitzer Prize for drama.

Like many shows today, *Next to Normal* had an unusually long, rocky road to Broadway. In an age of skyrocketing ticket prices and more and more non-English-speaking tourists in the audience, Broadway producers are rarely eager to take on a brand new show, especially one dealing with a topic as harrowing as mental illness. The show began its life in 1998 as a ten-minute workshop sketch called *Feeling Electric*. Writer Brian Yorkey had brought the idea to composer Tom Kitt (*High Fidelity*) while both were at the BMI Lehman Engel Musical Theatre Workshop, and Kitt wrote a rock score for the piece. Both Yorkey and Kitt moved on to other projects, but they kept returning to their ten-minute piece, eventually expanding it to a full-length musical. This version went through several workshops as the team kept working on it.

In September 2005, an abbreviated version of the full-length piece was part of the New York Musical Theatre Festival, where it attracted some attention. Second Stage Theatre workshopped the piece in 2006 and 2007, featuring for the first time the woman who would give the brilliant, startling, visceral performance at the heart of the story, Alice Ripley; with director Michael Greif (*Rent*, *Jane Eyre*, *Grey Gardens*) at the helm.

The show moved to off Broadway in 2008, now retitled *Next to Normal*, where it ran barely a month. Still, it won the Outer Critics Circle Award for Outstanding Score, and it was nominated for two other Outer Critics Circle Awards (including Outstanding New Off Broadway Musical), three Lucille Lortel Awards, two Drama League Awards, and two Drama Desk Awards. The *New York Times* said, "As befits what is surely New York's first mainstream musical about manic depression, *Next to Normal*, which opened Wednesday night at the Second Stage Theater, is apt to produce bipolar reactions in anyone who sees it. How could it be otherwise with a show that suggests a hybrid of fractured-family soapers like *Ordinary People* and the Who's *Tommy*, the 1969 rock opera of illness and nonconformity?

"To watch this tale of a haunted housewife (beautifully played by Alice Ripley) and the household she in turn haunts is to ride a speeding roller coaster of responses. One minute you're rolling your eyes; the next, you're wiping them. When the show ends, you're probably doing both at the same time." New York's *Daily News* said the show "is audacious, original and—like its heroine—has issues . . . In the end, the show is exactly like Diana—always unpredictable, never fully balanced. But if you're looking for something that'll shake you up, *Next to Normal* is just what the doctor ordered."

Perhaps it could have stayed that way, flawed but fascinating. It worked for *Rent*. But the team kept working, focusing like a laser on the emotions of the family. What musical theatre does best is emotion, after all, and Yorkey and Kitt's rock score was almost unbearably emotional. Yet another new version of the show was then given a regional theatre production at the Arena Stage in its temporary theatre in Crystal City, Virginia, from November 2008 through January 2009. Greif returned as director. Ripley and most of the off Broadway cast participated, but Brian d'Arcy James remained in New York to play the title character in *Shrek the Musical*, and he was replaced by J. Robert Spencer.

Finally, though no one might have expected it, the little six-actor rock musical that could began previews on Broadway in March 2009. This time, the *New York Times* said, "No show on Broadway right now makes as direct a grab for the heart—or wrings it as thoroughly—as *Next to Normal* does. This brave, breathtaking musical focuses squarely on the pain that cripples the members of a suburban family, and never for a minute does it let you escape the anguish at the core of their lives. *Next to Normal* does not, in other words, qualify as your standard feel-good musical. Instead this portrait of a manic-depressive mother and the people she loves and damages is something much more: a feel-everything musical, which asks you, with operatic force, to discover the liberation in knowing where it hurts. Such emotional rigor is a point of honor for *Next to Normal* . . . With an astounding central performance from Alice Ripley as Diana Goodman, a housewife with bipolar disorder, this production assesses the losses that occur when wounded people are anesthetized—and not just by the battery of pharmaceutical and medical treatments to which Diana is subjected, but by recreational drugs, alcohol and that good old American virtue, denial with a smile." *Rolling Stone* called it "the best new musical of the season—by a mile."

The first Broadway show to embrace social media, about six weeks into its Broadway run, *Next to Normal* began publishing an adapted version of the show over Twitter. Over the course of a month, this serialized version of the show was "performed" 140 characters at a time, presented as if the characters themselves were tweeting about their day-to-day activities in real time. In between these tweets, the show would periodically post a link to an audio file of a song from the show to move the story forward. This Twitter feed, designed to build a community around the show, eventually racked up more than a million followers. The Twitter "performance" culminated in a new song written by Kitt and Yorkey, based on suggestions from Twitter followers, who helped decide details about which characters are performing the song, where it takes place in the story, and also provided structure and lyric suggestions. The song was then publicly performed at a special event in New York. The producers also announced a "fan mashup" on YouTube, in which fans of the show recorded their own interpretations of songs from the score.

The show's investors recouped their initial investment of four million dollars a few days after *Next to Normal*'s one-year anniversary on Broadway, proving that new, challenging work can succeed on Broadway, but also that it rarely originates there anymore. Late in the run, real-life married couple and Broadway veterans Marin Mazzie and Jason Danieley took over the two leads, while Alice Ripley went on tour with the show. The Broadway production closed in January 2011 after 754 performances.

Edges

There have been more than thirty productions at colleges around the US, and more than a hundred productions around the world of this show that has never played Broadway or off Broadway. But chances are any musical theatre fan under twenty-five knows these songs. It's a song cycle called *Edges*, written in 2005 by University of Michigan sophomores Benj Pasek and Justin Paul, about the coming of age, the self-discovery, and the fear of the future that four twenty-somethings face. Its best-known song, "Be My Friend," has become known as "the Facebook song."

Unhappy with the musicals their school was producing, the two students took artistic matters into their own hands and wrote their own show, becoming the youngest recipients to date of the $20,000 Jonathan Larson Award, established by the family of the *Rent* author and composer to encourage composers, lyricists, and bookwriters at the start of their careers.

Modeled on Jason Robert Brown's breakthrough work, *Songs for a New World*, Pasek and Paul's musical explores four lives that "have succumbed to the definitions that they are forced into by their social surroundings," according to the authors, people who "question whether they are simply stuck being who others want them to be, or whether they can indeed break through to discover their own potential." The music is a mix of Broadway pop and old-fashioned show tunes, though the content is clearly contemporary.

Many of the show's songs are sometimes uncomfortably similar to the *Songs for a New World* score, in content, in vocal arrangement, and in many musical devices in the accompaniment—the introduction to "Lying There" quotes the first few notes of *Songs for a New World* almost exactly—but it's still a strong maiden effort by two new young writers, especially considering the obvious craft in both the music and lyrics. While *Songs for a New World* had a central, overriding metaphor uniting all its songs, making the show a concept musical rather than just a revue, *Edges*' songs are less unified and so the piece as a whole is more revue than musical; and to be fair, the authors themselves call it a song cycle. Though these songs sometimes tend to sound like college exercises in imitating the current Broadway pop sound, the score also frequently reaches beyond that impression through the sheer talent and artistry behind the work. Most young writers borrow from the writers they love as they learn their craft, and here it's clear who Pasek and Paul admire: Jason Robert Brown, but also, perhaps surprisingly, old-school show tune composers like Jerry Herman and Jerry Bock. The song "Be My Friend" would be at home in an off Broadway revue from the 1950s or '60s. And the quirky love song "I Hmm You" starts off by directly quoting Richard Rodgers's "If I Loved You" as its introduction, making the sly connection between these two love songs that never say "I love you." And this reaching back to the roots of serious musical theatre, this invoking of the elders, lets us also see the show as a valentine to musical theatre from two loving fans. It's the kind of smart-alecky self-awareness—in addition to its honest, heartfelt emotion—that has allowed this song cycle to win over its considerable fan base, theatre kids who love all the new rock musicals but also have great affection for the great theatre scores of the past. In some ways, *Edges* explores (perhaps unintentionally) the evolution of the art form from the point of view of its youngest artists.

Though *Edges* may be more derivative and less mature than the other shows discussed here, it's still a skillfully wrought piece, worthy of serious consideration. Where *Songs for a New World* explored lives already underway, choices already made, regrets already in place, *Edges* acts almost as a prequel to the other show, exploring lives just starting out, kids becoming adults, identities just forming, trajectories figured for the first time. Like *Rent* and *bare*, this is a show with flaws, but it's those flaws that lend authenticity and youthful passion to these songs.

Spring Awakening

No one expected a new alternative rock/pop musical based on a controversial German play from 1891 about sexual and intellectual oppression. Taking a page from Brechtian musicals like *Company* and *I Love My Wife*, pop composer Duncan Sheik and bookwriter and lyricist Steven Sater created a fascinating, powerful, often thrilling new musical out of Frank Wedekind's *Spring Awakening*. Set in late nineteenth-century Germany, the story follows a handful of teenagers first discovering their own sexuality, along the way grappling with masturbation, abortion, homosexuality, rape, child abuse, and suicide. At the center are three friends, Moritz, the haunted, troubled, abused misfit; Melchior, the good student whose existential questions will take him to very dark places; and Wendla, Melchior's sweetly innocent girlfriend. Despite the setting, Sheik and Sater made the bold choice to ignore period musical sounds and instead to make this story sing with the youthful rebellion and emotion of contemporary rock and roll. The kids of *Spring Awakening* are close cousins to the kids of *Grease*—the biggest difference is just one of tone—and any other music would have seemed emotionally false for audiences in the new millennium. This was the sound of full, heartfelt emotional authenticity, something Broadway only heard occasionally.

The show was groundbreaking in a number of ways. Physically, it was extremely minimalist, using only chairs to delineate scenes. In its content, it rivaled the most daring shows on or off Broadway, mining the complex, baffling emotions of the transition from child to adult, and never shying away from the darkness, the tragedy, the damaged sexuality, and the pain of these characters. Musically, Sheik and Sater took big risks. Beyond their refusal to use period sounds, their songs almost never grew organically out of the action. The songs commented on the story, acted as context and subtext, and, more than anything else, transformed this long-ago story into a contemporary, relevant piece of theatre. But because of this intentional and often illuminating disconnect between script and score, listening to the cast album only barely hints at the story or the real artistry of the score. By themselves, the songs all work as interesting pop and rock songs; but in context, they take on surprising weight and complexity that isn't apparent on the CD.

The show's creators showed us (or maybe just reminded us) that a theatre score can work in many different ways, that the conventions of Broadway must continually evolve and be challenged, and that musical theatre as an art form is incredibly flexible and ever moving forward, even despite the commercial pressures of Broadway and off Broadway.

As is common practice these days, *Spring Awakening* began its life through several workshops over seven years, hosted by the La Jolla Playhouse in San Diego, and the Roundabout Theatre and Lincoln Center in New York. Under the loving guidance of actor-turned-producer Tom Hulce, the show finally opened off Broadway at the Atlantic Theatre Company in May 2006, under the direction of Michael Mayer (who would later go on to direct *American Idiot*), with choreography by modern-dance icon Bill T. Jones. It received nearly unanimously favorable reviews. Charles Isherwood wrote in the *New York Times,* "It is disorienting to find the 19th-century German schoolboys in the new musical *Spring Awakening* yanking microphones from inside their little woolen jackets, fixing us with baleful gazes and screaming amplified angst into our ears. It is also exhilarating. When was the last time you felt a frisson of surprise and excitement at something that happened in a new musical? For that matter, when was the last time something new happened in a new musical?"

The show closed off Broadway in August and transferred uptown to the Eugene O'Neill Theatre in December 2006, where it ran about two years and over nine hundred performances. The critics still loved it. *USA Today* said, "Beautiful, messy, exhilarating, awkward, vital: They're all adjectives you might use to describe first love. So it's fitting that you could also readily apply them to *Spring Awakening*, the imperfect but transcendent new musical . . . But *Spring* is at once a less polished and more resonant work [than *Rent*]. Where *Rent* creator Jonathan Larson both embraced the bombast of rock-era theater and aspired to a more conventional sophistication, Sheik approaches the stage with the fresh eyes and open mind of an artist accustomed to an entirely different tradition." New York's *Daily News* said, "Great news for theatergoers who have craved a new musical with attitude, youthful exuberance and a fresh, gutsy sound. A serious show that raises provocative issues. And if Broadway audiences are lucky, it will run for many seasons to come."

Spring Awakening was showered with awards, just as *Rent* had been a decade earlier. The show was honored with eleven Tony nominations, winning eight, including Tonys for Best Musical, Best Book, and Best Score. The show also won four Drama Desk Awards, including Outstanding Musical, Outstanding Music, and Outstanding Lyrics. It won Outer Critics Circle Awards for Outstanding Musical and Outstanding Score. The cast album even won the Grammy for Best Musical Show Album. The London production also won four Olivier Awards.

Then *Spring Awakening* conquered the rest of the world, with productions over the next several years in Sweden, Helsinki, Budapest, Vienna, Malta, Tokyo, Brazil, the Philippines, the Czech Republic, South Korea, Norway, Argentina, Israel, Scotland, Ireland, Australia, and elsewhere. There is talk of a film.

Passing Strange

It's not often that a new musical has a philosophical manifesto, but *Passing Strange* has something close. Co-creator Stew (born Mark Stewart) wrote on his show's website:

> We have G. W. Bush to thank for this play. Seriously. When I found out that he had never been to Europe in his youth (or in his adulthood until he became prez!!!) I immediately knew I wanted to write a play about a kid who wanted to go to Europe. That fact about Bush said a lot to me about America's lack of interest in anything foreign except that which it can exploit (always to exploit—never to learn from). Can you imagine an uber-privileged billionaire's son from any other country that would not have been curious enough to travel to a

> foreign country or two or three or twenty? Especially when you're talking the kind of money where you already own a few airplanes yourself? As someone whose experience abroad informed and shaped my very being and consciousness about everything from sexuality, politics, culture, language and human nature, I became obsessed with this factoid and decided this incuriosity was at the heart of the war. I realized that we are actually suffering the results of Bush's and his cronies' incuriousness . . . their dimwitted foreign policy time and again shows that beneath it all these fuckers don't even care about trying to understand the world they wish to dominate.

Conceived and written by singer-songwriter and performance artist Stew and his collaborator, Heidi Rodewald (their band is called The Negro Problem), *Passing Strange* is a rock musical about a young black man searching for meaning and authenticity in this contemporary world. Loaded with soulful lyrics and overflowing with passion and ironic humor, this daring musical takes us from stultifying middle-class Los Angeles to morally adventurous Amsterdam to politically subversive Berlin and beyond, on a journey toward personal and artistic authenticity, across boundaries of place, identity, and theatrical convention. Like *Spring Awakening*, the set consisted of little more than chairs, with the band onstage. That's all it needed. The artifice of traditional scenic design had no place in these new rock musicals.

A popular performer at Joe's Pub in New York, Stew was commissioned by the Public Theater to develop this heartfelt, funny story of a young bohemian who charts a course for "The Real" through sex, drugs, and rock and roll. Its title a quote from *Othello*, the show first premiered in October 2006 at the Berkeley Repertory Theatre in Berkeley, then opened off Broadway at the Public Theatre in May 2007, under the direction of Annie Dorsen. It closed off Broadway in June and reopened uptown at the Belasco Theatre in February 2008. After 165 performances, it closed in July but was preserved on film by Spike Lee.

The critical establishment fully embraced this weird, original musical. Charles Isherwood wrote in the *New York Times*:

> Although it is far richer in wit, feeling and sheer personality than most of what is classified as musical theater in the neighborhood around Times Square these days, its big heart throbs to the sound of

> electric guitars, searing synthesizer chords, driving drums and lyrics delivered not in a clean croon but a throaty yelp. A rock 'n' roll autobiography of an artist in search of himself, *Passing Strange* is bursting at the seams with melodic songs, and it features a handful of theatrical performances to treasure . . . But please don't call it a Broadway musical. You could scare away too many people who might actually enjoy it. Call it a rock concert with a story to tell, trimmed with a lot of great jokes. Or call it a sprawling work of performance art, complete with angry rants and scary drag queens. Call it whatever you want, really. I'll just call it wonderful, and a welcome anomaly on Broadway, which can use all the vigorous new artistic blood it can get.

Newsday said, "Let's not get too distracted figuring out how to categorize *Passing Strange*, the stranger-in-a-strange-land original passing for a Broadway musical at the Belasco Theatre. What's important is that the thing—part indie-rock concert, part boho-art project, part coming-of-age black-identity crisis, part hipster travelogue—is all smart and all enjoyable and all very good for the theater."

The show was nominated for seven Tony Awards, including Best Musical and Best Score, and it won the Tony for Best Book of a Musical. It was nominated for seven Drama Desk Awards and won three, for Outstanding Musical, Outstanding Music, and Outstanding Lyrics. The show also won the New York Drama Critics Circle Award for Best Musical, and lots more.

Love Kills

Charlie Starkweather, infamous spree killer of the late 1950s, and his underage girlfriend, Caril Ann Fugate, have inspired so much American art and pop culture, maybe because their story holds some vital truths about America's tumultuous, disorienting transformation from the enforced, stifling conformity of Eisenhower's '50s to the complicated political and sexual freedom of the '60s. For one historical moment, all of America's anxieties were wrapped up in the person of Charlie Starkweather; he was Marlon Brando in *The Wild One* and James Dean in *Rebel Without a Cause*, every middle-American parent's nightmare come to frightening life. But long after Charlie's execution, his murder spree inspired films as varied as *Badlands*, *Kalifornia*, *Natural Born Killers*, *Murder in the Heartland*, *The Sadist*, *True Romance*, and *Wild at Heart*. They also inspired Bruce Springsteen's song "Nebraska."

Charlie and Caril Ann's story served as a launching pad for Kyle Jarrow's daring, aggressive emo-rock musical *Love Kills*, based on historical fact, though fictionalized in some of its details. An abbreviated version of the show was presented for six performances at the New York Musical Theatre Festival in 2007. It was significantly retooled and had its world premiere at New Line Theatre in St. Louis in October 2009, followed by other productions across the country. This final version of the show toyed with chronology, with time and place, and with audience expectations, portraying these teenagers alternately as scared innocents and as brutal, ice-cold killers—at first, we think Caril Ann has been Charlie's unwilling hostage, then we start to think she committed at least one of the murders herself, and finally we're left swimming in the complexity of these damaged kids, their fractured psyches, the undeniable horrors they committed, and their passionate, emotionally distorted relationship. It's an intermissionless roller coaster ride that leaves its audience shattered by its unflinching truthfulness even more than by its sensationalistic details.

Jarrow's musical is populated by just four characters—Charlie, Caril Ann, Nebraska sheriff Merle Karnopp, and his wife Gertrude—as it takes us back to Nebraska in 1958 (the kids in *Grease* would graduate high school just one year later), and we witness as the world closes in on these two child lovers who are charged with committing eleven murders in the course of a week. Under pressure to confess by dawn, facts blur and loyalties shift back and forth, and the kids have to ask themselves—and the show asks us—how far will you go for someone you love? Today, in a world of frequent public shootings and escalating violence on American streets, in a time of international terrorism, in a time when violence can be so random, but also in a time of accelerating medical advances in the study of crime and the human brain and the discovery of actual physical defects that disable impulse control and empathy, how do we make sense of it all?

Today we may be refighting the great cultural and political battle between the 1950s (conservatism) and the 1960s (progressivism), but in 1958 that battle was raging for the first time, and Charlie was at the heart of it. The *Omaha World-Herald* published an editorial shortly after the arrests:

> If Charles Starkweather were a case apart, a biological accident, a monstrous freak of nature, then today all Americans could take a deep breath of relief and give thanks that his mad career of murder

> had been brought to an end. But although his crimes were of a violence beyond precedent, nevertheless there was a certain flavor to the Starkweather story which brought back to mind a thousand others which have been told in recent years to an unbelieving America. The sideburns, the tight blue jeans, the black leather jacket—those have become almost the uniform of juvenile hoodlums. And the snarling contempt for discipline, the blazing hate for restraint, have become a familiar refrain in police stations and juvenile courts throughout the land. To a greater degree than ever before, influences are pulling some youngsters away from the orbit of the home, the school, and the church, and into the asphalt jungle. That is the problem.

The truTV website offers more cultural context: "This was the country that had elected Eisenhower and Nixon for a second term in 1956 and where the FBI's J. Edgar Hoover was firmly entrenched as the national policeman. This was also a country that was undergoing unsettling cultural changes. Frightening and offensive symbols of rebellion emerged and thrived: Elvis Presley, James Dean and the whole rock 'n' roll culture focused on a new generation that challenged the status quo of the sterile 1950s. The country that uncomfortably watched James Dean's *Rebel Without A Cause* in 1956 now saw a Dean-like figure in Charles Starkweather to make them *really* uncomfortable. What was the world coming to? Were the violence and the alienation of Starkweather just the beginning of some uncontrollable trend that would destroy the fabric of society?"

But *Love Kills* isn't really about the murders. We see none of the crimes take place. Instead we find ourselves in a Lincoln, Nebraska, jail where Charlie and Caril Ann have been brought after their extradition from Wyoming, where they had been caught. The action takes place over one night—a kind of Walpurgisnacht, a night of exorcism—as Merle tries to get Charlie to confess and Gertrude does the same with Caril Ann, before their lawyers arrive in the morning. We follow two time lines simultaneously; waiting through the night with Charlie and Caril Ann in (almost) real time, but also flashing back every other scene to important moments in the progression of their budding relationship. The horror of the crimes remains offstage. The point here is not to shock the audience with gore and violence, but to seduce the audience into caring for these psychologically and emotionally crippled teenagers. But the show is also about the relationship between Merle and Gertrude, a relationship never before examined by them; and once that door is opened it can't be closed again. Merle and Gertrude have had their eyes opened by these two teens, even if it's been against their will. And by the end of the show, we realize that this isn't a show about murder or even murderers; it's a gripping dissection of two very different relationships, their unlikely parallels, their commonality, and their opposite trajectories.

Jarrow's script is smart, raw, complex, minimalist. As with Sondheim's *Assassins*, you come away realizing (to your horror) that these murderers aren't all that different from you. Like *Assassins*, the show doesn't really judge Charlie and Caril Ann, both of whom are childlike and scared one moment and full of murderous rage the next, and that lack of moral judgment is what's most unsettling about the show. Charlie tries to be a man, even a gentleman, but he only understands the most superficial aspects of those roles; he's utterly unable to understand what lies beneath the manners and conventions of polite society, boiling with still unsatisfied rage. He is a feral animal, only pretending to be a man. Caril Ann is a total innocent, a tabula rasa, emotionally shut down, and thanks to her dead mother and distant (abusive?) father, she has never learned the necessary life lessons. She, too, is a child, only she doesn't pretend to be anything else.

The powerful emotion of the story comes from the rowdy, visceral emo-rock score, bursting with dangerous energy and complicated, unmanageable emotions. Every song in the score is about connecting. Only the show's emotional theme song, "Love Never Dies," dabbles in period doo-wop style; the rest of the score ranges from the driving, angry "Concrete Walls" and "When I Could Feel," to heartrending ballads, like Gertrude's disturbing lullaby, "Float," and the sheriff's introspective emo waltz, "Hard Man," in which he questions the very definition of manliness by which he has steered his entire life. As with *bare*, many of the chords in the *Love Kills* score are ambiguous open fifths, leaving us wondering about the subtext of the lyrics, stripped of some of the musical cues that would normally convey underlying emotion. These people have walls up. *Love Kills* is a story about trying to break through those walls and find human connection, a theme found at the heart of *Sunday in the Park with George*, *Assassins*, *Bat Boy*, *The Wild Party*, *Hedwig and the Angry Inch*, and many other shows. But this is no Broadway-rock score; it's *real* rock and roll. And like very few other musicals, it doesn't even have a piano in the band, just guitar, bass, and drums.

Like some of the other great composers working in musical theatre today (Bill Finn, Larry O'Keefe, Adam Guettel, Tom Kitt, Jason Robert

Brown), Jarrow knows how to use a rock/pop vocabulary in the theatre. The songs in *Love Kills* have the repetition and surface simplicity of real rock, but they also have the continually unfolding complexity and communication of important information that theatre songs need to do good storytelling. Dozens of tiny, subtle moments elevate these artful lyrics and slyly give us clues about these kids' fears, desires, loneliness. So often, where there is repetition, there is also subtle variation that changes the emotion or context just enough that it moves us forward dramatically and sometimes lets us in for a closer look. In Charlie's inarticulate, driving, teenage primal scream, "The Funny Thing," he sings:

> You stare at the newspaper pictures
> They shock like a kick in the crotch
> But I know you like what you're seeing
> I know you love to watch
> It's like watching a movie
> And we're the stars of the movie
> And it's a comedy movie
> And it's terribly funny
> And it's terribly funny how
> Now the roads all run with blood
> From the people we killed
> And the countryside could flood
> With all that we spilled
> 'Cause we did it all for love
> And we'd be doing it still . . .
> That's the funny thing.

About Jarrow's other stage work, both musical and non-, the *New York Times* had said, "Kyle Jarrow is New York's hipster playwright," and *Curtain Up* had written, "Jarrow's writing is messy, giddy, and poignant, and at its best, all three at once. Most importantly, Jarrow's work continues to prove that he is not afraid of playing with fire." The *New York Sun* wrote, "Kyle Jarrow's songs are dangerously catchy." The *New Yorker* said, "Mr. Jarrow is the kind of writer that likes to provoke people."

In St. Louis, the critics raved. Paul Friswold wrote in *The Riverfront Times*, "*Love Kills* is a gripping and fascinating evening [but] not a comforting evening, not by a long shot. Identify too much with one couple or the other and you're bound to feel bad about yourself. But Jarrow keeps feeding you moments in which you want the four of them to achieve everything they desire, even when the characters are at cross-purposes. The end result is much like navigating love—how do you give yourself to someone else and hold on to yourself at the same time? Life is long; if you're lucky, long enough to figure it out." Chris Gibson wrote on BroadwayWorld.com, "It would have been easy for Kyle Jarrow to score his tale of killer Charlie Starkweather and Caril Fugate's incarceration, *Love Kills*, to a more conventional and period accurate 1950s-flavored beat, but that would have softened his characters and weakened the emotional impact overall. Jarrow opts instead for a harder edge that suits the material much better, after all, Charlie isn't Danny Zuko, he's a murderer." As of this writing, *Love Kills* has not yet had a full New York production.

Glory Days

The four-character rock musical *Glory Days* followed in the footsteps of *Songs for a New World* and *Edges*, in this case focusing on four high school friends who return a year after graduation only to find how far they've grown apart and how little they now know their best friends. With music and lyrics by twenty-three-year-old Nick Blaemire and book by twenty-four-year-old James Gardiner, both only eighteen when they started writing it, the show premiered first at the Signature Theatre in Virginia, in February 2008. The Signature's artistic director Eric Schaeffer, had met Blaemire and Gardiner in 2005 when he was teaching at the Kennedy Center in Washington, DC. They played one of their *Glory Days* songs for him and he decided to produce it at the Signature.

Peter Marks wrote in the *Washington Post* that the show "swiftly, tunefully and yes, authentically latches onto the rhythms of late adolescence and plays them back to us as the music of wrenching transitions . . . It is a show that reminds us that even in comfortable suburbs, you can't really go home again." James Howard wrote on BroadwayWorld.com, "It's about that elusive thing—real emotion between grown men. Perhaps that is the greatest glory of this terrific new musical." Paul Harris said in *Variety*, "This charming little pop musical about adolescent innocence comes from two experts on the subject . . . [it] should register with legions of like-minded souls on the threshold of adulthood."

A few months later, in May 2008, the show was opening on Broadway at Circle in the Square, to the great surprise of industry insiders. This was a show seemingly in tune with the musical theatre zeitgeist, following young adults trying to navigate the big, cold world they see laid sprawling in front of them, trying to move from childhood to adulthood, unsure where they've been and where they're going. But *Glory Days* suffered from both inexperience and mediocrity, with a pleasant though very conventional rock/pop score that sounds like the pop musicals of the mid-1990s, lyrics that aren't bad for a twenty-three-year-old rookie, and a script that offers only the limited insights of its twenty-four-year-old author. And three of the four young actors were making their Broadway debuts. An audience full of only twenty-three- and twenty-four-year-olds would probably love this show, but that audience doesn't buy hundred-dollar theatre tickets. The show closed after seventeen previews and only one regular performance.

On Broadway, the show's inherent flaws could not be ignored. *Variety* said, "An irritating offshoot of the digital revolution is that it's democratized the filmmaking process, opening the floodgates for kids straight out of school with no life experience and no stories to tell to start making navel-gazing movies. Beyond the small-time local level or the ubiquitous solo show, theater is mostly spared that indignity because it costs more, requires more collaborators and demands an audience. But occasionally, one such immature self-indulgence slips through, such as *Glory Days*, which slipped all the way through to Broadway." In the *New York Times*, Ben Brantley wrote, "The show and its characters are gawky, sincere, tentative, self-contradictory and given to home truths that are expounded on as if they were discoveries of new planets. This means that the production manages to seem fresh and seriously stale at the same time." He went on to say that the producers "have done this little, hopeful show no favors by dragging it into a spotlight that invites close and unforgiving inspection." The *Daily News* said, " 'Who cares, who cares, who cares?' That's a line from a song in *Glory Days*, which opened last night at Circle in the Square. It's also the sentiment that sums up this undeveloped post-high-school musical whose own backstory is more fascinating than what's onstage."

Sadly, this was not a show that belonged on Broadway. But it has found limited further life in a few regional theatres. Younger audiences don't have Brantley's problem with the show, because the truths discovered in the show are truths most teens and twenty-somethings are still in the midst of discovering. For older audiences who discovered those truths many years ago, the show may seem inconsequential and a bit silly. As with many shows, it's all about expectations and the experiences audiences bring with them into the theatre.

Rooms: A Rock Romance

Rooms: A Rock Romance begins in 1980 New York, then flashes back to 1977 Glasgow, where Monica, a middle-class Jewish singer/songwriter meets Ian, a working-class Catholic and stagnating punk rocker. The two quickly become involved both artistically and romantically. Their music takes them to London and then New York, where they discover the burgeoning punk music scene. But Ian's self-destructive side reveals itself as success comes knocking, and the two part ways. As the show ends, Ian returns, having conquered some of his demons, and he and Monica start to write together again. Will it last this time?

With music and lyrics by Scotsman Paul Scott Goodman (who wrote the fascinating *Bright Lights, Big City* score), and a book by Goodman and his wife Miriam Gordon, the show made its debut at the New York Musical Theatre Festival in 2005 (along with an early version of *Next to Normal*). In 2008, *Rooms* was produced at Metro Stage in Washington, DC. Washington's *City Paper* called it "a speedy, scrappy new rock musical about wannabe rock musicians, all drive and neurosis, noise and naked ambition." The cast album describes the score as "part Sex Pistols, part early U2, part Frank Loesser," and that's pretty accurate. In some ways it feels like a companion piece to *High Fidelity*, often using a similar musical vocabulary. Where *High Fidelity* explores the people who consume rock and roll, *Rooms* shows us the people struggling to make that music to which Rob, Barry, and Dick live their lives.

Like many of rock musicals of the current golden age, *Rooms* is about searching for human connection through the emotional language of rock and roll, and like several other shows, most notably *Sunday in the Park with George*, it's also about the tension between living life and making art. But because the show uses only two actors, there is an intimacy here that is sometimes missing from more ambitious shows.

In 2009, *Rooms* opened off Broadway under the direction of Scott Schwartz, where it ran less than two months before closing, but it still got a cast album. The *New York Times* said, "The story told in *Rooms: A Rock Romance* is 100 percent surprise-free; you always know exactly where it's going. That means the stars of this modest musical at New World Stages need to be very good for the thing to stand a chance of holding your attention. Fortunately . . . the two actors are strong enough that when the musical takes a turn into not-very-convincing melodrama, you stick with them and their characters anyway." New York's *Daily News* said, "*Rooms: A Rock Romance* transcends the obvious answer and shopworn opposites-attract plot seen everywhere from Broadway to big-screen with bang-up, big-hearted tunes and a small-scale construction that lets a two-actor cast strut their stuff. Strut they do."

American Idiot

The catalog musical continued to evolve, with exciting results. Back in 2003, the American punk rock band Green Day had decided to write and record their own rock opera, inspired by the Who's *Tommy*, *Jesus Christ Superstar*, and *The Rocky Horror Show*. Their concept album, *American Idiot*, followed the life of Jesus of Suburbia, a sort of antihero created by band front man Billie Joe Armstrong, who goes on a journey of self-discovery. The album was released in 2004, selling fourteen million copies, almost six million in the US, and it won the Grammy Award for Best Rock Album.

From early on, the band hoped to turn the album into a stage piece or a film. Director Michael Mayer (*Spring Awakening*) approached the band about creating a Broadway musical, ultimately enlisting composer Tom Kitt (*High Fidelity*, *Next to Normal*) as music supervisor and orchestrator. In 2009, the show was produced at the Berkeley Repertory Theatre in California, where it became the highest grossing show in their history, extending its run twice. From its first words, "Don't wanna be an American idiot," the musical proved both its originality and its serious intentions. *American Idiot* was the next logical step in the art form after *Rent*. While *Rent* still has traditional musical theatre in its roots, *American Idiot* doesn't. It works physically much like *Rent*, using a basically empty stage, with the band on stage but even more integrated into the action than in *Rent*. The sophisticated score is full of driving punk anthems, aching emo ballads, and complex, extended musical scenes, as skillfully wrought as any Rodgers and Hammerstein wrote.

The show opened on Broadway in April 2010 and looks poised for a healthy run. Some of the reviews were mixed, but many critics were excited by this smart, angry, exhilarating show. The *New York Times* review was titled "Stomping Onto Broadway with a Punk Temper Tantrum," and critic Charles Isherwood wrote, "Rage and love, those consuming emotions felt with a particularly acute pang in youth, all but burn up the stage in *American Idiot*, the thrillingly raucous and gorgeously wrought Broadway musical adapted from the blockbuster pop-punk album by Green Day. Pop on Broadway, sure. But punk? Yes, indeed, and served straight up, with each sneering lyric and snarling riff in place. A stately old pile steps from the tourist-clogged Times Square might seem a strange place for the music of Green Day, and for theater this blunt, bold and aggressive in its attitude. Not to mention loud. But from the moment the curtain rises on a panorama of baleful youngsters at the venerable St. James Theater, where the show opened on Tuesday night, it's clear that these kids are going to make themselves at home, even if it means tearing up the place in the process." Some reviews called these characters slackers, but that trivializes the richness of their individual hero-myth journeys.

As reconceived for the stage by Mayer and Armstrong, *American Idiot* chronicles a year in the life of three friends who are lost in the labyrinth of modern-day American suburbia. As the story begins, Johnny, Tunny, and Will decide to head for the big city, but Will stays home with his pregnant girlfriend, and after getting to the big city, the depressed, desensitized Tunny decides to join the army. Now off on his own, Johnny conjures up the mythic drug dealer St. Jimmy, who leads him down a road of sex, heroin, and rock and roll, while Johnny pursues a mysterious woman he calls Whatsername. Ultimately, Johnny tells Whatsername that he's leaving her to follow St. Jimmy, but Whatsername tells Johnny that St. Jimmy is "a figment of your father's rage and your mother's love," and she leaves. Johnny abandons St. Jimmy and takes a soul-killing office job. All three friends ultimately find their paths unfulfilling, and they end up back home, much the wiser, accepting the demons and complexities of adult life. They may still be lost, but they are self-aware now in a way they had not been before.

In some ways, this is a classic story built on the hero myth, and while there are echoes of *Rent* here, there are also many echoes of *Tommy* and *Rocky Horror*, and other works (like Act II of *The Fantasticks*), yet it is still very much its own very original work, with a distinctive, authentic rock voice that Broadway doesn't often hear. Far from being just a rock album on stage, this is a fully realized rock musical with some interesting things to say about our culture and our times—from the show's opening video montage of very dark, depressing news stories, to the only partly resolved finale. Steven Hoggett's powerful, athletic, intensely aggressive hip-hop choreography in the Broadway production equaled the tone and intensity of the material. The walls of the set were covered with newspaper, rising all the way up past the proscenium, dotted with TV screens, and here and there the word *OBEY* was written across the papers.

There were those who hated *American Idiot* for not being a normal Broadway musical, for not having a more detailed, conventionally plotted story. But this is real rock theatre, not a Broadway musical that just uses rock as its vocabulary. Its aesthetics are different, its language is different, its goals are different. Rock theatre often tells much more primal tales. Like *The Odyssey*, the Passion story in the New Testament, *The Wizard of Oz*, *Star Wars*, and many other stories, *American Idiot* is a hero myth, a twenty-first century fable, as each of the three lost friends has to take his own journey and face his own obstacles, each crossing into the "underworld," learning something about himself, and returning to his people with his new knowledge. Johnny even has to face his own evil wizard in the person of St. Jimmy, and like Luke Skywalker on Dagobah, Johnny finally realizes he is his own evil wizard.

The tragedy of the show's ending, despite its uplifting feel, is that these three friends are still lost. They've gained some understanding and self-knowledge, but that's not enough in our oppressive, overstimulated, overly combative world. To its credit, there are no easy answers or resolutions at the end of *American Idiot* because, like *Hair*, it's telling the truth, and there are no easy answers or resolutions in real life.

Bloody Bloody Andrew Jackson

A brilliant, smartass, and decidedly original emo-rock musical about the founding of the Democratic Party by our country's first populist president (and lots more), *Bloody Bloody Andrew Jackson* began life (long before anybody thought the populist Barack Obama would ever become president) at the experimental theatre company Les Frères Corbusier (named for Le Corbusier, the legendary pioneer of modern architecture), where the show's thirty-two-year-old director and co-writer, Alex Timbers, is artistic director. With a score by Michael Friedman, the show had workshop productions in 2006 at the Williamstown Theatre Festival and in May 2007 at the New 42nd Street Studios in New York, where Benjamin Walker took over the lead that would eventually make him a Broadway star (at least temporarily). The musical premiered as a fully produced show in January 2008 in Los Angeles at the Kirk Douglas Theatre, where its press materials described the show this way:

> Shootouts, smallpox and scalpings—growing up on the American Frontier was killer! Hoping to kick some British butt and bitch-slap the Spaniards, thirteen-year-old Andrew Jackson joins the Army and grows up to become America's first populist president and greatest rock star since George Washington.

The critics loved it. *Backstage West* said, "Writer-director Alex Timbers and composer-lyricist Michael Friedman join forces for this wildly exhilarating theatrical ride. Their debuting emo rock musical views the life and career of controversial 19th-century American president Andrew Jackson through two disparate lenses. The production suggests the historical tomfoolery of a zany Monty Python spoof while conjuring an edgy seriocomic irony that recalls Stephen Sondheim's *Assassins*. It forges its own blazingly original artistic identity, pulsating with wit, melody, energy, and dazzling theatricality." The *Los Angeles Times* called it "goofy, daring . . . The product of sensibilities shaped by the topical ironies of Jon Stewart and the profane zaniness of *South Park* . . . Imagine *Avenue Q* with a master's degree in American history. Or Brecht for people who secretly find him a bore."

In May 2009, *BBAJ* (as its fans like to call it) opened in New York, in more of a concert staging, as part of the Public Theatre's Lab Series. It then had a full-fledged off Broadway run at the Public, from March through June of 2010. The Public's artistic director Oskar Eustis wrote about the show in the cast album's liner notes:

> I think *Bloody Bloody Andrew Jackson* is an experiment appropriate for our times. It may be about our seventh president, but it tackles the core of American populism—that ebullient, sentimental, no-nonsense, self-pitying, anti-intellectual, rowdy energy that is at the core of our national identity—with a precision and wit that speaks totally to our moment. The show invokes reactionary pleasures in order to savagely criticize them. It is a dangerous game, but Friedman and Timbers play it brilliantly. This is who we are, and if it's horrifying, it can also be a lot of fun. What a contradiction, America.

Eustis finished his notes with, "Who says political theatre can't rock?" Who indeed.

Ben Brantley wrote in the *New York Times*, "You're going to shake, rattle and roll when he makes you the ultimate promise, the one you truly want to hear from anyone who aspires to lead your nation: He solemnly swears to give you the best sex you've ever had. Thus does the man known as Old Hickory, poured into a pair of tight black jeans and fiercely embodied by a microphone-riding Benjamin Walker, take the stage in the rowdy, dopey and devastatingly shrewd *Bloody Bloody Andrew Jackson*, which opened on Tuesday night at the Public Theater. Produced there last spring in a concert version, Alex Timbers's and Michael Friedman's emo-rock musical—which makes the case that this country's relationship with its president is always deeply and irrationally personal—has returned to stake a claim as the most entertaining and most perceptive political theater of the season."

In September 2010, the show moved uptown and began previews at the Bernard B. Jacobs Theatre, where it officially opened in October, with most of the cast from the off Broadway production intact, especially Benjamin Walker in an electrifying performance and the tightest jeans on Broadway. *BBAJ* got rave reviews but was sometimes subverted by the sometimes self-indulgent original cast, several of whom didn't always serve the material as well as they could have, mugging and begging the audience for laughs. Still, the *New York Times* said, "Sometimes a funhouse mirror is more accurate than the one in the bathroom. There's not a show in town that more astutely reflects the state of this nation than *Bloody Bloody Andrew Jackson*, the rowdy political carnival that is sprawled all over the Bernard B. Jacobs Theater." *Variety* said, "Call it provocative anarchy, a 21st-century equivalent to the Marx Brothers' *Duck Soup*. At one point, van Buren, Jackson's veep and successor in the Oval Office, complains that Andrew is being 'laissez-unfair.' The authors are inarguably and entertainingly laissez-unfair to the Founding Fathers, tea-bagging Republicans, right-wing populists, handicapped narrators in motorized wheelchairs wearing sweaters with dancing bears, Native Americans, and just about whatever targets dart past their flyswatters."

The authors claim that absolutely everything that happens in the show is true, including Jackson's penchant for cutting himself. The show follows our seventh president, and founder of the Democratic Party, from birth to death, not incidentally including his systematic genocide of Native Americans. (Some historians today call him the American Hitler.) We witness both Jackson's greatness and his considerable darkness.

BBAJ's songs are outstanding and hard rocking, the lyrics both well crafted and consistently, hilariously surprising (the first song slaps us with "I'm Andrew fucking Jackson!"), the dialogue is smart, funny, and pointed, and there's as much subtext as there is surface action. Not only does the show give us a history lesson, it also says some very interesting things about these times we live in now, very often operating on two levels at once. The show tells its story in today's vernacular, in terms of today's pop culture (one political sign in the show reads, "Emocracy!"), and with dozens of sly, subtle references to both George W. Bush and Barack

Obama. When Jackson warns of the dangers from terrorism in our homeland, danger on the border, etc., we realize that the show's modern language and references aren't just stunts or cheap laughs. The writers are saying something serious: *those who do not learn from history . . .*

But as *Variety* predicted, this wild, fearless, emo-rock musical didn't interest the uptown audience, with its anachronistic dialogue, moral gray area, and its scathing subtextual commentary on today's more ridiculous political movements. The show closed in January 2011, after only 120 performances. Costing $4.5 million, it closed at a substantial loss to its investors.

Unfortunately, one of the reasons the show didn't succeed may be that the original Broadway production didn't entirely rise to the quirky brilliance of the material, despite Timbers doing double duty as writer and director. The show was infected with the same virus that killed *Cry-Baby the Musical* and that made the rock musical *Toxic Avenger* even worse than it already was: the misguided belief that nothing's funnier than intentionally "bad acting," in giant ironic quotes, followed by mugging to the audience, mouth agape, to make sure we know how funny that bad acting was. Like *Bat Boy*, *Urinetown*, *Spelling Bee*, *Little Shop of Horrors*, and other shows, *BBAJ* worked best when its actors played it deadly serious, with extremely high stakes. Timbers and Friedman wrote a completely overwhelming show, so crazy, so intense, so fast moving, that it's thrilling to be in the audience, and it doesn't need "help" being funny. Luckily, Benjamin Walker and several of the other leads did not succumb to the "hamming" bug; they played it sincerely and honestly, though also big and outsized, and as a result, their performances were funnier than the others, and also emotionally engaging in a way that the others weren't.

Populism, Yeah, Yeah!

Though some of these rock musicals succeeded commercially and others did not, it's clear now that rock music is no longer a particularly subversive or rebellious choice in the musical theatre. Just as rock has become part of the fabric of everyday American life, so too has the use of rock music in musicals become unsurprising. The musical theatre has almost always spoken in the voice of American pop music—ragtime in the 1910s, jazz in the '20s and '30s, the foxtrot in the '40s and '50s. But rock and roll had a hard time getting a foothold. There have been rock musicals since the 1960s, but until the mid-1990s they were the exceptions, maybe because those who grew up with rock weren't yet solidly in control of our culture. But finally, theatre music and popular music are coming together again. And that can only be a good thing for this uniquely American art form, no matter what the older generation may think.

One result of that is a whole new generation of musical theatre lovers, high school and college students who got hooked by *Rent*, *Spring Awakening*, *Hedwig*, *Songs for a New World*, *Bat Boy*, *Next to Normal*, *bare*, *Edges*, the 2009 revival of *Hair*, and other shows, as well as Disney's *High School Musical* and its sequels. Not only has this millennial generation given us a whole new audience for musical theatre, but they're *writing* new musicals, too, and that's very exciting. People are always predicting the death of the musical theatre, but it's never been more alive than it is right now.

The possibilities are endless.

CREDITS

Look At Me, I'm Sandra Dee (Reprise)
Those Magic Changes
from GREASE
Lyric and Music by Warren Casey
and Jim Jacobs
© 1971, 1972 WARREN CASEY
and JIM JACOBS
© Renewed 1999, 2000 JIM JACOBS and
THE ESTATE OF WARREN CASEY
All Rights Administered by EDWIN H.
MORRIS & COMPANY, A DIVISION OF
MPL Music Publishing, Inc.
All Rights Reserved
Reprinted by permission of
Hal Leonard Corporation

Sexually Free
By Threes
From I LOVE MY WIFE
Music by Cy Coleman
Lyrics by Michael Stewart
Copyright © 1976 Notable Music
Company, Inc.
Copyright Renewed
All Rights Reserved Used by Permission
Reprinted by permission of Hal Leonard
Corporation

Lyrics from *Bat Boy* reprinted courtesy of Larry O'Keefe.

Lyrics from *High Fidelity* reprinted courtesy of Amanda Green. Lyrics by Amanda Green. © by Amanda Green and Tom Kitt.

Lyrics from *The Wild Party* reprinted courtesy of Andrew Lippa.

Lyrics from *Love Kills* reprinted courtesy of Kyle Jarrow.

The chapter on *Hair* reprinted from *Rebels with Applause: Broadway's Groundbreaking Musicals*, copyright © 2001 Scott Miller. Published by Heinemann, a division of Reed Elsevier, Inc., Portsmouth, NH. Reprinted with permission from the publisher.